Understanding the Whole Student

Holistic Multicultural Education

Clifford Mayes, Ramona Maile Cutri,
P. Clint Rogers, and Fidel Montero

ROWMAN & LITTLEFIELD EDUCATION
Lanham, Maryland • Toronto • Plymouth, UK
2007

Published in the United States of America
by Rowman & Littlefield Education
A Division of Rowman & Littlefield Publishers, Inc.
A wholly owned subsidiary of The Rowman & Littlefield Publishing Group, Inc.
4501 Forbes Boulevard, Suite 200, Lanham, Maryland 20706
www.rowmaneducation.com

Estover Road
Plymouth PL6 7PY
United Kingdom

British Library Cataloguing in Publication Information Available

Library of Congress Cataloging-in-Publication Data:

Understanding the whole student : holistic multicultural education / Clifford Mayes . . .
[et al.].
  p. cm.
Includes bibliographical references and index.
ISBN-13: 978-1-57886-669-4 (cloth : alk. paper)
ISBN-10: 1-57886-669-3 (cloth : alk. paper)
ISBN-13: 978-1-57886-670-0 (pbk. : alk. paper)
ISBN-10: 1-57886-670-7 (pbk. : alk. paper)
1. Holistic education. 2. Multicultural education. I. Mayes, Clifford.
LC990.U53 2007
370.117—dc22   2007020477

Printed in the United States of America

∞™ The paper used in this publication meets the minimum requirements of American
National Standard for Information Sciences—Permanence of Paper for Printed Library
Materials, ANSI/NISO Z39.48-1992.

To our students

Contents

Part I: Foundations of Multicultural Education

Part II: The Four Domains of Multicultural Education

Acknowledgments

Cliff wants to thank his wife and best friend, Pam, and their children, Lizzie, Josh, and Dana, for their constant support, wisdom, and love—and just for making life exciting and fun.

Ramona thanks her husband, Christopher, and her two children, Tiare and Atticus, for helping her prove that mommies can do anything.

Clint would like to thank his parents for creating an environment that taught him to love education, to take risks in exploring the world, to believe in himself, and to be of service.

Fidel thanks his wife, Nancy, for her support, and his children, Maeva and Tane, for reminding him of the important things in life. He also thanks his parents, Fidel and Imelda, for their sacrifices that made it all possible.

We express our gratitude to the *Journal of Curriculum Studies* for permission to reprint sections from "The Psychoanalysts' View of Teaching and Learning: 1922–2002," which is now in press. We express our gratitude to *Multicultural Education* for permission to reprint sections from "First-year Latino Teacher," which appeared in 2004. We also extend our heartfelt thanks to Dr. Thomas Koerner, vice president of Rowman & Littlefield Education, for his wisdom, faith, and encouragement regarding this book.

Each of the authors would also like to thank their students, who have played such crucial roles in helping the authors refine their views and practices regarding multicultural education. We are especially grateful to our research assistants—Elizabeth Mayes, Laura Wyatt, Danielle Churchill, Sarah Lynn Zavoral, and Stephanie Judd—for their very kind and competent help.

Above all, we wish to thank the Lord for His guidance, patience, and tender mercies in our individual and collective efforts.

Introduction

WHAT IS HOLISTIC MULTICULTURAL EDUCATION AND WHY SHOULD IT MATTER?

This book rests on the assumption that the best educational practices are those that acknowledge and nurture every aspect of a student's being—the physical, emotional, social, cognitive, ethical, and spiritual. If that assumption is correct, then it makes sense that the best approach to multicultural educational issues should also be holistic. However, most books that deal with multicultural education fundamentally do so with an overriding emphasis on the *sociopolitical* nature of these issues. Sometimes their tone is contentious, which tends to exacerbate the culture wars that are raging in our society. What is this sociopolitical approach which, although very important, can be problematic when it is the *only* lens that is used to view multicultural educational issues?

The purpose of the sociopolitical approach is to examine the assumptions that shape pedagogical practices and institutional structures in the schools. For (it is argued) these practices and structures operate in ways that are academically unproductive and politically disempowering for students from lower socioeconomic realms and minority ethnic groups. According to these theorists, these unfair practices sometimes result from a conscious strategy on the part of school people while at other times they happen in a less conscious way as school people—despite their good intentions—uncritically engage in educational and administrative practices that favor some students and cast others to the margins. But (the sociopolitical approach goes on to argue) whether these teachers, principals, and policymakers are acting consciously or unconsciously, they are more or less ensuring that children from

1

the privileged realms of society will do well and that those from the outer realms will continue to live on the edges of school and society.

This political critique of schooling—stemming from two interrelated socioeconomic analyses of schooling known as *Reproduction Theory* (Bourdieu, 1977) and *Critical Theory* (McLaren, 2003)—sets out to show how schools do not so much provide *knowledge* to students as they provide *different kinds of knowledge, using different ways of teaching, different curricula, and different levels of per-pupil expenditures*, depending upon a student's socioeconomic status (Apple, 1990; Morrow & Torres, 1995; Sadker & Sadker, 2004). By this interpretation, children from the more privileged groups in society have a much greater chance of success in their elementary and secondary years than do children from the less privileged groups, both because of the enriched environments that they have grown up in and because of the fact that schooling favors them in all sorts of ways, some blatant and some hidden (Oakes, 2000). All of this combined privilege prepares the more socioeconomically favored students to quite literally "talk the talk" that will allow them to score well on college entrance exams and move on to universities, even to prestigious ones (Bernstein, 2000). From there, the most favored students will continue steadily and securely onward and upward to professions that are socially and financially rewarding, where they will then become comfortably settled in as the dominant groups in society who can lord it over the "dominated" groups (Spring, 2000). This whole process then repeats itself again with *their* children. In this way, socioeconomic advantage *reproduces* itself through the politically *uncritical* practices of teachers, administrators, and policymakers. Reproduction Theory and Critical Theory propose ways of identifying and addressing this problem.

Now, although we want to take a much broader approach to multiculturalism in the schools than a political one, we also want to acknowledge upfront that this critique of schooling is powerful, rests on a considerable body of research, and (if it is used as one of many ways of approaching the issue of multiculturalism in the schools) can help us understand how to create more truly democratic forms of education (Bowles & Gintis, 1976; Kozol, 1991; McLaren, 2003). What is more, the sociopolitical approach casts considerable light on the sad fact that the greatest predictor of how a student will do on college entrance exams is his or her parent's socioeconomic status (Berliner & Biddle, 1995). It would be a mistake to minimize the political side of these issues or sugarcoat the conflicts that they involve.

However, it would be an even bigger mistake to look at multicultural issues *only,* or even *primarily*, in political and "politically correct" terms. A student's cultural identity is much more than a political fact. It is an existential fact. By that we mean that it is interwoven throughout his or her entire being—

physically, psychologically, cognitively, ethically, and spiritually. Also important to the authors of this book is the idea that multicultural education should not simply be about children from disempowered groups (although, to be sure, it must never lose sight of those students' very special needs and challenges). For, *every* student comes from a culture—or, more precisely, a variety of subcultures—that shape that child and prepare him or her to *see* schools and *be* a student in certain ways. *Every student* is multicultural and this fact affects *every aspect* of the student's life from the sensorimotor to the spiritual. Multicultural education should aim to engage *every student* at *every level* of his or her existence, and it should provide students many ways to communicate about their different ways of being, seeing, and doing in the world.

In short, *holistic multicultural education is simply good education—and it is for everyone.* This is an especially important fact to keep in mind, it seems to the authors of this book, in a society that is now so extremely diverse as is ours. For students who come from socioeconomically marginalized groups, holistic multicultural education is not only socioeconomically empowering but also physically, emotionally, ethically, and spiritually nurturing. For students who come from privileged groups in society, holistic multicultural education will help them see and respect multiple cultural perspectives, thus expanding their inner world and making them more sensitive citizens in a pluralistic democracy.

WHAT IS HOLISTIC EDUCATION?

To talk about holistic multicultural education requires that we first understand some of the basic principles and practices of holistic education in general.

Holistic education stems from the simple yet powerful notion that education, to have profound, healthy, and lasting effects in a student's life, must try—to the extent practical in any given educational setting with its political and institutional constraints—to address various aspects of that student's being. A person is not just a stimulus-response mechanism, a member of a politically marginalized group, or a passive vessel into whose head facts and theories are to be dispassionately poured. Rather, the student is a complex creature (indeed, the most complex of all creatures!), and he or she will grow more and more detached from the teacher and the curriculum if this complexity is ignored. For as John Dewey correctly observed almost a century ago, deep and durable learning—the kind that will stay with and influence a person throughout his or her lifetime and will not be forgotten after the next test—occurs only when a student finds the curriculum relevant to his or her life situation (Dewey, 1916). Educational practices, therefore, that take into account the student's physical nature, emotional dynamics, sociopolitical commitments, styles of learning, ethical convictions, and spiritual commitments will have a much greater chance of capturing the student's interest than those that just address one aspect of the student's being—and, too often, do not even address *that* aspect with any particular finesse.

Of course, teachers cannot know everything about every student, nor would it be appropriate for them to try to do so. But the holistic educational tradition maintains that teachers should know as much as *is* appropriate and possible about their students, honor the fact that every student *is* a complex person, and design their curricula and instruction accordingly by including a wide variety of perspectives and addressing a wide variety of learning styles. Doing so helps to create classrooms that are inviting to all students, that address the many facets of the living diamond that each student is, and that will encourage the exploration of many different ways of seeing the world and acting in it.

In sum, the key concept in holistic education is *integration*—integration of all aspects of a student's being into a harmonious whole; and *integration* of various students' perspectives, needs and abilities in a classroom into a truly cooperative "learning community" (Brown, Collins, & Duguid, 1988). Such things are important because they assist in the growth of healthy, intelligent, compassionate, contributing members of a local, national and global community. Although we are certainly concerned with students' intellectual capacity and growth, we are equally concerned with fostering their identity, their physical, psychological, and social health, and their spiritual well-being and compassion—all of which things will simultaneously stimulate and allow them to grow intellectually.

Holistic Categories

But what are these "aspects" of a student's being—and how can they be categorized? Two of the best categorizations in the holistic education literature come from Brown and his associates (1988) and Miller (1983).

Brown felt that education should be pictured as consisting of four concentric circles that correspond to the four major components of an integrated person. The first circle dealt with essentially psychological issues such as self-actualization, self-esteem, and motivation; the second circle, the interpersonal, dealt with relationships between the teacher and student as well as between student and student in the classroom; third was the extra-personal circle, which dealt with the student's understanding of and roles in the culture(s) in society of which that student was a member; finally, Brown and associates postulated a transpersonal circle, which embraced the spiritual purposes of education. Miller, using slightly different terms, discussed how teachers needed to attend to behavioral, cognitive, social, developmental, academic, ethical, and spiritual implications of what and how they teach to foster the maximum holistic growth in themselves and their students. Both of these systems evidence the holistic emphasis on addressing the multifaceted needs and potentials of teachers and students as they discover themselves and each other in the integral context of the classroom.

This is also the purpose of the holistic categorization that we offer in this book, which posits the following four domains of teaching and learning: (1) sensorimotor, (2) psychosocial, (3) cognitive, and (4) ethicospiritual.

The Four Holistic Multicultural Domains

The first domain is the *sensorimotor domain*. It involves issues relating to the student as a developing physical, "sensing" being. As two centuries of physical and cultural anthropology have shown, there is no such thing as a human being whose ways of sensing, responding to, and negotiating the world on a physical basis have not been strongly influenced by the culture in which he or she has matured.

Second is the *psychosocial domain*. Typically built upon (neo) Freudian and (neo) Jungian foundations (about which we will have much more to say later), this domain is concerned with the deep psychological dynamics that are at play, both consciously and unconsciously, in the relationship between the student and the teacher. Although this domain includes many different issues that have been discussed in other books by one of the authors (Mayes, 2001a, 2005), in this book we will study such topics as the cultural construction of emotions (especially the student's feelings about different ways of teaching and learning); the student's natural emotional commitments to his or her culture and how this plays out in both positive and problematic ways in the classroom; the inherently emotional nature of teaching and learning in every culture; the development of self-esteem in the student; and the classroom as a place for addressing the emotional traumas that many students have experienced, some (but not all) of which are the result of political and economic factors.

In the *cognitive domain,* which comes third, we discuss how there is often considerable cultural variation in what constitutes a conceptual "problem," what qualifies as "evidence" to solve that problem, and cultural differences in how one (individually and in concert with others) should go about "solving" that "problem." In short, this chapter will deal with cultural variations in cognition and interpretation—obviously very important issues when dealing with the strictly "academic" side of the curriculum.

Fourth and finally, there is the *ethicospiritual domain.* Here, we provide a case study of a minority teacher in a middle school with a varied ethnic student body to consider how a teacher's spirituality and pedagogical practices in a multicultural setting can enrich each other in a wide variety of ways. In other words, we examine: (1) how the teacher's ethical and spiritual commitments can deepen his or her commitment to the cause of providing sensitive multicultural education as well as (2) how that sense of caring can deepen his or her ethical and spiritual commitments.

The book is divided into two parts. Part one, comprising chapters one and two, provides the reader with the fundamental terms, concepts, and theories in the field of the cultural foundations of education. Knowing about the cultural foundations of education in general is, we believe, essential to understanding the more specialized issues that arise in the field of multicultural education in the United States today. Chapter two deals with the most important facts, models, and controversies in the field of second-language acquisition, with a special focus on the acquisition of English as a second language. Although very few books in multicultural education reserve a special chapter for these linguistic issues, we believe that the reader will enjoy and benefit from a discussion of them and will become a more sensitive and effective teacher and citizen in considering them in the depth and detail which we have attempted to provide. The chapters in part two each deal with one of the domains of multicultural education discussed above.

Holistic Multicultural Goals

In order to clarify some of the points we wish to make and part of what we hope you gain from this book, perhaps we should start by stating what we are *not* trying to do.

Things we are *not* trying to do:

- Encourage the belief that the individual is completely determined by his or her culture.
- Encourage the relativistic view that all cultural perspectives are equally healthy and equally valid in all respects.
- Give a complete list of all the cultural differences that teachers should be aware of or expect that teachers can know all the cultural differences that their students bring with them to the classroom.
- Pretend to provide a complete, foolproof list of how to approach each student's cultural differences.
- Make statements about how one culture might be considered "better" than another.

- Say that teachers do not already care about these things or already respond to some cultural differences in healthy ways.
- Help only minority students.

Some of the things we *are* trying to do:

- Challenge many traditional and often unstated assumptions about learning and education that follow what is known as the "scientific-management," "corporate," or "industrial" view of the purpose of education as the "shaping" and "control" of students as social "units" to be used for merely economic or military purposes.
- Offer an approach to teaching and learning that puts primary emphasis on the agency and holistic needs and potential of students as physically, emotionally, culturally, politically and spiritually rich beings.
- Propose that holistic multicultural education is important for *all* students and teachers.
- Argue that there are culturally variable yet equally valid ways of viewing what it means to teach and learn.
- Demonstrate the importance to teachers and educational leaders of recognizing and honoring valid cultural differences in their students (even if those teachers and leaders cannot, of course, be expected to know precisely what *all* those differences are) and be willing to explore those differences and encourage students to do the same thing.
- Give examples of when these cultural differences tend to matter most in educational settings.
- Insist that if teachers are not aware of these differences and do not approach them holistically and sensitively, they can misinterpret and mislabel student behavior (categorizing a student as "cognitively deficient," for instance, when in fact she is merely "cognitively different") and thus treat these students in a way that alienates them and incites behavior and attitudes that are damaging to both the student, the teacher, and the school culture.
- Assert that if teachers strive with students to become as aware as possible of the valid cultural differences that exist, and honor and celebrate alternative ways of knowing and learning (all the while avoiding a morally destructive relativism), then they will help create an enriching classroom environment that is more physically, emotionally, ethically, and spiritually nurturing and even therapeutic for *all* students.
- Provide theoretical models and concrete examples of how teachers can most productively approach multicultural issues in their classroom by: (1) examining their own cultural assumptions, beliefs, and biases through

a process which we will later define and discuss called *cultural reflectivity*; (2) joining with their students in becoming "anthropological investigators" of each other's cultures; (3) recognizing both the influence of culture and also the great variability within a culture due to intracultural differences and individual choices; (4) honoring multiple ways of reasoning and promoting multiple means of teaching and assessing students in order to accommodate cultural variability; (5) teaching the dominant culture's norms while leaving room for critique of those norms; (6) taking an "additive" view of bilingualism as a potential advantage to be appreciated and cultivated, not a "subtractive" view which sees linguistic differences as a social pathology to be "cured"; (7) creating classrooms that are a "holding environment"—an emotionally safe space where students will not only succeed but can also be allowed to encounter difficulties—and occasionally even to "fail"—so that they can lovingly be shown how to regroup in order to grow; (8) developing an "authoritative" teaching style, which involves both high degrees of care for students *and* high expectations of them; (9) knowing it is not necessary to be a perfect teacher to be a successful one but simply to be one who is continually striving to discover how to better teach from a holistic multicultural perspective of care and love for one's students.

- Recognize and honor the fact that teachers generally *do* care, knowing that (precisely because teachers do care so much) they are anxious not to misunderstand their students or engage in types of teaching that might in some way damage those very students whom they want to help. We want to find ways to recognize what is good in so many classrooms and encourage more of it!

One final technical note. In order to avoid sexist pronoun usage, we have used the female and male pronouns as the general pronominal referents in alternating chapters. Some chapters thus use "she" to refer to individuals in general and some use "he." We believe this is fair and avoids the frequent stylistic dilemmas caused by the rhetorically unwieldy "he or she," "he/she," "his/her," and so on.

I

FOUNDATIONS OF
MULTICULTURAL EDUCATION

1

Core Issues in the Cultural Foundations of Education

WHAT IS CULTURE?

Shade (1989) has defined culture in very broad terms as:

a group's preferred way of perceiving, judging, and organizing the ideas, situations, and events they encounter in their daily lives. It represents the rules or guidelines a set of individuals who share a common history or geographical setting use to mediate their interaction with their environment. As such, culture might involve adherence to a specific religious orientation, use of a certain language or style of communication, as well as preferences for various expressive methods to represent their perceptions of the world, i.e., in art, music, or dance. Culture also determines the guidelines individuals within groups use to select the specific information to which they attend as well as the interpretation given to that information. (p. 9)

Berger and Luckmann (1967), offering a similarly wide definition of culture, have claimed that all cultures have five basic characteristics: (1) there are some more or less universally shared assumptions among all the individuals; (2) individuals incorporate shared experiences of the social world in their individual biographies—that is, they tell the stories of their lives in terms, settings, roles, life stages, and ethical values that their culture provides; (3) a culture involves rules and roles—a body of transmitted "recipe knowledge" about how to act in certain situations; these are the parameters regarding when, how, and why one should behave as one does in various settings; (4) individuals internalize more or less the same elements of their shared social world; and (5) individuals share a language (pp. 63–64ff.).

A culture organizes itself around certain values. These provide the culture with a widely (although not necessarily completely) agreed upon set of criteria within the culture that enables one to determine what conduct is obligatory, what forbidden, and what simply acceptable; these criteria are the standards by which a person or a group within the culture decides which situations and events are desirable and which undesirable, and what to do to restore order when order has (for whatever reason) been upset or violated. These criteria—which determine the "average expectable" or "normal" way of seeing, being and acting in the world, and which offer ways of coping with destabilizing forms of deviance—are called *normative values* (Williams, 1987).

A culture's normative values typically exist in the form of a hierarchy—some being more central to a culture's understanding of itself and enactment of its reality, and some being less so (Rokeach, 1979; Williams, 1987). Bruner (1996) has pointed out how these values in their original form are typically expressed as the sacred stories—the foundational "myths"—upon which a society originally arose in the misty beginnings of its history. As the great modern ethicist Alasdair MacIntyre has said, mythology as a moral exemplum is at the very heart of a culture and represents a primary mode of education into the virtues (1985, p. 216). Many American children learn about the virtue of honesty, for example, hearing the story about George Washington as a boy, how he cut down a cherry tree and finally admitted to this bad behavior because he "could not tell a lie"—or about courage by hearing about Rosa Parks and her bravery in refusing to sit at the back of the bus as was required of African Americans in the 1950s. Explicit moral instruction, inspirational poetry, and religious allegory are similarly employed to make a culture cohere (Berger & Luckmann, 1966, p. 69). When the values that are implicit in these sacred stories become explicitly systematized in a set of abstract principles that are used for determining what is acceptable and what is unacceptable behavior in a culture, then that culture has *a legal system.*

Of course, it is not always the case that everyone in the culture *adheres* to its values or that there are not individuals or groups (*subcultures,* which we will discuss presently) within the culture that *object* to some of the culture's values and even wish to introduce alternative values. However, whether one is defending or attacking cultural standards, it is precisely that culture's *normative values* that are the subject of discussion and conflict—and that are at stake in how the tension is resolved. These cultural tensions involve both the mind and the heart of the disputants since human values have both cognitive and affective aspects. Interestingly, the older the individual, the stronger the link is between values and behavior (Williams, 1987).

Hofstede (2001), after amassing an enormous body of data regarding different cultures' values systems, added a great deal to the understanding of the structural dynamics of cultural values. He concluded that most cultures' values are built around five basic axes—or sets of issues. Any culture tends to be located at or somewhere between the poles of each of these five axes, which are as follows: (1) *Power distance* refers to the degree to which the less powerful members of the society agree upon and accept the fact that power is distributed unequally—the acceptance of power inequality in the society. (2) *Uncertainty approach/avoidance* is a measure of how comfortable or uncomfortable members of a culture are in unstructured situations; how much the society accepts the novel/surprising/unknown versus how much it tries to control it. (3) *Individualism/collectivism* represents the poles in the balance that a society chooses to strike between the requirement that individuals take care of themselves versus integrating into groups. It is also the degree to which "social referencing" is encouraged—that is, whether the individual identifies strongly with a group and is indivisible from it or whether the individual primarily sees herself in self-defined terms, separate from group identity. (4) *Masculinity/femininity*, the width of the divide between gender-based roles, is the degree to which biological differences are expected to be reflected in social and emotional roles. (5) *Long-term/short-term orientation* is the degree to which members of a society are expected to be able to accept delayed gratification of material, social, and emotional needs; persistence and thrift are aspects of this continuum.

Is there a normative American culture? According to Spindler (1963) there is. He argued that the traditional values that make up the core of the Anglo-American culture encompass: (1) a Puritan morality, particularly regarding the establishment of a family and sexual fidelity of spouses, (2) a belief that hard work will lead to success, (3) a premium placed on individualism, (4) an orientation of one's efforts towards socially and financially rewarding achievements, and (5) a future-time orientation—that is, seeing one's present activities and situations in terms of their future yield, as if the present were a constant investment in the future (p. 134–136). In 1992, Spindler and Spindler added the following as core values of mainstream American society: (1) equality of opportunity, (2) the value of honesty (as an expedient best policy), (3) a belief in the openness of the American socioeconomic structure that can be penetrated by personal commitment and hard work, and (4) a sociable, get-along-well-with-others orientation (p. 37).

Learning a Culture

Typically, an individual *learns* about her culture-of-origin from the beginning moments of awareness. In the very first touches, sights, sounds, smells, and tastes that she experiences, she is being *shaped by, getting information about,* and *becoming an influence on* her environment. The textures and caresses, schedules and spaces, and motions and emotions that she experiences in her burgeoning field of awareness are often phenomena that are typical of her culture and are even, in some instances, quite specific to her culture (Wade, 1996).

Even the breast-feeding infant is being educated into her culture by learning the protocols of nursing. An infant from Culture A may be nursed in discreet privacy on a very regular schedule every day for a certain amount of time in each nursing session. She will then be put in her crib in a softly lit, quiet room with a colored, slowly revolving mobile above her from which soothing nursery music streams. In and around the crib, a mother has placed picture books in order to pique her growing baby's interest in them as she gets older. This baby girl is learning at the somatic ground level of her being many lessons about time and space, sights and sounds, bodily rhythms and interpersonal relationships, action and rest, and constraint and possibility.

These are different experiences than a child in Culture B—which has different nursing practices—is having during the same day. That culture's nursing practices may include nursing the child whenever it seems hungry, offering the baby the breast quite openly, often in a noisy public square or in the fields while the mother is engaged in chatting and laughing aloud with other nursing mothers and workers. After nursing, the child may be strapped again to the working mother's back or passed around from person to person between feedings—to another mother, then a few minutes later to a doting sister or complaining brother, an hour later to find herself gathered up in the capacious embrace of a loudly laughing "auntie" or softly singing grandma. All the while, this baby girl is registering the complex, sometimes even cacophonous, sounds of animals, family, and friends. She is also taking in the varicolored images of shifting clouds at sunset and the pungent odor of fruiting crops in the evening. Probably she is alternately delighted by and apprehensive about the physical and emotional ups-and-downs of what must, to her, sometimes seem like riding on a perpetual wave! This infant is obviously taking in radically different lessons about time and space, sights and sounds, bodily rhythms and interpersonal relationships, action and rest, and constraint and possibility than is the baby in the first example.

The point here is not to examine in depth the cultural variation in early mother-child interaction, what the psychiatrist D.W. Winnicott (1992) has called the fascinating "romance of the nursing couple." Rather it is to suggest by a simple example how learning and culture are integrally connected from the very outset of a person's life—*and* at every level of her being, from the most minutely neurological to the most broadly spiritual. Even in this simple example, it is clear how the two baby girls are learning distinct lessons about what it means to hear, see, touch, smell and taste in the world; about how to *act upon* and *interact in* the world; about the rules and roles and prohibitions and possibilities that all combine to create an embracing context for their lives. In short, they are being *differentially acculturated.*

As the child grows, she continues to learn mostly through interactions with those who are closest—typically the mother. To take but one example, when American mothers play with children, they tend to ask questions about objects and supply information about these objects. This contrasts with Japanese mothers who tend to ask questions that are about feelings, employing feeling-related words when children misbehave: "The farmer feels bad if you did not eat everything your mom cooked for you." "The toy is crying because you threw it." "The wall says 'ouch'" (Nisbett, 2003, p. 59–61). Additionally, American mothers teach their children to adopt a "transmitter" orientation towards communication, in which the speaker is responsible for clearly communicating messages; however, Asian mothers teach their children to adopt a "receiver" orientation toward communication, in which it is the hearer's responsibility to understand what has been said. Because of this difference, Americans tend to find it difficult to "read" Asians, who assume that their point has been made with subtle finesse and that it is the hearer's responsibility to now "decode" it. Asians, on the other hand, often find Americans brutally direct, leaving so little room for the hearer's interpretation that it seems to them that the speaker is being rude, even condescending (Nisbett, 2003).

In an experiment conducted by developmental psychologists Fernald and Morikawa (in Nisbett, 2003), Japanese and American mothers were asked to present a toy to their child. The researchers observed that American mothers used twice as many object labels as Japanese mothers (i.e., "piggy," "doggy," "kitty") whereas Japanese mothers engaged in twice as many social routines teaching politeness norms (empathy and greetings, for example). The typical American mother might say: "That's a car. See the car? You like it? It's got nice wheels. Look at the engine!" The typical Japanese mother, on the other hand, might say: "Here! It's a *vroom vroom.* I give it to you. Now give it to me. Yes! Thank you." In sum, while "American children are learning that the world is mostly a place with objects, Japanese children are learning the world is mostly about relationships" (Nisbett, 2003, p. 148–150).

And all of this learning is occurring at the earliest ages and around the simplest acts. With each new circumstance and event, with each new cast of characters and complications that she experiences—some delightful and some terrifying, some boring and some intriguing, some gratifying and some frustrating, and some just routinely neutral—the child is learning more and more about what it means to be a human being in the world. With each new task that she confronts and each new tool (from a hoe to the prepositional system of her native language) that she is consciously and unconsciously learning how to employ, she comes to understand how she fits into the world and into the universe.

In more categorical terms than our poetic examples provide, Fay (2000) has identified six ways that a culture shapes an individual or group of individuals. First, culture *enables* the person or group by providing necessary resources. Second, culture *constrains* the person or group by limiting the range of the person's or group's options. Third, culture *selects* as most desirable certain types of outcomes resulting from the actions of the person or group. Fourth, culture *mediates* action by shaping the ways *in which* and the limits *to which* people or groups are allowed to affect each other. Fifth, it *prevents* the person or group from going too far with certain actions or ideas by thwarting certain kinds of change that might otherwise occur without those social constraints. And sixth, culture *determines* much about the individual's concrete and social reality simply by the fact that it gives the names and defines the purposes of *objects* and the roles of *people.*

In short, it is quite impossible to think about being human without also thinking about her being in a culture. Furthermore, the very idea of culture is so intimately interwoven with the idea of learning that it is usually difficult, if not impossible, to tell where one stops and the other starts. From the cradle to the grave, we are cultural beings engaged in acts of learning. Indeed, not only our lives but also our deaths make sense to us largely because of the terms which our cultures have provided for us. As one of the greatest sociologists of the twentieth century, Peter Berger, has written:

> every human society is, in the last resort, men banded together in the face of death. The power of religion depends, in the last resort, upon the credibility of the banners it puts in the hands of men as they stand before death, or more accurately, as they walk, inevitably, toward it. (1967, p. 52)

Culture in the Individual, the Individual in Culture

All of this is not to say, however, that *every* individual's *every* experience and thought, aspiration or value, is *merely* a product of her culture and that there is, therefore, no truth outside of cultural truth.

This view, known as *cultural relativism,* takes the cultural influence too far, in our opinion, because it allows little or no room for the operation of individual agency or the possibility of universal truths that transcend culture. Rather, we believe, along with the cultural anthropologist Levi-Strauss (1987) as well as the psychologist Carl Jung (1978), two of the most impor-

"despite the categories we may all fit into or that are assigned to us, the combination of these affiliations is what makes everyone unique" (p. 54). Again, it is important to remember that most individuals are a mix of subcultures, which means that most individuals are multicultural—some more so than others, of course, but it is a very rare person in today's world who is "purely" a "single" culture.

Borders and Boundaries

Within a culture, subcultures are delineated—that is, distinguished from each other—by cultural *boundaries* or *borders*.

A cultural boundary refers to "the presence of some kind of cultural difference" (Erickson, 2001, p. 40). The term "boundary" simply captures the fact of some variation(s) between Subculture A and Subculture B. These variations need not be problematic. Indeed, they can, if handled in a constructive and compassionate spirit of mutual edification, become the basis for all sorts of rich communication and interaction that not only spans the boundaries but may even creatively reshape them. There are, as we will see throughout this book, various ways to honor and cultivate the presence of subcultural borders in the classroom so that teachers and students will all be psychosocially and intellectually richer for the experience.

But things are different when subcultural variations—whether in a classroom or in a nation—are viewed and treated as *borders,* for borders are "a social construct that is political in origin. Across a border, power is exercised, as in the border between two nations" (Erickson, 2001, p. 40). In a border situation, subcultural differences are treated as threatening, the *status quo* is jealously guarded at all costs, interchange is discouraged, and "power is exercised" (by the more powerful subcultural group(s) to dominate the other subculture—or at least to forcefully keep it at bay. Too often, border maintenance in the classroom may lead to educational inequity by privileging some sets of students and marginalizing others in both explicit and implicit, and conscious and unconscious ways— an issue that will concern us a great deal in the following chapters.

However, all of this is not to imply that every subcultural variation is legitimate and that it is always a good thing to try to "dialogue" with it in either a microsocial setting like the classroom or in terms of macrosocial public policy. For instance, the authors of this book believe there is nothing to learn, either in the classroom or in the formulation of policy, from the tenets of the American Neo-Nazi parties. Keeping that subculture and its branches under constant surveillance and control is a good thing—indeed, a morally necessary thing—as probably most Americans would agree. This instance of a legitimate enforcement of cultural borders is relatively straightforward.

The problems arise—both in the classroom and the society at large—in knowing how to handle a certain subculture whose beliefs and practices are not so clearly egregious as those of Nazis but whose beliefs and practices *other* subcultures nevertheless interpret as socially destabilizing and even ethically wrong. When that is the case, such questions as the following begin to arise: *How much variation from more generally agreed upon cultural norms should such a subculture be given in promoting its beliefs and engaging in its practices? Should its beliefs and practices be given any latitude at all or simply be defined as "deviant," even punishable by law?*

The postmodern American landscape is rife with such *culture wars*, which get resolved (when they *do* get resolved) in a variety of ways, including: how different print and electronic media choose to portray the subculture in question; public debate, in forums ranging from the neighborhood bar to nationally televised "town hall" meetings; hiring, promotion, and firing policies (both overt and covert) in businesses; the differential influence of political action groups in favor of or opposed to the existence of that subculture; patterns of interaction and avoidance between individuals or groups of individuals; and, ultimately, in a society such as ours, by the decisions of the legislatures, the pronouncements of the courts, and the enforcement thereof by the executive branch. Looming in the background, of course, is always the possibility of police and military measures to ensure that democratically agreed-upon policies are carried out. A particularly dramatic example of the use of such draconian military measures by both sides of a culture war in U.S. history was President Eisenhower's deploying the 101st Airborne Division to Little Rock, Arkansas, in 1957 to enforce the U.S. Supreme Court's 1954 decision in *Brown v. Topeka Board of Education* to integrate the public schools. Governor Orval Faubas had been using the 153rd Infantry of the Arkansas National Guard to successfully keep African American students out of Central High School in Little Rock. Here the military force of one subculture (southern segregationism of the 1950s) was pitted against the military force of the larger culture (a federal commitment to integration). As is always the case, the more powerful cultural agenda was victorious.

In the liberal democracies that currently prevail in the major industrialized nations in the West, the goal (which derives from eighteenth-century Enlightenment political philosophy and ultimately from the Judeo-Christian emphasis on individual rights) is to promote social cohesion and maintain normative values while, at the same time, allowing the maximum liberty to subcultures that is consistent with defending society's normative values (Rawls, 1999). This is a tricky balancing act, an ongoing sociopolitical project, and one that, as we shall have occasion to note from time to time below, has manifold implications regarding what will be taught in the schools and how it will be taught.

In short, the goal of a pluralistic democracy *and its educational system* is to honor (to the maximum degree possible) the existence of boundaries, to learn from each other in doing so and thus become a richer culture, and to avoid whenever possible the exercise of power by the dominant group(s) because a subculture's existence is seen as being too destabilizing. To attain these laudable goals has been the ideal of public education in the United States for at least the last century (Cremin, 1988; Dewey, 1916).

Cultural Competence

To achieve the goal of promoting intercultural communication generally requires what we call *cultural negotiators.* A cultural negotiator is a person who can act as a facilitator to help members from different cultures or subcultures communicate positively with each other. A cultural negotiator—anyone from a young child translating for her immigrant parents, to a concerned neighbor, to a diplomat—can help the parties involved view and use their differences as boundaries across which they can move back and forth in order to interact with and even enlighten each other—not as xenophobic borders which breed suspicion and even fear. Obviously, a cultural negotiator must have a good working knowledge of the cultures involved. Multicultural students are often highly adept cultural negotiators because they have developed sophisticated cultural competency skills involving various linguistic and cognitive skills. As we will see in part two of this book, these skills can directly tie into classroom work under the guidance of a well informed administrator or teacher. Cultural negotiators are, therefore, people who have a high degree of *cultural competence* and use it to help people cross boundaries. Why is cultural competence particularly important currently?

Today's world is characterized by the daily and dizzying growth of new means of electronic communication, the explosion of transnational corporate capitalism in the new "global village," the shrinking of time and space through inexpensive and increasingly swift means of transportation, by what seems to be the almost daily tragedy of large groups of people being displaced to new geographical areas and even new nations because of political conflict and economic distress, and the unprecedented rate of the disappearance of old nations and the creation of new ones (Friedman, 2000). As Giddens has ominously noted, we live in a "runaway world" (2002). Multiculturalism is, indeed, not only *an* important issue; it is arguably *the* important issue of our time (Fay, 2000).

In such a dynamically diverse, ever-shifting set of ideological, political, financial, and social landscapes—both within and among nations—the development of cultural competence becomes an issue of paramount importance. This is true in many fields—ranging from nutrition to advertising, sports to manufacturing—but it is particularly the case in the service-oriented professions such as medicine, law, therapy, and teaching, where deep, nurturing, and effective communication between a "practitioner" and "client" are of the utmost importance—and can only occur if there is mutual respect and cultural sensitivity. For as Kohl (1995) has noted, "to agree to learn from a stranger who does not respect your integrity causes a major loss of self," resulting in what Carol Locust has aptly termed "wounding the spirit" (cited in Nieto, 2002, p. 20).

Although different fields involving human services have varying definitions and practices regarding cultural competence, they tend to emphasize the following three criteria. A practitioner should: (1) gain an awareness of her own cultural assumptions, beliefs, and biases—a process known as *cultural reflectivity*, (2) cultivate knowledge of the worldviews of culturally different others, and (3) develop appropriate strategies and techniques for promoting intercultural awareness and cooperation in others (Sue et al., 1996).

The purpose of this book is to help teachers and educational leaders develop holistic cultural competence in school settings, and we will have a great deal to say in part two about what holistic cultural competence means for a teacher. At this preliminary juncture, however, let us rely on Slowinski's (2002) criteria for cultural competence, which, developed in the context of Teaching English as a Second Language (TESOL), offers standards that all teachers would do well to attend to. Slowinski's model encourages teachers to be able to: (1) identify and understand their own culture(s), (2) effectively and positively communicate with others in culturally appropriate ways to better meet student needs, (3) understand the effects their students' first languages and cultures have on their acquisition of English (a topic that we address in depth in the following chapter), and (4) create positive multicultural environments for learning and understanding (p. 6–7).

Moreover, in being a cultural negotiator—whether it is at a social gathering, on the block where we live, in the classroom, in the halls of justice, or even in a world forum—it is good to keep in mind the social theorist Brian Fay's (2000) "Principle of Charity" and "Principle of Humanity" regarding intercultural relations. According to the Principle of Charity we should "count others like us unless there is clear reason not to." We should be neither fooled nor distracted by surface differences so that we cannot see our common humanity and the archetypal similarity of most of our shared hopes and fears, loves and antipathies. We are, after all, all humans. The Principle of Humanity enjoins us to "count others intelligible in their own terms unless there is clear reason not to." Where there *are* substantial differences between one's own culture and another's, it is the most humane course to assume that those differences make sense and even promote health within that other culture in ways that are valid for members of that other culture even though they may be obscure to us.

But note the phrase: "unless there is clear reason not to." A recent example of this important caveat that has been brought to the attention of the world is the brutal and dangerous practice of "female circumcision," which is really nothing other than genital mutilation of young girls for reasons that are grossly sexist and gruesomely damaging. In the case of such cruelty, there is "clear reason" not to honor this practice as culturally valid or morally permissible. Indeed, there seems to be "clear reason" to call for its immediate prohibition in international political forums and through international political means. *There are limits to cultural tolerance.*

One final note is that cultural competence should never be viewed as something that one either has or that one does not have. We are constantly growing in competence and as a result must continually focus on what we can learn from the current situation and from those around us. As one example of how one matures in cultural awareness, Milton Bennett (1993) has developed six ethnocentric stages that people normally go through in viewing cultural differences.

Bennett's (1993) first stage is "Denial." In this stage, people avoid interacting with others and disbelieve that there are any real cultural differences. Even if people go to another location and culture, they do not realize that they are still seeing things through the same cultural lenses that they had back home. They think everyone sees with their cultural lenses. Indeed, it never really occurs to them that there *are* different lenses. The second stage is "Defensiveness and Denigration." In this stage, the tendency is to see the world as "us and them" with the assumption being that "we are superior." In this stage, the person engages in broad negative stereotyping based on categories such as race, cultural group, age, and so on. The third stage is "Minimization." In this stage people treat cultural differences as if they do not matter. The problem with this stage is that it too conveniently allows people to hold fast to their ethnocentric beliefs and not deal with cultural differences, covering those differences over with the naïve belief that "everyone is really the same." Cultural differences are comfortably ignored. A characteristic of this stage is *transcendent universalism*—the idea that "We are all God's children" and that cultural differences therefore do not really matter. Although the authors of this book firmly believe that we are all God's children, we assert that the problem with this form of transcendent universalism is that it does not face some important differences among those children—differences which, if left unaddressed, can result in some of those "children" continuing to be unfairly advantaged and others of those "children" to be unfairly disadvantaged.

In passing through the first three stages, individuals can shake off a good deal of their ethnocentrism. In the next three stages, people can then move more vigorously toward greater intercultural sensitivity. Bennett's (1993) fourth stage is "Acceptance." Individuals in this stage accept and respect cultural differences in a wider variety of contexts. They see the world and its cultural variety in more nuanced terms, and they understand more about how to navigate through these varieties in a way that is sensitive to others and healthy for themselves. In the fourth stage, people begin to use and show diverse verbal and nonverbal communication styles and different customs, tones, and nonverbal gestures. The fifth stage, "Adaptation," typically takes from five to seven years of immersion in a new (sub)culture. People in this stage are not assimilating to the new culture, but they *are* developing new skill sets, knowledge, and empathy as they move more adroitly from their own "frame of reference" to that of others. Bennett says that in this stage, "culture is understood as a process and not an object. One does not have a culture. One engages in it." In the last stage, "Integration," some people have been exposed to so much change or cultural differences that they must go through a process to create a new identity! They may feel lost and confused about their identity and how to behave because they no longer identify with any one culture (Bennett 1993). They are able, however, to use and integrate a variety of worldviews. Successfully integrating all of the healthy cultural perspectives and practices that they have embraced, such people can develop a new identity that is psychologically rich, morally wise, and socially efficacious.

Bennett's stages are just one way to look at the process of developing cultural competence, but they are quite useful in highlighting the need for us to be cautious of feeling that "we have arrived" at some impossible ideal called "perfect intercultural competence." They help us see that developing cultural sensitivity is an ongoing process for everyone—a lifelong process.

THE TEACHER AS A CULTURAL NEGOTIATOR

Culture and Education

We believe that one of the major roles for a teacher in today's classroom is to be a cultural negotiator who can help students explore their own and each other's cultures in a variety of ways that will enliven discussion and enrich the curriculum. It is vital that teachers see that teaching is, by its very nature, a profoundly cultural act. There is no such thing as "culture-free" teaching or learning. Not only is education central to most societies; cultural norms are central to how teaching and learning are practiced and what is seen as appropriate material for students to learn. Culture and education are inextricably related—so much so, in fact, that, in a sense, they "define" each other. As Pai and Adler (2001) observe:

> the processes of teaching and learning are influenced by the core values, beliefs, and attitudes, as well as the predominant cognitive and communication styles and linguistic patterns, of a culture. Further, the educative process, whether formal or informal, is equally affected by the socioeconomic status of the learner, peer pressures, the nature of the relationship between dominant and minority groups, and the impact of technology on the society. Regardless of how education is defined, from a cultural perspective it can be viewed as the deliberate means by which each society attempts to transmit and perpetuate its notion of the good life, which is derived from the society's fundamental beliefs concerning the nature of the world, knowledge, and values. These beliefs vary from society to society and culture to culture. (p. 4)

An excellent example of this is Heath's (1983) seminal study of the psychosocial development of three groups of children from birth to elementary school in an Appalachian community: lower-SES (socioeconomic) African American children, lower-SES Caucasian children, and middle-SES children from both Caucasian and African American families. She concluded that, even before they first walked through the doors of a school to begin their formal education, each group of children had already learned very different things about the nature and value of printed words, rules of conversation, patterns of self-assertion and obedience, storytelling conventions, and, of course, how to speak English. What Heath discovered was that both the black and white middle-class children were primed for academic success whereas the lower-class children, black and white, were not. We will look at Heath's important study again later in this book. For now, it must suffice to make the simple point that since classrooms are embedded in a society whose norms they reflect, students from cultures other than the dominant one(s) may be more or less primed for academic success, depending upon the degree of "cultural continuity" between their culture and that of the school (Erickson & Mohatt, 1982; Gee, Michaels, & O'Connor, 1992; Hewitt, 1984; Woods, 1992).

"Individuals have predisposed notions of how to respond to questions, solve problems, and so forth" (Solano-Flores & Nelson-Barber, 2001, p. 38). Barbara Spronk (2004) asserts that a culture's view of education:

> involves beliefs and values, ways of seeing the world, and ways of knowing, thinking, doing, and relating to the cosmos and to society. These beliefs, values, and practices are learned from infancy onward, and are . . . . very much bound up in the process of defining one's identity, or better, identities . . . (Spronk, 2004, p. 171)

Gauvain (1995) has identified three ways in which a society impresses upon the developing child what teaching and learning "mean": (1) Any teaching and learning situation rests upon a foundation—sometimes only implied, sometimes made explicitly clear—about what kinds of goals and activities a culture values; (2) the culture provides the teacher and learner with tools and materials to meet the goals and support those values; and (3) there exist "high-level cultural structures" (e.g., scripts, routines, and rituals) that are considered appropriate and useful to implement the goals and values in socially harmonious and reinforcing ways. These three subsystems, Gauvain asserts, both assist and constrain the cognitive development of the child, show her what it means to teach and learn, and channel her thinking in ways appropriate to and supportive of her culture.

Gauvain (2001) has also shown how culture-specific messages shape the developing child as she: (1) learns "*problem solving skills*" (strategies to use and the knowledge base to develop in order to recognize and approach and negotiate a problem); (2) develops "*memory*" (which entails absorbing cultural values in the form of memories of "exemplary situations" and learning specific strategies for remembering); and (3) learns the rules for "*planning*" (learning how to coordinate one's own actions in order to reach goals as well as the rules for how to coordinate one's plans with those of others). Where there is cultural congruity between a teacher's and student's worldview in these respects, there is a much greater chance that the child will succeed in her schooling than there is for a child whose worldview is less congruous, and even might conflict, with that of the teacher.

In other words, a child who has learned to define certain things as problems that are consistent with what a teacher considers to be a legitimate problem, who has a knowledge base and memory that "fits" her teacher's, and who coordinates her own and others' activities in ways that the teacher approves, will usually be much more successful in the classroom than a child who comes from a culture that has different definitions of what constitutes a problem and how to go about solving it. It is not that the child from the dominant normative culture is brighter necessarily. It is simply that her cultural worldview is more consistent with the worldview of the teacher and school than is the cultural worldview of the child from the minority culture.

Another kind of "cultural congruity" between teacher and student—a "fit" between a teacher and student from the same minority group in a basically majority-culture school—has often happened to one of the authors of this book, Fidel Montero, whose Latino cultural background often prompts immigrant Latino/a students to feel an instant sense of connection with him. Also, without knowing him personally at the beginning of a school year at his mostly white school, many Polynesian students approach Fidel when they learn that his wife is Polynesian.

Of course, teachers—many of whom come from the dominant culture and all of whom are more or less required to teach a state-mandated core curriculum—must attend to the normative values of the society in which the school is embedded. There are institutional, district, state, and federal requirements—all of which embody cultural norms—that teachers simply cannot ignore. Nor should they ignore them. For, it would be disempowering for minority students if the teacher did *not* teach students the dominant bodies of knowledge and the official "languages of success" that will ultimately allow these children to have increasingly vibrant and influential voices in the ongoing cultural conversations about how we all choose to define ourselves as a society (Ravtich, 2000). Along with Macias (1987) in his study of Papago children on the reservation in Tucson, Arizona, we feel that for a pedagogy to be both politically realistic and culturally responsive, it must: (1) teach the "official curriculum" that constitutes the "language of power," (2) do so in a way that is as consistent as possible with the students' culture, and (3) also include the students' culture (in both what is taught and how it is taught) to the maximum degree possible, and in a way that will encourage students to politically and ethically analyze and even critique the dominant culture.

In other words, we believe that education can be richer—and students from minority cultures can learn the language and perspectives of the dominant culture most effectively and positively—if the teacher, the school and the society at large include in substantial and meaningful ways the cultures of other students in the classroom. What does "substantial and meaningful" mean? Perhaps the best way to answer that question is to say what it does *not* mean. It does not mean the "Tee Pee and Fry Bread Approach" to a minority culture, in which the culture is seen as a mere curiosity that the class will study for fifteen minutes every Friday at the end of the day—once all the "important" material has been covered. It also does not mean simply a "Heroes and Holidays Approach," in which a culture is examined only in terms of some of its major heroes (i.e., Martin Luther King) and special days (i.e., "MLK Day" in January). Such an approach to multiculturalism arguably does more harm than good in the last analysis because—even with the best of intentions on the part of a well-meaning teacher—it perpetuates the assumption that minority groups are "odd" (even if interesting) and "marginal" ("We will study 'those *other* people once we cover all the 'important' material—as a sort of colorful 'addition' to the *real* curriculum").

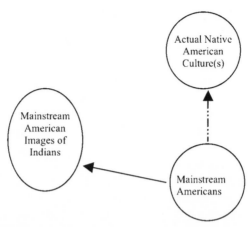

Figure 1.1. Interaction Between Mainstream Americans and Images of Indians as a Cause of Misidentification

In her study of the Kumeyaay people, a Native American tribe, Kampf (2005) depicted the traditional interaction through these types of approaches between the mainstream Americans and this minority group (figure 1).

In other words, the mainstream American image of the American Indians, reinforced by "Tee Pee and Fry Bread Approach" in schools, results in misidentification due to the fact that perceptions of the other culture are so far removed from its reality. "The habitual way of thinking, that may be stereotyped or otherwise distorted/biased, are more prone to cause problems in intercultural encounters than perspectives which have been questioned and critically reflected" (Lindh et al., 2003).

Kampf (2005) argues that we need to find more ways to facilitate rhetoric as a dialectic process, helping to reduce rhetorical distance by fostering a stronger connection to each group's own *evolving identity* and promoting *an increasingly accurate understanding of another culture*. The second figure (figure 2) represents the dialectic process by which awareness of one's own perceptions and more accurate identification with other cultures comes about.

Reducing the distance between our own and our students' perceptions of others and the reality of others while in the classroom settings can help include the cultures of other students in a "substantial and meaningful way."

A multiculturally sensitive teacher endeavors whenever possible in her classroom to: (1) encourage study and discussion of various cultural perspectives on an issue, (2) honor culturally specific ways that different groups of her students have in engaging in activities or performing tasks in the classroom, and (3) teaches the dominant culture's norms while leaving room for critique of those norms. Holistic multicultural education can accomplish

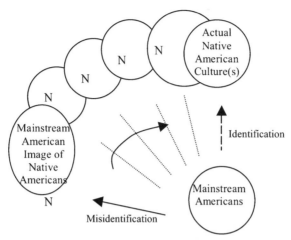

Figure 1.2. **Reducing Distance by Moving from Misidentification to Identification**

these goals, enriching students', teachers', and administrators' school experiences and their lives in general. Indeed, it can create a win-win situation in which students, teachers, and administrators engage in the rewarding experience of being cultural negotiators. The practical benefits of such a situation is that teachers and administrators will now be able to spend more time and effort on academics, less time dealing with unproductive and unnecessary cultural conflicts in the classroom, and students will find what they learn in the classroom to be more pertinent to their lives.

We will now turn in the following chapter to an examination of the crucial role that language plays in the creation of cultures, the process of cultural negotiation, and the multicultural dynamics of the classroom. Following that, we will move on in part two to detailed explorations of the exciting dimensions of holistic multicultural education—the sensorimotor, psychosocial, cognitive, and ethicospiritual.

2

Language and Education

One of the primary tools in the formation, operation, and transformation of a culture is its language.[1] Because of the central role of language in thought and action, it is extremely helpful for teachers to understand the emotional and cognitive processes experienced by their students who are learning to communicate and operate in a second language.

If students feel ridiculed or even simply marginalized during the intellectually, socially, and emotionally challenging process of acquiring a second language, they will likely suffer psychological damage in the form of lowered self-esteem, confused identity, and enmity towards the dominant culture and language. On the other hand, if teachers are more sensitive to honoring and even celebrating both the native language and the second-language-acquisition processes of various students, the environment of emotional support will be as beneficial to the minority-culture student as the exposure to and positive experience with other languages will be to the native English speakers.

In most classroom settings, language is the primary vehicle of teaching—teacher talk—and of demonstrating knowledge—student talk. Teacher and student talk is often conversational as well as instructional, permeating and shaping the entire "culture" of the classroom. Because it is such a dominant component of classroom life, language must be carefully examined in any analysis of how teachers teach and students learn, but this is especially crucial when multicultural students, whose native language may not be English, are involved. It is

---

1. Edith A. McGee, a doctoral candidate in the Department of Educational Leadership and Foundations and the principal of Butler Elementary School in Cottonwood Heights, Utah, was instrumental in writing this chapter.

even an important issue for multicultural students when English *is* their native language but not the language that their parents primarily speak at home.

Teachers can therefore benefit greatly from knowing about the history and theory of language policies and practices in the classroom. This will enable them to act as informed professionals making enlightened decisions about second-language acquisition in their classrooms regardless of the stormy political winds that always seem to be blowing around this topic. This does not mean that teachers will ignore whatever language policies in the schools happen to be current at a certain time (and they are historically quite changeable) but, rather, that they will know how to negotiate those policies within the four walls of their own classrooms in ways that are most humane and beneficial for their students.

LANGUAGE, THOUGHT, AND CULTURE

So essential is language to the existence of a culture that the linguist Edward Sapir (1929, p. 207) claimed that the way one sees the world depends upon the language one speaks. "Human beings," he said, "do not live in the objective world alone, nor alone in the world of social activity as ordinarily understood, but are very much at the mercy of the particular language which has become the medium of expression for their society."

Along with the anthropologist Benjamin Lee Whorf, Sapir would later formulate what has come to be known as the *Sapir-Whorf Hypothesis*, which is the assertion that we can experience our world *only* in the way that the structure of our language allows—a position called *linguistic determinism* because it makes all human cognition dependent upon the words, grammatical structures, verb-based processes, and semantic categorizations that a language allows. The Sapir-Whorf Hypothesis asserts "that language is not simply a way of voicing ideas, but is the very thing which shapes those ideas. One cannot think outside the confines of their language. The result of this process is many different world views by speakers of different languages" (Amy Stafford, 10/29/06: http://www.mnsu.edu/emuseum/cultural/language/whorf.html).

A corollary of the idea of linguistic determinism is *linguistic relativity*. According to the doctrine of linguistic relativity, a person who speaks Language A will see and interpret the world in roughly the same way as a person who speaks Language B to the extent that Language A and Language B are more or less the same. However, to the extent that Language A differs from Language B, then person A will correspondingly experience the world differently from person B. For instance, if Language A provides six terms for shades of blue while Language B provides only three terms, then according to the Sapir-Whorf Hypothesis, person A will actually be able to perceive more shades of blue than person B can. Similarly, if a language has only two verbal tenses, such as Hopi, which has a "manifested" tense and "becoming manifested" tense, then a speaker of the Hopi language will experience the phenomenon of time quite differently from someone whose native language is English, which divides time into past, present, and future—along with the progressive and perfect forms of each of those tenses.

Does this mean that a native-English speaker will experience time differently than a native Hopi speaker does? According to the Sapir-Whorf Hypothesis, the answer to that question is a resounding "Yes!" Carroll (1956) has offered one of the clearest formulations of the Sapir-Whorf Hypothesis: "We dissect nature along lines laid down by our native language," wrote Carroll, going on to assert that "we cut up nature, organize it into concepts, and ascribe significances as we do, largely because we are parties to an agreement to organize it this way—an agreement that holds throughout our speech community and is codified in the patterns of language" (p. 212–214). What are we to make of this extreme statement of linguistic relativity?

It is undoubtedly true that one's language figures prominently into how one perceives the world. We owe Sapir and Whorf a great deal in highlighting this fact and offering us specific examples from various cultures and languages of how this process occurs. However, most linguists and anthropologists today would probably agree that linguistic relativity goes too far in proclaiming that we are imprisoned by our language, that we can see the world only in such-and-such a way that our language allows—and in no other. If this were so, it would, by definition, be impossible for people from Language/Culture A to ever be able to communicate in any significant ways with people from Language/Culture B if their languages were radically different. If the Sapir-Whorf Hypothesis were strictly true, then the fact of linguistic differences would trump the fact of our common humanity—an emotionally counterintuitive and politically dangerous assumption.

The question arises, too, how a person who speaks Language A could ever even *learn* another Language B, especially one that was radically different from the speaker's native Language A, since speaker A's Worldview A would be so completely and insurmountably determined by his native language that he would have few or no points of reference that would allow him to "bootstrap" himself out of Worldview A into the completely foreign perspectives of Worldview B. In fact, however, all sorts of people seem to be able to learn to speak all sorts of languages that bear very few similarities to their native languages.

There is undoubtedly merit in the Sapir-Whorf Hypothesis about the importance of language in perception, emotion, and cognition. However, a weaker form of the hypothesis is necessary, and that is precisely what many anthropologists and linguists now put forward. The reconstructed Sapir-Whorf hypothesis—one which is supported by a considerable body of research (Bloom, 1981)—concludes that *language and culture are inseparable and that they influence each other.* Thus, the "strong" Sapir-Whorf Hypothesis—that a given language makes some forms of thinking obligatory or impossible—has yielded to a more intuitively agreeable, "weaker" version—namely, that *a given language makes certain ways of thinking easier or more difficult* (Weiten, 1998).

An interesting example of this is the difference between person-oriented and status-oriented styles of discourse (Ting-Toomey, 1999, p. 106–107). Person-oriented, or *informal,* communication reflects a democratic, egalitarian worldview that deemphasizes the differences in individuals' status and prescribed roles. In this mode, informal verbal expressions are used without complex codes of behavior or ritualized language. Further, each individual's uniqueness rather than social or professional status is recognized. For this reason, communication often occurs on a first-name basis. This informality characterizes the communication styles of both African American and Anglo American groups (Grossman, 1995).

Unlike the informal style, the formal, or status-oriented, style such as one finds in many Asian languages uses verbal and nonverbal expressions that are prescribed as appropriate for honoring individuals' status and roles (Shade, 1989, p. 207). This means that, although both native American English speakers and native Japanese speakers can be formal or informal in their discourse, American English speakers will tend to be less formal, reflecting the egalitarian worldview and social organization that prevails in their culture; Japanese speakers, on the other hand, will tend to be more formal, reflecting a more hierarchical worldview. For example, the English verb "to give" must be rendered by two different words in Japanese, depending upon whether the speaker is describing a situation in which one is giving something "up" to a social superior or "down" to a social inferior.

Another way of approaching the crucial issue of the intimate interaction of thought and language is to try to formulate a thought without talking to yourself, either silently or audibly. Our guess is that you can't do it! Why can a person not think unless he is also consciously or unconsciously talking to himself?

The reason is that *thought is internalized speech*—or, at least, that *a fully formed thought cannot take place in the absence of such internalized speech.* We do not *have* a thought—at least not a "complete" one—until we are able to *say* that thought. But *saying* a thought implies saying it to *someone.* Often, that *someone* is an actual person with whom we are engaging in an actual conversation. Yet often enough, that *someone* is *not* in the external world but is rather an internalized "audience" whom we are "addressing," an internal "other" to whom we are "presenting" our formulations.

George Meade called this "person" the *Generalized "Other"* and pointed out that thinking, as an internal conversation, is, by definition, a type of social process because it rests upon the dynamics of conversation (see also Berger & Luckmann, 1967). And what is true of thinking is (by this view) also true of feeling, for "we only fully experience an emotion when we name it" (Hewitt, 1984, p. 68). This is undoubtedly why so many poets say that they do not really know how they feel about something until they have written a poem *about* those feelings, and why so many composition teachers continue to insist to their students each term that "You can't really know what you think about a subject until you've expressed your thoughts in a cogent essay!" Hewitt has put the point well: "Men must talk about themselves until they know themselves" (Hewitt, 1984, p. 39).

"As a child moves through childhood," Hewitt further observes, regarding the role of language in the growth of the child's understanding of himself and his world,

> he or she learns not only his or her own name, gender, and relationship to others but also the names of objects recognized by the group to which the child belongs. The child learns the names of tools, ideas, places, buildings, activities, plants, vehicles and myriad other objects that constitute the surrounding culture. (p. 83)

Furthermore, the child learns not only one language in common with his overarching macrosocial group (i.e., American English) but also the language of other groups to which he belongs and into which he is being acculturated linguistically (i.e., upper-SES, East-Coast American English; Southwest U.S. "Spanglish"; inner-city Midwest Black English; Appalachian rural English; and so on).

The assumption that *language enables thought* underlies a theory of cognition known as *social constructivism,* which, in its strongest forms, is another instance of the "nurture" side of the "nature/nurture" controversy. It asserts that since thought is internalized dialogue and, further, since dialogue is a social act, then all of our thought is fundamentally social in nature—a function of the forms of the language that our culture provides us as our birthright. According to social constructivism, *language enables thought.* The research of the Soviet psychologist Vygotsky (1986) provided the foundations of social constructivism, which gained considerable popularity in academic circles in the United States in the late 1970s and early 1980s (Wertsch, 1985) and continues to be quite influential (Rogoff, 2003).

On the other side of this question is the strict *cognitive constructivist* argument about language (Mayes, 1998). It is the "nature" side of the debate—the assertion that certain innate cognitive, emotional, and ethical structures must mature in the psyche first, *before* an individual can then express his growing awareness in his language(s). By this view, which was more popular in the 1950s and 1960s than it is today, *thought enables language* (Chomsky, 1968; Piaget & Inhelder, 1969).

Language, Thought, and Culture—Nature AND Nurture

Here again—this time in psycholinguistic form—is the nature/nurture conundrum that we have already confronted: "Does language enable thought, or does thought enable language?"

Again our position is that the answer lies somewhere in the middle. *Thought and language depend upon each other* in such subtle and manifold ways that the most we can assert with any real certainty is that thought cannot exist without language, nor can language exist without thought. We will probably never know the exact nature of the interaction between thought and language. We may never be able to solve, once and for all, the conundrum of whether language determines thought, thought determines language, or—as is most probably the case—thought and language are so interwoven that it is impossible to tell where one leaves off and the other starts. But this much is certain: *thought and language are inseparable in the individual's psyche; and language and culture are indispensable to the person's sense of identity.*

Strip a person of his culture and its language, or even ridicule or simply marginalize them, and you will probably do considerable psychosocial damage to his ability to develop cognitively, establish a healthy sense of self-worth, and maintain an appropriate pride in his culture's integrity. Conversely, if you honor a person's language and culture, you stand a good chance of being able to: (1) help him develop cognitively, (2) nurture in him a robust sense of self-worth, (3) foster in him an appropriately positive view of his own culture, and (4) provide him with reason for taking a generous view of your culture, too (Lee, 1997).

The best teachers will generally try to be sensitive to the fact that their students' cognitive, emotional, and spiritual identity, potential, and growth are inseparable from those students' native cultures and languages.

THE ACQUISITION OF ENGLISH AS A SECOND LANGUAGE

We have looked at the centrality of cultural-linguistic issues in education as a general principle. These issues are even more visible, dramatic, and pressing in examining the issue of the increasing number of Limited English Proficient (LEP) students in the contemporary American classroom—somewhere in the neighborhood of 3.5 million students and growing daily (Anyon, 2001). Some estimates predict that by 2040 one out of every three residents in the United States will be an immigrant or a child of immigrants (Nieto, 2002, p. 80). In some states this situation is particularly pronounced—California, for instance, having an ethnic minority between 40 and 50 percent, with over 50 percent of its school population consisting of ethnic minorities (Ovando, 2001). Clearly, no outline of the cultural foundations of education in twenty-first-century American education—especially public school education—should omit a discussion of the learning of English as a second language.

Contrastive Analysis

An important concept in second-language pedagogy is that of *contrastive analysis* (Rivers, 1978). According to the principle of contrastive analysis, a speaker of Language A will have the most difficulty in learning Language B at those points where the two languages differ—the degree of difficulty corresponding to the degree of difference.

For instance, in Spanish syntax, the order of words in simple declarative sentences tends to adhere to the following pattern: Subject (which can in some instances be implied and therefore omitted in actual speech) + Object + Verb. In English, the syntax is slightly different: Subject (which is never omitted except in special colloquial contexts or in the use of the imperative) + Verb + Object. English, being a Germanic language in its structural origins, is often syntactically much closer to German than to Spanish, which is a Romance language (i.e., Latin—"Roman"—in origin). Hence, a German declarative statement also follows the English Subject-Verb-Object pattern. Now, take the simple English statement: "He knows me." By the principle of contrastive analysis, it should be easier—everything else being equal—for a native English speaker to learn to render this statement in German ("Er kennt mich") than to render it in Spanish ("El me conoce") because the word order in German in the same as in English whereas the Spanish word order is not.

The principle of contrastive analysis is useful at other levels of a language as well—not only at the syntactic level of word order in a sentence. For instance, at the phonological level—that is, the pronunciation system in a language—it is generally harder for a native English-speaker to pronounce the Spanish "d"-sound, which is rendered in phonetic script as [ð], than to pronounce the "d"-sound in both English and German, which is rendered as [d] in both cases. The difference in the phonological symbols used indicates that the Spanish "d" is produced by very lightly placing the tip of the tongue behind the two front teeth and making a vibrating sound. The English and

German "d," however, are very similar in that they are more "explosive" sounds, produced by the speaker heavily laying a large portion of the tongue on the ridge behind the front teeth and then making a "plosive" sound when lifting the tongue. Thus, it is usually easier for a native English-speaker to pronounce the "d"-sound correctly in the German word for "your"—"dein"—than it is for him to pronounce the "d"-sounds correctly in the Spanish word for "adequate"—"adecuado."

Bear in mind that the above examples involve three very closely interrelated Indo-European Languages—English, German, and Spanish. As the principle of contrastive analysis correctly predicts, the difficulties for a native Language A speaker in learning Language B increase proportionally as the disparities between Language A and Language B increase.

A native speaker of Thai, for instance, which is a Sino-Tibetan language, will have greater inherent linguistic obstacles in learning English, which is an Indo-European language, than will a native speaker of Spanish, for Spanish is also an Indo-European language with many syntactic structures and phonological elements that parallel those in English. Thus, in teaching students whose native language is not English, it is important for the teacher to keep in mind that the "proximity" of the student's native language to English is an important factor in how quickly or slowly that student learns the new language.

Of course, the degree of difficulty that a student who speaks Language A encounters in learning Language B is not *merely* a function of the amount of difference between the two languages. There are other factors that will also come to bear in determining how easy or hard it is for Speaker A to learn Language B. We will look at those factors below. For now, we will mention only some of the most obvious of those factors, which include: the ability of the teacher, the emotional support that Student A feels from others in the classroom environment and surrounding society, the native language-learning ability of Student A, his emotional readiness to learn another language, his previous exposure to other languages, his socioeconomic status, and the quality of education he received in his native culture.

Despite the varying degrees of similarity and difference between and among languages, it is important to avoid the error of proclaiming one language or one form of a language as being "superior" to other languages or language forms. As Pai and Adler (2001) have noted,

> notwithstanding the tremendous differences in speech forms, phonetic patterns, and dialect variations in ancient and modern languages, the findings of anthropological linguistics reveal that, in general, all languages seem to do their job. That is, all languages are capable of expressing thoughts and feelings that the society considers appropriate. Hence, no language or language group should be

regarded as inherently superior to any other. But this does not imply that all languages are equally functional; some may be better equipped to express logical and analytical thoughts, whereas others might be better suited to communicating more global or aesthetic thoughts and feelings. (p. 9)

Different languages, in short, have different strengths. For instance, we looked above at egalitarian and hierarchical conversational styles—each of which suits its unique social purposes quite well.

Another difference—also related to conversational styles—is the one between what is called "direct," or low-context communication, and "indirect," or high-context communication. "Direct" communication refers to the mode in which the speaker expresses his thoughts and intentions directly in explicit verbal messages. This style, often known as "straight talk" is sender-oriented in that the speaker is responsible for delivering clear, accurate, and convincing messages. On the other hand, in "indirect," or high-context, communication the speaker uses indirect verbal and nonverbal expressions to convey his messages. Here, the receiver is responsible for accurately interpreting the hidden meanings of the verbal messages. "Reading between the lines" is often required in this process (Pai & Adler, 2001, p. 206). Americans, with their focus on individual assertion and immediate action, tend to favor direct speech, while the Japanese, with their prizing of group harmony and the avoiding of giving offense, tend to favor indirect speech. Which is better? Neither! Or rather, one is better than another depending upon the context in which it is being used. We will examine this issue in considerable depth later in the book.

For now, it is enough if you have grasped the main points that: (1) languages are generally quite similar in that they all serve their purposes, (2) many of those purposes are the same across cultures, and that (3) languages are also different in important ways that imply different strengths and weaknesses depending upon the contexts in which they are used. These are important points for the contemporary American teacher to keep in mind as he deals with and honors the linguistic traditions of the various students who make up his classroom in the increasingly diverse American school.

Second-Language Acquisition: Facts and Models

Although linguists who study second-language (L2) acquisition have greatly expanded our base of knowledge over the last sixty years about how someone learns another language, there is still a great deal that we do not know (Chomsky, 1968; Cummins, 1995; Halliday, 1975; Krashen, 2003; Lado & Fries, 1958). What we do know for certain is that "the processes of [L2] learning and acquisition are enormously complex" (Hinkel, 2005, p. 413); that L2 learning is not something that can be rushed too much since it is a "protracted affair, taking much longer than is commonly assumed" (van Lier, 2005, p. 202); and that "the study of second language acquisition impacts on and draws from many other areas of study, [including] psychology, psycholinguistics, sociology, sociolinguistics, discourse analysis, conversational analysis, and education, to name a few" (Gass & Selinker, 1994, p. 1).

Not all teachers will necessarily be directly involved in teaching English as a second language to their students, but it is a rare teacher indeed who will not in the course of his career have students—and possibly *many* students— who are involved in the cognitively, emotionally, socially, and even spiritually challenging process of acquiring English as a second language. This makes it incumbent on every teacher to know at least the fundamental theories and facts about second-language acquisition.

Stages of L2 Acquisition

L2 acquisition seems to take place in some fairly predictable stages. According to some researchers, those stages are marked by the student's ability to produce spoken utterances and are as follows: Silent/pre-production; early production; speech emergence stage; intermediate language proficiency stage; advanced language proficiency stage (e.g., Ernst-Slavit, Moore, & Maloney, 2002; Haynes, 2005). Another way of measuring the growth of a student's ability with a second language is in terms of the order in which he grasps the structures of the language. Krashen (1981), one of the leading researchers in the L2 field, notes that "grammatical structures are acquired (not learned) in a predictable order. Certain structures tend to 'come' early, others later" (p. 51).

Note Krashen's insistence on the use of the term *acquisition,* not *learning,* in describing the L2 mastery process. This is because of the many cognitive, psychological, and social differences between *learning* a native language and *acquiring* a second one. Clearly, there are similarities between L1 and L2 mastery but there are differences as well regarding such things as: (1) the interpersonal settings in which they occur, (2) the types of positive and negative reinforcements that a person experiences in the two processes, (3) the motivations that come into play in the two processes, (4) the deep emotional dynamics involved, (5) the socioeconomic stakes of one's success or lack of success in the mastery process, (6) the uses to which one will put the mastered language, and so on.

Interlanguage

As a person acquires a second language, he will speak and write different "versions" of the language as he advances from Stage A (at the beginning) to

Stages X, Y, and Z (as he attains high levels of proficiency that increasingly resemble the way native speakers speak L2). These "versions" are called *interlanguages.* An L2-interlanguage is not the same thing as the L2 itself, of course—although as the student becomes increasingly proficient in L2, his interlanguage comes more and more to resemble the native use of L2.

However, it would not be accurate to dismiss interlanguages as merely "incorrect" versions of L2. For, what second-language-acquisition researchers and teachers have found is that interlanguages tend to have their own internally consistent systems of pronunciation, vocabulary, and grammar, which the speakers of those interlanguages robustly employ with each other. Interlanguages are "composed of numerous elements [in which] the learners themselves impose structure on the available linguistic data and formulate an internalized system" (Gass & Selinker, 1994, p. 11) For, although students who are roughly at Stage E, say, of learning English do not speak English in a fully fluent way yet, they are nevertheless speaking a rule-governed "language"—a version of English that is "on the road" to becoming the L2. As such, speakers of L2/Stage E, will often be able to communicate among themselves quite robustly in ways that their L2 teacher may not be able to totally understand.

Another aspect of interlanguage development is that of speakers who consciously choose to maintain their interlanguage rather than move on to a higher level of English proficiency. Such a choice may sometimes result from the sense of identity associated with the interlanguage that they and their peers speak. Often, when acquiring another language, young people find themselves in the precarious situation of straddling two languages and cultures without finding full acceptance in either.

For example, an immigrant youth from Mexico living in the United States may not be fully accepted anymore by his Mexican culture as his Spanish and customs become more and more "Americanized." Yet, the same youth may now find as well that he is not fully accepted by the U.S. culture because his English is not completely fluent, because he has not adopted all of the U.S. customs, and because, after all, there still are certain prejudices that continue to exist against minorities among some Americans. Thus, just as his language is considered an interlanguage—one suspended between his L1 and L2—so his identity and culture can be considered a type of interculture, or *mestizo* culture. A *mestizo* culture is formed when a person, positioned between two or more opposing cultures, is left to work out an identity drawn from those cultures, none of which fully embraces or includes him. The development of such an identity and interlanguage often requires courage and creativity and should be acknowledged and treated sensitively by administrators and teachers.

One of the authors of this book, Clifford Mayes, was often surprised and amused in his fifteen years as an EFL (English as a foreign language) teacher in the United States, Asia, and Central America to hear a group of students, who were at about the same level of English proficiency, speaking to each other quite passionately about a topic of mutual interest and even sharing jokes in their shared interlanguage version of English while he could only catch the highlights of what they were talking about—and sometimes not even that! It would have been frustrating to both him and his students if he had viewed their use of English as simply "wrong" and a problem to be strictly addressed in order to "correct" their "mistakes."

A much more accurate, satisfying, and humane view of that situation was that these students were speaking an evolving form of English—one that is systematic; functional, to a degree, in its own way; and evidence of the student's progress in and ongoing commitment to learning English. By taking this more generous view of their interlanguages, he was able to be of much greater benefit to his students in their linguistic development than if he had simply seen their current use of English as a "problem."

A teacher can develop even more patience, even delight, regarding his student's dynamic evolution as an L2 speaker by honoring the fact that his student is engaged in a profoundly complex task—one that typically involves the daunting challenge of mastering four interrelated but still different language skills: reading, writing, listening, and speaking (Ellis, 2005). This entails a set of related challenges regarding *phonology* (the sounds of the language, how it is pronounced), *syntax* (word order in sentences, what grammatical elements must go where), *morphology* (how elements of words can be combined, such as adding an "-(e)s" in the third-person singular present tense of a verb, or adding "un-" to signify the negative of an adjective); *lexicon* (the actual vocabulary of a language), *semantics* (the different meanings, and the often extremely subtle shades of meaning, both in words, phrases, and sentences); and *pragmatics* (the contextual uses of language, what kinds of statements are appropriate in what situations and what are not, body language that tends to be employed by L2 speakers in various situations, and so on (Gass & Selinker, 1994).

With all of this in mind, we as teachers often have many causes to celebrate the victories, both small and great, that our LEP (limited English proficiency) students make in our classrooms every day as they acquire English as a second language. This is true whether we are actually teaching English as a second language in the classroom or are simply using insights from that field to help LEP students learn and interact better in English. Such an attitude about and approach to LEP students allows us to find greater satisfaction in our work and, what is more, transforms us into ever more loving and (therefore) more effective facilitators for our LEP students in their linguistic, academic, and social development.

Three Important Researchers in L2 Acquisition

Three of the most important researchers in L2 acquisition today are Stephen Krashen (2003), Jim Cummins (1997), and Virginia Collier (1995).

Krashen's Five Hypotheses about L2 Acquisition

Stephen Krashen's five hypotheses about how a second language is acquired have been highly influential in the training of ESL teachers for decades.

Krashen's first hypothesis, which we have already encountered, is the *Acquisition-Learning Distinction*. He claims that language acquisition is a subconscious process. Those acquiring the language are usually unaware that they are actually acquiring a language; rather, they are simply aware that they are using the second language for communication. He uses the term "learning" to identify the conscious knowledge of the language. Included in learning are knowing grammatical rules and being able to talk about them.

The second hypothesis, which we have also touched upon above, is the *Natural Order Hypothesis*. Simply stated, this "hypothesis claims that grammatical structures are acquired (not learned) in a predictable order. Certain structures tend to 'come' early, others later" (Krashen, 1981, p. 51).

Krashen's third hypothesis is the *Monitor Hypothesis*. This is perhaps the best known of Krashen's hypotheses. It adds more information about the acquisition-learning distinction discussed above by positing that in most cases:

> acquisition "initiates" our utterances in a second language and is responsible for our fluency. Learning has only one function, and that is as a *monitor* or *editor*. Learning comes into play only to make changes in the form of our utterance, after it has been "produced" by the acquired system. (Krashen, 1982, p. 15)

The "monitor" can become a problem if a student is so overly concerned about the "correctness" of every utterance that he ties himself up in knots of self-vigilance! It is important for a teacher to bear in mind that, although the goal is for the student to become near-natively fluent, this will happen most smoothly and quickly if the teacher does not "overcorrect" the student to such an extent that the student begins to overcorrect himself. Learning a language requires taking risks and making mistakes—sometimes rather embarrassing ones—in a variety of speech situations and social contexts. If a student is always monitoring himself perfectionistically, he will not take those risks and thus will become fluent, if at all, in a much slower and more painful way than if he did take risks. Ironically, in L2 learning, the desire to speak perfectly can be the greatest obstacle to progress.

Krashen maintains that his fourth hypothesis, *the Input Hypothesis,* is the most important of all five because it answers the question how language is acquired. How does an individual move from understanding something in L2 at level X to understanding something at the next level of competence in the L2, Level X+1? The answer is that he must be able to comprehend *most* of the input that is contained in utterance X. The rest of the utterance—that is, the new, +1 part of the utterance—can be understood and then learned by the language learner by his piecing together various kinds of clues that reveal the +1 meaning.

In other words, if the learner understands *most* of what is being said in an utterance—if the *input* is *comprehensible*—then he can generally draw fairly accurate inferences about the part of the utterance that he does *not* understand from the context provided by what he *does* understand. Says Krashen, "we use more than our linguistic competence to help us understand. We also use context, our knowledge of the world, our extra-linguistic information to help us understand language directed at us" (p. 21).

Everyone who has ever learned a second language has experienced this. You may not understand a certain word in a sentence that someone speaks to you; however, because you understand the other items in the sentence and also because of the speaker's tone or gestures or expression, you are able to piece together what the unknown word means. The implication for L2 teaching is that it is best to present the learner with new texts and utterances that are *just above* (that is, +1) his present level of development. If he is presented with something that is more than that, he may easily become frustrated or discouraged. However, if he is presented with a +1 challenge, he not only *can* learn but will generally be excited about learning because it is a challenge that he can successfully meet.

The *Affective Filter Hypothesis* is Krashen's final hypothesis. This hypothesis explains how emotional factors such as motivation, self-confidence, and anxiety affect the process of SLA (second language acquisition). We will take up this key point in chapter three, in which we deal with the psychodynamic factors that influence learning. At this point, let it suffice to say that if the teacher, classmates, the school as an institution, and the society at large help and take a positive view of students who are attempting to learn English as a second language, those students—sensing that nurturance—will learn English more quickly and joyfully than if they are meeting with suspicion, criticism, and fear. Learning a second language in a new culture is a highly emotional thing, and it requires emotional support. As teachers, we need to be in the front line of offering that support and helping the community understand why it should support our LEP students, too.

Cummins' Basic Interpersonal Communication Skills, Cognitive Academic Language Proficiency Skills, and Common Underlying Proficiency

According to Cummins, there are three aspects of L2 proficiency.

First is conversational fluency. Cummins uses the phrase *Basic Interpersonal Communication Skills* (*BICS*) to describe this phenomenon. It takes approximately one to two years for a student to develop BICS.

Second is discrete language skills. These "reflect specific phonological, literacy, and grammatical knowledge that students acquire as a result of direct instruction and both formal and informal practice (e.g., reading)" (p. 65). Discrete skills develop early, at the same time that BICS are developing.

Third is *Cognitive Academic Language Proficiency Skills* (*CALPS*), which refers to the form of L2 that a student must master in order to succeed in the classroom. While BICS are acquired within one to two years, CALPS require anywhere from four to seven years to develop. Van Lier explains the differences between BICS and CALPS:

> when English language learners reach a stage in their schooling (from fourth grade upward) when cognitive and academic language skills become of paramount importance, they hit a wall of complexity [that is, the CALPS level] that their basic conversational skills cannot penetrate, and at that point they fall further and further behind . . . unless specific steps are taken to develop their academic-linguistic competence. (2005, p. 202)

This distinction is crucial. The classroom teacher needs to understand that just because a student may be able to converse energetically in the cafeteria, on the playground, or during a school outing, this does not necessarily mean that the student has mastered the forms and levels of English that are necessary for academic success. The language of the classroom is a specialized discourse—one that requires a good deal longer for a nonnative English-speaking student to master than the language of everyday social interaction.

A final component of Cummins (1994) theory is the *Transfer Hypothesis*. According to this idea, "prior knowledge and skills in the home language transfer to the new language" (Ovando, 2001, p. 272). This is so, Cummins argues, because if a student learns how to perform a task in his native L1, he can transfer those skills to solving a similar task in his new L2. A student who has learned to set up, carry out, and then report on a chemistry experiment in Spanish will be able to use that same set of conceptual skills to perform another experiment using English. His chemistry experiments in Spanish and English rely on a *Common Underlying Proficiency* (*CUP*) (Cummins, 1994, p. 164).

The point here—and one that is crucial in the argument for bilingual education—is that what is learned in a student's L1 is not lost in the process of the student learning an L2. Quite to the contrary, a student learns an L2 all the more quickly and correctly if his L2 instruction builds upon—and does not neglect or negate—his L1 experiences, proficiencies, and psychosocial attachments. This argument is eminently sensible in the light of findings in cognitive psychology that students learn new concepts and skills by building upon ones that they have already mastered (Chi, Feltovich, & Glaser, 1983; Driver, Asoko, Leach, Mortimer, & Scott, 1994; Posner, Strike, Hewson, & Gertzog, 1982; Vosniadou, 1991).

Conversely, depriving a student of his L1 so that he will be "forced" to "learn" an L2 is not only emotionally traumatic and culturally insulting, it is simply bad pedagogy for it does not use the student's L1 as a basis upon which to most efficiently and humanely build his ability to perform well in the L2 as well. How long and to what extent the student's L1 should be used in his education in an L2 culture is a question of considerable debate. What is not in question, however, is the fact that, to the extent a student's L1 is honored, preserved, and used as a ongoing tool in his education, his L2 development will be all the more rapid, complete and satisfying.

Collier's L1-Maintenance/L2-Development Pedagogy

Collier's (1995) work is in many respects a synthesis and extension of Krashen's and Cummins' work.

Like Krashen, Collier believes that there is an "affective filter," which is a combination of social and emotional factors, that is central to how, and how well, a student will learn. If a student feels emotionally and socially validated by his teacher, classmates, and institution, he is much more likely to be successful in his academic performance and general social involvement in the school. These psychosocial factors "may include individual student variables such as self-esteem or anxiety or other affective factors" (Collier, 1995, p. 2). If a student feels emotional warmth and cultural respect from his teacher and peers, he has a much better chance of succeeding in the classroom than if he does not.

Like Cummins, Collier feels that what a student learns in his L1 will transfer into his L2—not only with no loss but with considerable gain since: (1) the student is learning to be competent in two different languages and (2) the skills that the student possesses in his L1 can enrich his performance in his L2 in various ways, just as the skills he learns in the course of his mastery of his L2 can enrich his understanding of and performance in his L1. It is common, for instance, for someone to say, "I never really understood the gram-

mar of my own language until I learned the grammar of a foreign language!"
This is an example of L2 proficiency heightening L1 sensitivity and enhancing L1 use in a native L1 speaker.

Collier points out that as a student's grade level increases, so, of course, do
the "vocabulary, sociolinguistic, and discourse dimensions of language"
which that student is compelled to confront (p. 3). Collier is here alluding to
Cummins' BICS/CALPS dichotomy. The problem, she goes on to point out,
is that the rapidly increasing cognitive and linguistic demands on a student as
he moves from grade to grade may be faster than his L2 development. When
that happens—and it very often does, even for the best of L2 learners—then
the nonnative English-speaking student, despite his most valiant efforts, will
fall behind the other students in his academic development, which will, in
turn, have a depressing effect on his L2 acquisition.

Thus, Collier argues for what are called "maintenance bilingual education
programs"—so called because they *maintain* the student's L1 and continue to
provide much, if not most and sometimes even all, of his classroom instruction in the L1, while helping him with his L2 development at other times in
the school day. It is essential that we provide nonnative English-speaking students with such programs, Collier claims, because if a student is trying to
learn English at the same time as he is learning academic content in English,
he must inevitably fall behind his peers, which will begin a downward spiral
of decreasing academic success that will end catastrophically in general academic failure.

Some might ask why such special provisions are needed for LEP students in
our schools. "My great-grandfather came to this country and learned English
while going to school and he was successful! Why do immigrant students need
such special accommodations?" To this question, the answer is threefold.

First, that person's grandfather arrived in the United States at a time when
a high-school education or less was still probably enough to allow him to be
relatively successful in American society—something that is clearly not the
case today. Second, grandpa did not have to reckon with the massive bodies
of information, rapidly expanding number of academic disciplines, subtle
technological skills, and new global economic conditions and imperatives
that today's youth must confront. And third, that person needs to consider
how much better grandpa *would have learned* English if he had, in fact, had
access to such innovative bilingual education programs—and how much
richer his life might have been, professionally, intellectually, and emotionally,
if he could have benefited from such things. Collier writes:

[W]e have found that the most significant student background variable is the
amount of formal schooling students have received in their first language. . . .

[F]rom fourth grade on through middle school and high school, where the
academic and cognitive demands of the curriculum increase rapidly with each
succeeding year, students with little or no academic and cognitive development
in their first language do less and less well as they move into the upper grades.
. . . But the difference in student performance in a bilingual program, in contrast
to an all-English program, is that students typically score at or above grade level
in their first language in all subject areas, while they are building academic development of a second language. . . . Because they have not fallen behind in cognitive and academic growth during the 4–7 years that it takes to build academic
proficiency in the second language, *bilingually schooled students typically sustain this level of academic achievement and outperform monolingually schooled
students in the upper grades.* (Collier, cited in Ovando, p. 273, emphasis added)

Collier's most important contribution to the research in second-language
acquisition is in drawing attention to just how imperative it is that the LEP
student's linguistic and cognitive development be addressed equally so that
the student can rise to his full potential not only as an English speaker but, indeed, as an intelligent, informed, and creative contributing member of the society at large. Whatever the costs involved in bilingual education, the authors
of this book believe that the costs will be paid back to society with great dividends by having an increasing number of such competent and richly diverse
people in our society. Conversely, whatever the money "saved" by not providing such education will be consumed many times over, in both the near
and distant future, by the social costs to society of more and more undereed-
cated students whose potential will remain untapped and whose disappoint-
ment at an educational system that did not fully cultivate that potential will,
sadly, be all too understandable.

Maintenance Bilingual Education

The case for maintenance bilingual education is a strong one. Indeed, as Nieto (2002, pp. 90ff) points out, many, if not most, of the people in the world
are at least somewhat bilingual. In Switzerland, for instance, there are four
official languages of the nation, German, French, Italian, and Romansh. In
Canada, 10 percent of married couples are mixed-lingual. And in the United
States, about thirty-two million people (over 10 percent of the population)
speak another language at home: seventeen million speaking Spanish, two
million French, and combined one million speaking German, Italian, and
Chinese.

We need to take an "additive" view of bilingualism in society and the
schools, not a "subtractive" one. According to the additive view, bilingualism,
involving no loss of L1 while developing mastery of L2, generates many ben-

efits, including: (1) higher cognitive development for the student, (2) greater and more varied linguistic resources within the school and society, and (3) increased cultural interaction and understanding, leading to the mutual enrichment of the cultures involved.

In a world characterized by ever more sophisticated electronic technologies, more rapid and inexpensive forms of travel, and increasing migrations of various peoples for political and economic reasons across national borders that are becoming more and more "porous," it is easy to see how a multilingual society would—with English still as the dominant language, of course—be much better prepared to meet such challenges and reap many possible economic and cultural benefits than a society stuck in a xenophobic, "English-only" mentality that refuses to recognize or come to productive terms with the increasingly multicultural makeup of most of the industrially advanced nations around the world. The deficit perspective, or social pathology model of viewing minority groups contributes to the perpetuation of institutional racism and robs our society of richness. At the personal level, minority individuals are made to be ashamed of their ethnicity and cultural heritage.

Lambert has demonstrated how people who are bilinguals have various cognitive advantages over monolinguals, including: (1) more expertise in their own L1, (2) better selective attention to subtle aspects of language, (3) more awareness of the arbitrariness of names of items, (4) more sensitivity to nonverbal elements of communication, (5) better ability at following complicated instructions, and (6) enhanced performance on tests of creativity, concept formation, and spatial ability (cited in Grossman, 1995). One disadvantage that Lambert noted was that bilinguals are sometimes slightly slower than monolinguals in language processing speed—an important thing for teachers to keep in mind with administering timed tests to bilingual students, who may need a bit more time to complete the task. In general, however, research on bilingualism has shown it to represent an enormous "academic plus" if the bilingual program is a good and sustained one (Nieto, 2002).

If Not a Maintenance Bilingual Education Program, Then What?

With the 1968 Title VII Bilingual Education Act and the U.S. Supreme Court's *Lau v. Nichols* decision in 1974, it has been the law of the land that schools must find ways to address the needs of LEP students so that those students may progress toward having equal access to the nation's educational resources. What we have just discussed is Maintenance Bilingual Education (MBE). However, some schools, districts, or states may feel that they lack the money to institute MBE, or they may simply not wish to set up full-fledged

MBE programs in their schools for various reasons, ranging from the strictly pedagogical to the heatedly political.

Other alternatives that schools have chosen to try to address the needs of LEP students include Transitional Bilingual Education (TBE), Sheltered Immersion (SI), and English as a Second Language (ESL).

TBE is similar to MBE. It differs in two important ways, however. First, it is for a limited period of time in the student's public-school career—generally from two to four years. This is a problem particularly for older students—particularly from the middle-school years on—from other countries, for whom two to four years is not enough time to develop Cognitive Academic Language Proficiency Skills (CALPS). It is less of a problem for K–4 students, however, since it is at about fourth grade that an LEP student's English proficiency begins to be inadequate for him to perform to the best of his ability in the classroom.

Second, the focus on TBE is not on the preservation of the student's L1 but rather on moving the child out of his L1 into exclusive use of L2. This often sends the message to the child that his L1 is a "problem" that needs to be "fixed" as quickly as possible—an attitude that often increases the operation of the student's "Affective Filter" and "Monitor" so that he learns the L2 more slowly, and often less joyfully since the process is implicitly (and sometimes explicitly) riddled with negative messages about his L1.

SI keeps the LEP child in the English-only classroom but gives him special help in the form of such things as peer-tutoring, introducing vocabulary that he will need to complete an assignment before the assignment is given, the possible occasional use of his L1 in a very limited way in the classroom in conversations between him and the teacher if the teacher speaks the L1, and an interpreter (usually a volunteer or paraprofessional) who sits with the child and helps him participate in what is going on in the classroom (Ashbaker & Morgan, 2006).

The most common—and probably the least effective—way of trying to help LEP students is ESL. Here, a child is "pulled out" of a class or classes during the day to receive English instruction. Although better than nothing, there are two major problems with this approach. First, the child is being taken out of regular classes for a certain amount of time each day. Naturally, he falls behind regarding the material he has missed and becomes a less involved member of the "culture of the classroom" because he is regularly compelled to be separate from (and some would argue "segregated" from) it. Second, various studies suggest that the English that LEP students tend to get in ESL classes is lower order, conversational English—BICS—which, although important, does not significantly advance the child cognitively or academically (Collier, 1995; Nieto, 2002; Ovando, 2001; Pai & Adler, 2001).

Of course, most teachers are not bilingual education teachers. However, in our opinion, it is important in both the personal and professional development of teachers to develop the kinds of skills and dispositions that we have discussed in order to be of maximum service to their LEP students in the increasingly diverse American classroom. This includes: (1) having at least a basic familiarity with the nature of L2 acquisition (such as this chapter has provided), (2) learning about at least the highlights of the history of immigration and immigration policy in the United States, including specific groups, (3) developing the ability to adapt curriculum to LEP students' needs, (4) trying to relate personally to students and teachers of other backgrounds, and (5) being willing to try to communicate with parents of diverse backgrounds and socioeconomic statuses (Nieto, 2002, p. 208).

In this chapter, we have looked at some of the most fundamental research, theories, models and practices regarding second-language acquisition. The purpose has been to introduce the reader to this important and complex issue in many classrooms today.

We began by examining the inextricable links that exist between language, thought and culture. We then moved on to an examination of the pedagogical implications of this interrelationship. We argued that honoring a student's native culture and language to the maximum degree feasible increases the likelihood that he will learn the new culture and its language(s) quickly and with a positive, constructive attitude.

We also discussed the dynamics of L2 acquisition, discussing such ideas as contrastive analysis, the stages of L2 acquisition, and the phenomenon of "interlanguage."

The theories of some of the major researchers in the field of second-language acquisition and bilingualism were also introduced. We looked at Krashen's five statements about L2 acquisition: the *Acquisition-Learning Distinction,* the *Natural Order Hypothesis,* the *Monitor Hypothesis,* the *Input Hypothesis,* and the *Affective Filter Hypothesis.*

Also presented was Cummins' important distinction between Basic Interpersonal Communication Skills (BICS) and Cognitive Academic Language Proficiency Skills (CALPS) as well as his idea of the possibility of the transfer of skills between L1 and L2 because of a Common Underlying Proficiency (CUP). Collier's research into an L1-Maintenance/L2-Development Pedagogy was examined because it is essential to understanding the argument for bilingual education. We concluded by looking at the differences between Maintenance Bilingual Education, Transitional Bilingual Education, Sheltered Immersion, and ESL.

Now, armed with knowledge about the cultural foundations of education as presented in chapter one and the importance of language in the formation of culture and the life of the classroom as presented in chapter two, the reader is well prepared to move on to part two, in which we look in depth at the four specific domains of holistic multicultural education: the sensorimotor, psychosocial, cognitive, and ethicospiritual.

II

THE FOUR DOMAINS OF MULTICULTURAL EDUCATION

3

The Sensorimotor Domain

As we move into the first holistic domain, the sensorimotor domain, we begin by introducing a theme that will play out in many ways throughout this book. Good multicultural pedagogy, by addressing the perspectives and predispositions of diverse groups of students, is also simply good pedagogy because it holistically addresses each individual student in many dimensions of her being. At the sensorimotor level, different cultural groups tend to favor different senses in how they process information, act with others, and create "products" that demonstrate their learning. By creating curricula and teaching in ways that appeal to all the senses, therefore, the teacher is also responding to the special strengths of various groups of students.

We should make it clear at the outset, however, that *we do not believe that different racial and ethnic groups are born with substantially different sensory or cognitive capacities*. For instance, we do not believe that because one is born to Native American parents, one is genetically *programmed* to favor, say, visual learning styles. This is the kind of empirically shaky argument that is made in what we consider to be the politically and ethically dangerous claims of such researchers as Herrnstein and Murray (1994), who have claimed African American children tend to score lower on intelligence tests because they are, in fact, born with brains that are slightly inferior cognitively. Such "scientistic" racism (which abounded in theories of Aryan superiority, for instance, in Nazi Germany) can have very grave educational and political consequences (Richards, 2006).

Still, it is also clear that one's culture *does* affect how one perceives, conceptualizes, talks about, and acts upon the world—and this effect can (to some as yet undetermined extent) have physiological consequences on the child after it is born, which the emerging field of sociobiology is beginning to study (Dennen, 1999). The authors of this book assume that at the organic level all "normal" brains function roughly in the same way (within a broad range of individual differences, of course).

But as the brain matures, it develops *mental schemata* (or *conceptual maps*) that, at the physiological level, exist in the form of neurological pathways that are more and more deeply "etched" upon the brain with each similar, successive experience that the person's unique environment is providing her with. In this manner, data provided by the environment (including the sociocultural context) will, over time, probably change the neurological dynamics of the brain to some extent (Valsiner & van der Veer, 2000). Thus, although all "normally functioning" brains operate more or less the same at birth, neural pathways are likely forged thereafter in ways that are shaped by the environment—and this includes the sociocultural environment—and this is one of the reasons that children from certain groups may be disposed to favor certain ways of seeing, being, and doing. Again we see the extremely close interaction of nature and nurture.

At any rate, whatever the type and degree of interaction is found to exist between physiology and culture, it has been established by decades of research into culture and cognition that different groups of children *tend* to favor different physical senses in the educational process. We stress the word "tend" to make it clear that we do not believe that just because one is a member of a certain cultural group, one will inevitably favor the teaching and learning style of that group—merely that there is a tendency, taking the group as a whole, to favor that style.

TEACHING, LEARNING AND THE FIVE SENSES

Teaching in a way that both caters to and builds upon different senses is quite different from what happens in the typical public school classroom today. For in the standard classroom, 90 percent of all instruction is conducted through either lecture or lecture-discussion, although only 20 percent to 30 percent of school-age youngsters are primarily auditory learners, as Dunn, Dunn, & Price (1977) found almost three decades ago and as still seems to be the case today (Sardello & Sanders, 1999).

Complicating this dilemma is the ongoing cry among certain policymakers for more math, science, and English, at the expense of elective courses that target that other 70 percent of our students. Electives such as band, dance, theater, drafting, woods, metals, and so forth are suffering due to the escalating demands for more and more credits in the core content areas for graduation. This standard auditory-centered instruction, drawing upon only one sense, plays to the strengths of only certain groups of students at the expense of other groups and the other senses.

In other words, 90 percent of what happens in the classroom is focused upon the inborn inclinations and abilities of only about one-fourth of the students. Of the other three-quarters of the students in a classroom, approximately 40 percent are primarily visual learners, and the remaining 30 to 40 percent are either tactile/kinesthetic, visual/tactile, or some combination of these four senses. It is hardly surprising, then, that many students do not learn as well as they could, even acting out in various ways because of their boredom and frustration, for their primary sensory modes of learning are being marginalized or even excluded in the daily operations of the classroom (Holland, 1986, p. 173).

Why is hearing favored over the other senses in most classes—and why is this increasingly the case as a student proceeds into higher grades? The answer is because in the traditional classroom, especially in the upper grades, most of the activity revolves around a teacher who *talks*. Students are compelled to *listen*, usually quite passively or with occasional information-based questions, and then are further compelled to demonstrate how *well* they listened by showing the teacher on a test that they have not only *heard* but obediently *memorized* what she said. In other words, 90 percent of what happens in a classroom is auditory because students are generally forced to be a passive *aud*-ience ("hearers") for most of the day—a role that even the 20 to 30 percent of students who favor hearing probably find difficult to take as a one-course diet!

The holistic pedagogies of researchers like Schutz (1976) in his tellingly entitled essay "Education and the Body," Hendricks and Fadiman (1976) in their vision of a "Curriculum for Feeling and Being," Gardner (1999) in his insistence that education be sensitive to "The Seven Intelligences," and Sardello and Sanders (1999) in their concern for the "Care of the Senses: A Neglected Dimension of Education" represent attempts to bring the other senses into play and into balance in the classroom. When teaching and learning honor all aspects of the individual as a sensory being, they are simultaneously honoring various cultures' differential sensory preferences. In this way, both the individual student and groups of students will find that their strengths are sometimes emphasized (leading to a healthy sense of inclusion and empowerment) and that the areas in which they need development are emphasized at other times (leading to interesting challenges that cause one to grow in new and unexpected ways).

Native American Students and the Importance of Nonverbal Communication

According to Kaulback (1989) in his study of Native American childrearing practices and their educational consequences, Native American children learn things by being included in adult activities, observing what is going on in those adult settings, patiently practicing the skills and behaviors that they have observed before trying them out themselves in public, and getting feedback on their performance in many nonverbal ways from their adult mentors.

> Native children learn by observing and imitating the actions of their parents, elders and older siblings. Basically, in most Native societies, the child is a revered member of the family unit and, as such, is a welcomed spectator and participant to all types of family and community affairs. Indeed, it is not uncommon to see young Native children accompanying their parents (or siblings) to bingos, community meetings, church, or even to their places of employment. This constant and close proximity to the actions of others provides the child with a valuable opportunity to intimately familiarize himself with a multitude of tasks. (in Shade, 1989, p. 143)

In "learning how to learn," therefore, the Native American child discovers early on that much of the most important instruction and information that she will receive from her parents and other elders will be communicated nonverbally—through eye contact, body language, and even silence as a sign of approval or disapproval of the child's performance on a certain task. This is not to say that verbal instruction never occurs in Native American childrearing practices; however, nonverbal instruction is more common (More, 1989), which is not surprising given the fact that "the child's close proximity to the observable action makes instruction-giving quite redundant" (Kaulback, 1989, p. 144).

Furthermore, Native American children are generally not tested or questioned afterwards to see if they have mastered a task because, being treated like adults from early on, they are expected to self-test as an adult would (More, 1989, p. 159). The high degree of freedom that a Native American child typically receives from her parents, who include her as a valuable and responsible member of the family and community, is admirably nurturing to and respectful of the child. It fosters in the child a profound sense of responsibility to her family, a healthy measure of self-reliance, and a rich sense of the subtle dynamics of nonverbal communication.

However, in a classroom where the teacher's lessons and the student's demonstration of mastery take place in almost exclusively verbal ways, the Native American student may justifiably feel herself to be at a distinct disadvantage if her preferred nonverbal, observational, and performance-oriented ways of learning and demonstrating mastery are not also included and honored. In a typical public school classroom, therefore, a Native American student may run into both internal and external obstacles to learning because, based on her learning experiences growing up, she entered formal schooling "expecting freedom of movement, but discovered restrictive movement; where visual spatial kinesthetic learning was the mode, the verbal dimension is stressed; where direct experience had been the route for learning, now most experience is indirect, and so on" (Pepper, 1989, p. 37).

This does not mean that Native American students should not have to learn how to perform more effectively in verbal ways (as indeed all children should), for this is a skill that is essential to almost anyone's academic and professional success in contemporary American society. It does mean, however, that if the Native American's preferred mode of teaching and learning is honored at various times in the shared culture of the classroom, then not only will she benefit from it in many ways—some obvious, some not so obvious—but all other students will benefit as well in learning about the importance of self-initiative, subtle communication, and responsible performance. As is generally the case with holistic multicultural pedagogies, therefore, we see here a win-win situation in which a certain group's preferred educational modes are honored, that group's less preferred modes are developed, and everyone benefits from learning multiple ways of seeing, being, and doing both in and out of the classroom.

Another result of research (Kaulback, 1989) into Native American teaching and learning styles is that there seems to be great importance placed upon the sense of sight. This focus upon the visual should not be surprising in a culture where there is a premium placed on *observing* how elders do things and then *observing* the elders' body language and facial gestures regarding one's performance. "[N]ative children are able to efficiently and effectively process and retain information presented through visual formats" (Kaulback, 1989, p. 141).

Thus, many Native American students may often feel especially at home with classroom activities involving charts, graphs, and posters both in computer and paper form; paintings, sculpture and other visual and plastic arts; both watching and producing video and DVD presentations; and the use of dance and other physical forms of expression to demonstrate mastery. One of the authors of this book once had a Native American student who chose to do his final project as a sculpture instead of a final paper. The sculpture, of a Greek athlete, evidenced a profound understanding of the aesthetic, historical, and philosophical ideas about Greece that had been discussed in class throughout the term.

African American Students: A Classroom with "Verve"

Barbara Shade, one of the most prominent researchers of preferred learning styles among African American students, has written widely about what she calls "the kinesthetic preference" of many African American K–12 students (Shade, 1989). As she and other educational anthropologists have noted over the years, African American childrearing practices tend to be more physically dynamic than those in many white families. This dynamism is characterized by "spontaneity and ability for improvisation and rhythmic orientation which is shown in body movements, music, art forms, verbal, and nonverbal communication patterns, and other artistic expressions" (p. 26).

In *Ways with Words,* Shirley Brice Heath (1983) provided richly detailed and loving portraits of these highly energetic environments. Following a group of lower SES African American children from birth to their first years of schooling, she found that these children grew up in a kaleidoscopic world of vibrantly bright colors; the seemingly perpetual motion of constant activity—activities flowing out of the houses, into the community "square," and back again into the houses—in crisscrossing circuits of communication that linked everyone in the neighborhood in a vibrating web of communal action; and ongoing conversations overflowing with improvised poetry, singing, chanting, and the playful posing of mock challenges and exaggerated protestations of love. "'Rappin', 'stylin' out,' and 'shuckin' and jivin' are . . . calculated to please the hearer. What is said is not as important as the way it is said" (Cooper, 1989, p. 117).

Studies such as Heath's have led various scholars to the conclusion that African Americans tend to "differ from other groups in their preferences for a toleration of a high noise level and need for vividness and multiplicity of stimuli which Boykin refers to as 'verve'" (Boykin, in Shade, 1989, p. 19). The taste for "verve" among many African Americans in their discourse and interactions can probably be traced back to an African communicative pattern known as "Call-and-Response" which is a "participatory-interactive" mode of conversation and story-telling (Gay, 2000).

In "Call-and-Response," the speaker begins the conversational process by making some sort of assertion—often a rather bold one. This is the issuing of the "call." The listener shows that the call is meaningful to her and that she wishes to attend to it and engage the speaker in verbal intercourse by issuing a "response." Whereas in a good deal of standard white conversational interaction, the listener shows that she is polite by quietly listening until the speaker indicates that she has finished speaking, in "Call-and-Response" discourse the situation is quite the opposite. Here the listener shows politeness by immediately, sometimes even simultaneously, responding with statements that match the exuberance of the speaker and which may overlap the utterances of the first speaker.

Nor is the listener's response merely verbal. It is often accompanied by some kind of physical motion by the listener—from rhythmically moving the head to clapping to dancing—that signals a deepening involvement of the listener with the speaker and, in turn, may evoke similar physical responses in the speaker. Here we see the African roots of "the kinesthetic preference" of many African Americans in the physically lively protocols of interpersonal communication.

According to Boykin, important educational implications flow from all of this. African American children, he insists, tend to do best in classrooms where they are presented with information that is presented "at a constantly changing pace [because such students] seem to have little tolerance for monotonous or low-level activity. European American children, on the other hand, seem to be able to tolerate a more low-keyed and less varied type of activity" (Shade, 1989, p. 104). We have already seen how the auditory bias of many classrooms—favoring students who are more inclined to passively receive verbal information from a teacher—can be a problem for some Native American students because of their desire to observe and act. In the case of African American students, the auditory bias may be problematic not because there is too much verbal input from the teacher but, in a sense, because there is too little of it—or, at least, too little that is imagistically and physically exciting and (literally!) "moving" for either the teacher or the student.

Along with Hamlet in one of his most bored moments, certain African American students might well complain that the classroom is filled only with "words, words, words" that fail to inspire either emotional or physical stirrings in them. Indeed, in his study of the words that African Americans tend to employ in conversing with one another, Kochman (1972) found that there was a "preponderance of words which possess the quality of rapid and unrestricted movement or have the potential for such movement." On the other hand, "words which suggest static or impeded movement have unfavorable connotations" (cited in Shade, 1989, p. 100). Again, there are probably African roots discernible here. "Africans find a language 'wearisome' that does not tell a story," and this can be a conversational dilemma in discourse between an African and a European because the "European is empiric, the African . . . mystic and metaphysical. . . . African words are pregnant with images" (Cooper, 1989, p. 123). "Concrete imagery . . . drawn from everyday life" is what invests so much of African and African American discourse with its galvanizing beauty.

Of course, not everything that happens in a classroom can be so aesthetically and spiritually rich in kinesthetic "verve." But a classroom in which the discussions and activities never rise to such a passionate level will be tedious and alienating—and not only for African American students. Everyone needs spice in their inner and outer lives, and teachers and students are certainly no exceptions. Few things are more boring than a bland teacher delivering a bland lecture about bland facts. Honoring the kinesthetic learning preferences of African American students by authentically including kinesthetically based talk and tasks can help teacher and students become passionately engaged with any curriculum, from physics to physical education.

In one of the authors' classes, for instance, a student presented her evaluation of a chapter in a history text by "rapping" her understanding of the major points in the chapter. The student was white. Her "rap"—although definitely not destined to win any awards among real rappers—was nevertheless greeted by boisterous enthusiasm, good-natured kidding, and wild applause by the black and white students alike throughout the student's performance. It pays rich dividends for a teacher to deepen and enrich her teaching with "the pedagogy of verve."

THE EXPERIENCE OF TIME IN THE CLASSROOM

Another aspect of the teacher's and students' physical experience of life in the classroom has to do with time; for, how we perceive our physical surroundings, move within them, and act upon them is inextricably tied into the rhythms and schedules that prevail in them.

It might seem self-evident that time is a simple phenomenon. It might also seem that time in the classroom is a neutral, impersonal medium that everyone is experiencing and moving through in just the same way—like fish in the same pond. But time is a much more complex phenomenon than that.

The idea that time is a simple linear "entity" that moves in a straight line and can be divided into equal parts that can be mechanically measured is a relatively new idea historically. This so-called "objective" understanding and experiencing time is by no means universal; for, how time is understood, experienced, and used varies greatly across cultures, among individuals in the same culture, and within the same individual in different circumstances.

To understand more clearly how the current Western scientific notion of time is not the only important one, it is necessary to look briefly into the history of this view of time. We will see that this view is neither ancient nor universal. After that, we will discuss the educational consequences of this mechanical, linear view of time in the classroom which, as important as it undoubtedly is, too often prohibits other ways of experiencing time in the classroom—and thus can do psychosocial harm to both teachers and students for whom other ways of experiencing and enacting "passage" can be personally and culturally significant.

A Brief History of (Business-Oriented) Time

Most historians of Western conceptions of time agree that three interrelated events were especially important in the growth of the modern obsession with mathematical, impersonal time: (1) the emergence of capitalism in the fourteenth century, (2) the growth of towns, and (3) the invention of the mechanical clock (Aguessy, 1977; Boorstin, 1985; Whitrow, 1988). The rise of guilds signaled the emergence of early capitalism in Europe (Marx & Engels, 1978). Soon villages, growing larger and more complex in their economic organization, evolved into towns, some of which would eventually become the great industrial centers of Europe (Gurevich, 1976). But it was undoubtedly the modern clock—invented in this very early industrial context—that, more than any other single invention, symbolized and advanced this sea change in Western European culture (Whitrow, 1988).

The clock's effects were immediate and dramatic. It measured (and in measuring, radically changed) the *lived* experience of "passage." The clock became a teacher—and sometimes a hard taskmaster, making all people experience things in the same cadence and often for purposes that were defined by those in the upper echelons of society. "For generations, the town clock was the one complicated machine that hundreds of thousands saw every day, heard over and over again every day and night. It taught them that invisible, inaudible, seamless time was composed of quanta. Like money, it taught them quantification" (Crosby, 1997, p. 85).

The personally, poetically, and socially rich rhythms of existence that governed simple agrarian life were close to nature. It was not the sweeping minute and hour hands of the clock or watch against which things were measured. Rather, it was such events as the fruiting and decay of crops that were the major signposts of significant passage; the periods of the body in its cycles and maturation; the archetypal events that defined family life such as birth, baptism, marriage, and the death of the elders—all of which typically occurred in full view of all the members of the family; and cultural and mythic "times" in which ordinary daily events and tasks were seen in the context of sacred events, rituals, and feasts that lifted the individual, the family, and the culture into a sense of an eternal time beyond time. Life—individual, familial, cultural, spiritual—was lived in the complex counterpoint of all of these "passages" and purposes. *These kinds of time that defined most people's experience of time anciently continue to underlie many people's lives today in the nonindustrialized world.*

In the industrializing West of the clock and capitalism, however, these forms of time have been squelched—almost to the point of extinction—by mechanical time, which proclaims itself as not only the only type of time that *matters* but the only type of time that truly *exists* (Foucault, 1980). This largely happened because industry and the modern state in general increasingly came to rely upon

> more precise and standardized measurements of bodies and surfaces, space. Merchants needed to be able to cover the distance between trading centers more quickly. Entrepreneurs were anxious to produce as much as possible within a given time and to increase the length of working hours; small craftsmen and workmen were interested in seeing that the hours of work were precisely measured. (Gurevich, 1976, p. 240–241)

Little surprise, then, that from its advent in the early 1300s until the seventeenth century, no technology spread as fast as the clock (Nowotny, 1989).

The clock was inaugurating not only a new political and economic order but a cosmological one, and it would find full expression in the Enlightenment notion that *the universe is itself a clock* (Crosby, 1997)—a view of the universe that runs quite counter to that of many other cultures in the world, especially indigenous First World cultures, which see the universe as a living being, Mother Earth, whose organic rhythms must be respected, not made to conform to mathematical time. There is a world of difference in one's experience of time if the universe is seen as a cold lifeless machine or if it is seen as a wise nurturing mother.

While giving due credit to the many undoubtedly useful innovations enabled by industrial models of mechanical and mathematically manageable time, Nowotny (1989) also reminds us of the heavy toll its iron-fisted control has exacted in the marginalizing—even the eradication—of other ways of knowing and telling time (Ermarth, 1992, p. 6). For, "time" is much more than just a question about the periodicity of subatomic particles. It *is* that, of course, but it is also a political question: *Whose* time, organizing people in *what ways* in order to accomplish *which task* for the benefit of *which groups* of people (often at the expense of other groups of people)? These are not mathematical questions. They are ethical ones.

"With the responsibility for measuring time passing to the State, the State [begins] to proclaim its time as the only true time and impose it on all its subjects" (Gurevich, 1976, p. 242–243). This politically conditioned, "state-sponsored" type of time, where people are "efficiently" regimented to maximize their industrial "productivity," attempts to turn each individual into a cog in a corporate machine that is well greased by the profit motive. *This single-focused, economic vision and use of time is the basis of a theory of social organization known as "scientific management."* It began in the early twentieth century, and it had, and continues to have, profound (and sometimes devastating) effects on how schools are organized and how their purposes are defined. These effects have grown at an alarming rate over the last century.

The Corporate Classroom and the Physical Experience of Mechanical Time

The scientific-management view of how schools should operate has increasingly dominated national policy about public schools for the last century. The scientific-management approach to education has also dominated most colleges of education in the United States in their single-minded focus upon teaching teachers how to *efficiently manage* students and *scientifically deliver* a *standardized* curriculum devised by so-called educational *"experts"* (Popkewitz, 1997). The American educational historians David Tyack (1974) in *The One Best System*, Joel Spring (1976) in *Educating the Worker-Citizen*, and Lawrence Cremin (1988) in *American Education: The Metropolitan Experience* have traced in minute detail the rise, growth, and overwhelming predominance of this "corporate" view of education in industrial America in the twentieth century.

This view aims at the managerial control of teachers and students as if they were "workers" on an assembly line—workers whose "labor" is marked off by rigidly segmented class "periods" that are announced by the shrill sounds of bells that command students to move from Room A to Room B every forty-five minutes. In this industrial-model of schooling—which more or less defines most public schools in the industrialized world—"instruction" occurs in strictly managed segments of time, and "output" is monitored numerically in the scores that students receive on standardized tests. It is not surprising, therefore, that much current educational research refers to teaching as "input" and student performance as "output."

The mechanical-time/input-output model of education strips teaching and learning of subjective personal rhythms and needs. It is a model that runs roughshod over other personal needs and cultural visions regarding what kinds and cadences of activity people should engage in together, how they should interact with each other while doing so, and indeed what kinds of tasks matter in the first place. Probably the most extreme statement of the corporate, scientific-management view of the teaching and learning was made by the most famous behaviorist psychologist of the twentieth century, B.F. Skinner.

Skinner argued—in books ominously entitled *The Technology of Teaching* (1968) and *Beyond Freedom and Dignity* (1971)—that all people, not only students, should be seen as mere stimulus-response organisms. An organism's "behaviors" could be studied and controlled by mathematically formulating the correlations between changes in the type and intensity of stimuli applied to the organism (whether it was a tadpole or an eight-year-old child) and the corresponding changes in the organism's behavior. We need not bother ourselves about what was going on inside the child's mind, said the behaviorists, for it is impossible to see, measure, or mathematically manage subjective experiences.

Therefore, for all intents and purposes, subjectivity was seen as irrelevant, even nonexistent. This was very convenient for the behaviorists because caring about a teacher's or students' subjective responses was messy, "scientifically" unacceptable, and would get in the way of a truly "objective" approach to curriculum and instruction. Allow subjective experience and different cultures' ways of doing things into the picture, and you would destroy the equation! So intent was Skinner on erasing every element of culture and subjectivity from education that he argued that teaching-robots or teaching-machines would be better than human teachers (human teachers have messy emotions and bothersome ethics that make them less than optimally efficient). Skinner's dream was that teaching-machines would replace human teachers some day.

Skinner's theory of education offered the ultimate "scientific-management" model for controlling teachers and students, allowing "educational experts" to: (1) decide what knowledge was important for students to learn (and this was almost always the "knowledge" that would make them efficient and obedient workers in a corporate economy) and (2) measure how well teachers were teaching and how well students were learning this corporately defined knowledge by the use of tests whose impersonal and standardized nature mirrored the impersonal, standardized nature of the only kind of "time" that would now matter in the classroom—corporate, scientifically managed time.

Of course, *there certainly are important segments of the classroom day in which mechanical models or time, standardized instruction and assessment, and coordinated corporate activity among students are necessary to maintain order and get certain things learned and done.* As teachers ourselves, the authors of this book understand that this is a practical necessity in any classroom—especially a public school classroom where both parents and the State have invested considerable energy and money to make sure that certain things are taught and accomplished.

We are simply warning about the many types of psychosocial problems that inevitably arise for teachers and students when—as is overwhelmingly the case in modern American public schooling under the rigid, punishing fist of such policies as *No Child Left Behind*—there is no *time* for *any other* type of time: no *time* for subjective exploration, improvisation, and creativity; no *time* for teachers or students to probe deeply into the moral and spiritual implications of the material in the curriculum; no *time* to engage with others in socially and emotionally complex and growthful forms of interaction; no *time* for the students to explore each others' cultures in order to learn from each other and advance the cause of democracy; no *time* for living life in the classroom in ways whose rhythms are rounds that are enriched by worldviews other than that of the modern corporate obsession with amassing more and more data in order to produce greater and great profits in shorter and shorter "bites" of "time."

The psychological and cultural damage caused by the dictatorship of corporate time in the classroom is a serious emotional and ethical issue for both teachers and students. As the psychiatrist R. D. Laing (1967) pointed out several decades ago, people who lose touch with their body and bodily rhythms can become neurotically and even psychotically alienated *from* their bodies— *disembodied*—with the result that concrete reality becomes less and less real to them as they grow more and more lost in fragmented images that have no concrete foundation or reality. Macdonald has captured the significance of the physical realm in his discussion of "disembodied intellect" versus "sensorimotor presence" (1995, p. 124).

We do well, therefore, to heed the sociologist Anthony Giddens' observation that self time-zones are more psychologically significant than corporate time-zones, which "disembed" people from a healthy sense of themselves as physical beings who are naturally "embedded" in their cultures-of-origin (Giddens, 1990, p. 77).

Teaching, Time, and Talk in the Classroom

Much research has shown how ethnic minority students often physically experience and express their cultural sense of time and space in the classroom in differential ways. For instance, Au and Kawakami (1985) illustrated how Hawaiian children's classroom discourse is characterized by the South Pacific Islander propensity to "Talk-Story." "Talk-Story" is characterized by such conversational devices as the inclusion of tall tales (and the "taller" the better!); flashbacks and flash-forwards; repetition, variation, and embroidery for dramatic effect; multilayered digression; and people speaking excitedly at the same time. "Talk-Story" is definitely not mechanical or linear! Being able to "Talk-Story" in the classroom—at least occasionally—is how many South Pacific Islander students learn best.

But these nonlinear preferences in conversational patterns and story content often do not fit the conversational or instructional standards of the typical public school classroom, where teachers tend to value and reward student performances that are strictly sequential, going from A to B to C to D, using only the "facts" presented by the teacher or the text, in order to make an "objective" conclusion that is true precisely because it is *impersonal*. Nothing could run more contrary to the ethos of "Talk-Story," where the truth of a statement is inseparable from the speaker's and listener's passionate investment in the statement—an emotional investment that is inseparable from the listener's excited physical responses to statements.

Au and Kawakami found that "Talk-Story" was seen by the students' non-Hawaiian teachers as an unacceptable, even punishable, mode of interaction among students because it did not fit those teachers' white, middle-class preconceptions about how a classroom should operate and what constituted proper "decorum." The teachers saw the students' behavior when engaged in "Talk-Story" as inappropriate and disrespectful. But just the opposite was true! It was precisely when the students were *most* engaged with what was going on in class that they fell into "Talk-Story."

Au and Kawakami also found that when white teachers began to respect "Talk-Story" by allowing it an important place in the culture of the classroom, the students showed immediate and marked improvement in their reading. A strictly linear, non-Hawaiian approach to teaching and learning led to boredom, alienation, and failure in the Hawaiian students whereas honoring their nonlinear, "Hawaiian-time" ways of conversing and cooperating led to academic success.

Macias (1987) studied how Papago (also known as Tohono O'Odham) children of southern Arizona began to thrive academically in classroom environments where the more deliberative, less demonstrative rules and rhythms of interaction that set the pace of their culture also governed the relationship between the teacher and the student. The standard classroom expectation for a student to respond *quickly* and demonstrate her *individual* accomplishment and excellence violates the Papago way of thinking deep and long about a question, observing a master perform a skill, and then practicing it many times oneself before performing it in public, and never behaving in a way that selfishly calls special attention to oneself as better than others.

When the quick-fire rhythms and individual-ownership ethos of standard classroom instruction are aimed at Papago students, they may well come off looking dull, unprepared, and uninterested—an educationally devastating misimpression resulting from insensitivity to the Papago experience of time. Furthermore, classroom motivation often involves the future (e.g., schedules, deadlines, future uses of one's education). Using the future as the point of reference to motivate students may have quite different results with Indian and non-Indian children, whose sense of what the "future" is and how it should be "used" are quite different (Davis & Pyatowski, 1976, in More p. 159).

In another study, *Ways with Words,* Heath's (1983) classic sociolinguistic investigation of time, space, and relationship among three different groups of elementary school students and their families in an Appalachian community, the author looked at a low-SES African American community, a low-SES white community, and a middle-SES racially mixed community. Heath studied the linguistic growth of these children from the cradle to elementary school. She showed how each group's space and time assumptions shaped how they differentially viewed and used language, especially in the classroom.

Heath found that lower SES white parents, for instance, taught their children that there is only one correct order to things, both temporally and spatially, and that they must conform to that order unquestioningly. Kept on rigid play, sleep, and feeding schedules as infants, the children learned at the sensorimotor level from their first moments of consciousness that time is a taskmaster who brooks no deviation from the one "correct" order of things. Toys could only be taken down from the shelves at specified times, could only be used in approved spaces, and had to be returned to their approved slots on counters and in shelves when this particular unit of time had expired and the next scheduled space-time segment began. "A place for everything and everything in its place!" was the motto of this subculture.

Heath concluded that these parents were unconsciously preparing their children to be obedient workers in the low-paying assembly-line jobs, which they themselves had. Unlike their African American counterparts in this study, whose narrative experimentations with time and space were too flexible for classroom success, these children's discourse was too "stiff," leading their teachers to judge them cognitively deficient.

Despite these and other studies about how a student's personal/cultural times "fit" with the governing time of the school (Riordan, 1997), there is still a great need for more empirically rich and culturally specific research regarding cultural variation in the experience of time and its educational implications (Nieto, 2002). For example, Grossman (1995) concluded that some groups of students like to take things at a more leisurely pace: he mentioned especially African Americans, Filipino Americans, Hawaiian Americans, and Samoan Americans. On the other hand, Japanese Americans and Chinese Americans tend to prefer a quicker rhythm.

Of course, the teacher cannot be expected to understand all of her students' cultural temporalities. Nevertheless, knowing that such variations exist enables the teacher to help students explore their experience of time. In this way, the teacher can assist students in: (1) cultivating their ways and rhythms of doing things in some cases; (2) considering and experimenting with more mainstream alternatives regarding time in order to learn about how to gain power and recognition in mainstream society; and (3) being active and contributing members in a classroom community where different groups of students learn about and personally benefit learning about other ways of "being and doing in time." According to Heath (1983), the whole class can be drawn into the mutually enriching cultural project of exploring each other's sense of time. In this manner, teachers and students can, in a sense, become anthropological investigators of each others' cultures. Or, as Heath puts it, "teachers can become 'practical ethnographers' and students can become 'ethnographic detectives'" (p. 327. See also Gonzalez, 2001).

A teacher becomes a practical ethnographer when she begins to reflect on her own culture's time and space assumptions and how they may be affecting her practice. How does she divide up the day? How does she arrange and decorate her classroom? What kind of physical movement does this encourage or prevent in students? She can then use what is pedagogically fruitful in her cultural assumptions and discard or modify what is not.

Students can become ethnographic detectives by creating an environment for each other that is safe and open, and by fostering the innate curiosity in themselves and others. Tinney, Morgan, and Rogers (2006) encouraged teachers to have students work in groups as often as possible, especially with students from different backgrounds than themselves. Additional support and encouragement should be given to ensure that students help each other feel safe and valued, correcting immediately any situation that is demeaning to a student.

With the infusion of technology in the lives of students and in the classroom itself, teachers also have a great opportunity to invite students to be ethnographic detectives in connecting with others in their community and around the world in creative and valuable ways. It is quite simple to even have live discussions with anyone around the world using free and very user-friendly software. Some classrooms have used this to invite guest speakers to present from remote areas, and others have used it to connect with other students. For example, one of many international organizations called "Taking it Global" was "started by youth for youth" to connect with people from around the world in hopes of understanding each other better (http://www.takingitglobal.org/). To a great extent, the only limitations are those placed on us by our imaginations.

When one of the authors, Clint Rogers, was in South Africa (a very dynamic multicultural society) during the summer of 2006, he visited a rural school that intended to have students of all races and tribes use mobile phones to create "mobile wikis." Whereas a normal website can only be edited by certain people who have access, a wiki is a website or similar online resource which allows many users to add and edit content collectively. This school took the concept one step further to capture audio content.

The school was located in an area with a rich and poignant cultural heritage—tribal burial grounds, old concentration camps, and other historic locations. The idea was for students to have their parents and others in the community record memories at different locations. These recordings would later be accessed by the class members to stimulate discussion and an increased awareness about the various perspectives from the different cultural groups at the different locations. It was a novel opportunity for students to become ethnographic detectives using technology to involve the community and see the same sites through different eyes and multiple perspectives. But solutions do not need to be so high-tech or elaborate to be effective. For instance, simply requiring students to interview older people in a community made up of different ethnic or national backgrounds from those of the interviewers can provide fertile ground for cultural awareness, respect, and sensitivity.

Moreover, the teacher who is sensitive to and inclusive of various cultural rhythms can create a classroom environment that is healthier for *all* of her students. No student (or teacher!) can thrive intellectually or emotionally in an environment that is constantly in the grip of the hands of the clock. As both psychological and educational research is beginning to demonstrate, such violation of personal and cultural rhythms breeds a wide range of psychological disorders, ranging from the mildly neurotic to the fully psychotic (Block, 1997; Mayes, 2005b; Slife, 1993). Or, as the great curriculum theorist James Macdonald proclaimed, the "divorcement of the verbal from affect and psychomotor activity . . . [teaches] students to distrust their own values, emotions, and bodies as basic aspects of life and to this extent diminishes the full meaning of being alive" (1995, p. 124).

On the other hand, a classroom that is *multirhythmic* —one that honors and acts upon different cultural views of time—will not only be felt as affirming for minority students in the classroom *but will also contribute to the holistic health of each child* as she learns that she does not always have to be under the gun of impersonal, mechanical time in her life! In other words, the teacher who allows different types of time to inform the rhythms of the classroom provides the student with a *liberating environment* because the student learns in bodily ways there are varied and rich alternatives to the dictatorship of corporate, mechanical time.

Teaching as a Subversive Activity: The Politics of Time in the Classroom

With the mounting obsession on higher standardized test scores in the service of corporate profitability, children are being forced to acquire information and cognitive skills at breakneck speeds that interfere with healthy developmental and cultural rhythms. This collective national fixation upon high scores on standardized tests is particularly damaging when it comes to the very young:

> In the United States . . . the number of children with a diagnosis of attention deficit disorder (ADD) . . . combined with hyperactivity is growing rapidly. The drug Ritalin is often being prescribed for such children. Statistics vary but range from 1 million to 1.5 million children in the United States now receiving Ritalin. . . . Whereas some children genuinely need help because of constitutional problems in the nervous system, many others appear to need help primarily because they cannot accommodate to current educational practices. (Almon, 1999, p. 254)

There is a gender dimension to all this as well because, although both boys and girls are overmedicated to "quiet them down," this practice is probably more prevalent with boys, who, having ever higher testosterone levels as they mature, are forced to sit in chairs all day and memorize dry facts and figures so that they will "score well" on the next standardized test (Sommers, 2000). When both boys and girls are simply unable to deal with this form of physical torture and naturally begin to rebel, they are diagnosed as having an Oppositional-Defiant "disorder" or an Attention-Deficit-Hyperactivity "disorder."

Thus labeled as a clinical problem and drugged into submission, these students become the scapegoats of dictatorial corporate time in the classroom. Indeed, it has very recently become *illegal* for a child in a British classroom to refuse to take such drugs when they have been prescribed for her—as if the classroom were a state psychiatric ward. The political and ethical implications of the practice of drugging both boys and girls into submission to the inhumane rhythms of a corporate curriculum are chilling. The only way to stop these practices and the lifelong damage they create is to attend to the personal and cultural rhythms of the child—as indeed most teachers *want* to do and *continue* to do.

These teachers know that there are schedules and agendas defined by the institution and the state that they must obey. They understand that some of these schedules and agendas are useful and healthy. However, when these schedules and agendas become manifestly unhealthy, then, for the sake of their students *and* themselves, they must find ways to resist the dictatorship of the corporate clock in the classroom. This is not an easy thing for teachers to do, but it is, in our view, an emotionally and morally necessary thing for them to do. And when teachers do heroically find ways to honor the different personal and cultural rhythms of their students—when, that is, they are engaged in teaching as a holistic multicultural practice—then they are also teaching "teaching as a subversive activity!" (Postman, 1969).

Although this view of the teacher as something of a rebel may sound a bit shocking to the reader and although one will not find it in more mainstream "methods" classes in colleges of education, there is nothing new in it. Indeed, it stretches back as far as Socrates in the Western tradition and Lao Tzu in the Eastern tradition. Moreover, as the educational theorist George Counts (1932) declared, teaching is always a political activity whether the teacher consciously realizes it or not. Why? Because the teacher chooses either to *submit* to unhealthy agendas that are being imposed on her and her students (and thereby allows those agendas to prevail over her and her students) or to *resist* them (and thus becomes a political and ethical advocate for her students). Holistically including different kinds of cultural time in her classroom is a very important way that the teacher can be a champion for her students' personal and cultural integrity and health.

EMBODIED TRAUMA IN THE POSTMODERN CHILD

An increasing number of students in the public school classrooms have experienced a wide range of emotional, socioeconomic, and political traumas in their lives (Bullough, 2001). Such trauma "leaves its traces not just in people's minds but in their muscles and skeletons as well" (Fay, 1987, p. 146). Indeed, the trauma may first be registered at an unconscious neurological level before it takes on more conscious form as a "thought." As the psychiatrist Greenspan has put it in somewhat more technical language, "Somatic patterns are part of the experiences which eventually become internalized at a representational level" (1989, p. 234). More and more teachers are seeing these physical signs of oppression in their students.

For instance, a student from an inner-city ghetto may have personally witnessed one or even several murders by the time she is in junior high school. She may have been shot at herself. She may have never known her father but been raised by a teenage mother who herself was physically and sexually abused by a string of violent boyfriends throughout the child's young life. It is possible—even probable—that she was undernourished and malnourished *in utero* and has continued to be so throughout her life. Her mother may have been using, even addicted to, various drugs during her gestation. Cockroaches and rats are daily uninvited visitors in her "Project" apartment's living room and bedroom. She may herself have been physically or sexually abused by either her mother's boyfriends or gang members who not only roam but control the streets of her neighborhood. This is an extreme scenario, but it is not uncommon for children living in inner-city poverty to have experienced at least one or two of these horrors.

Such previous trauma in students' lives often results in misbehavior, low academic achievement, and low expectations for themselves. And it does not take a trauma as dramatic as witnessing a shooting to leave deep and lasting emotional scars. The frequent moving from place to place that many lower SES and ethnic minority children experience in addition to the high levels of stress associated with poverty also do considerable damage. Having to be the financial negotiator for the family (and sometimes at a very young and tender age) when parents, not understanding documents that they were signing, tied themselves to binding contracts, is also an enormous stressor on a child. It is also a trauma to constantly be told that one's goal should be academic success but not to have any models in the family or neighborhood of this. These are the "everyday traumas" that relentlessly beset so many of our lower SES students and students of color in our classrooms.

These traumas are all too prevalent in the life of "underclass" America where, despite our enormous wealth, the scandalous fact remains that one in five children grows up in poverty. And of course, physical/sexual abuse knows no socioeconomic or geographical boundaries but is an equal-opportunity monster who is devouring more and more children in his diabolical work. Naturally (or, rather, *un*naturally), these psychological traumas engrave themselves on the body of the child as a wide range of physical symptoms such as: facial and bodily tics; hyperactivity; panic attacks; physical clinging to adults and exorbitant neediness, on one hand, or physical and emotional detachment from and unresponsiveness to adults, on the other hand—a condition known as "flat affect"; behavior that is either too defiant or too submissive; sexual promiscuity and perversion; physically aggressive behavior against classmates; overly suggestive clothing sexually; scarification of the body with excessive piercing and tattoos; and detachment from the body in order to escape into an inner world of schizoid delusions.

These are but a few of the consequences of the many somatic maladies that result from the psychological and socioeconomic oppression of children in postmodern America (Bullough, 2001). And with more and more children coming into the United States and its schools after fleeing areas where wars and racist programs of "ethnic cleansing" endangered their lives on a daily basis and have claimed the lives of people in their immediate family, the physical consequences in children of trauma now have a geopolitical side to them as well.

Added to this are the physical consequences of what we call the "*Victoria's Secret* Syndrome." Little girls learn from early on that they are sexual objects and that to be desirable, they must conform to an image of femininity that is really nothing more than male corporate executives' fantasies about what constitutes "sex appeal." Only a certain body type qualifies as the right "look." To get this "look" an increasing number of girls will torture their bodies into stylish proportions, develop eating disorders such as anorexia and bulimia or take amphetamine-type drugs that perilously accelerate their metabolism. Anything to look like the women in the *Victoria's Secret* catalogue. And, on the other side of the fence, boys put their lives at risk with steroids so that they can look and perform like the athletes whose home runs or rushing yards are superhumanly high because they are also killing themselves with performance-enhancing chemicals.

What can the teacher—who, after all, is neither a therapist nor a social worker—do to help children who suffer from such problems? One answer lies in helping the teacher create a classroom environment that is physically therapeutic.

THE CLASSROOM AS PHYSICALLY THERAPEUTIC

In this chapter, we have examined three major aspects of the physical domain of holistic multicultural teaching. First, we have seen that there are differential sensorimotor preferences in how certain groups of students tend to learn best. Second, we discussed how certain groups of students' differential senses of time, manifesting themselves in physical ways, can either be a plus or a minus in the classroom, depending on how sensitively the teacher perceives those various rhythms and how adroitly she incorporates them in the daily life of the classroom. Third, we mentioned a few of the physical embodiments of trauma that beset so many students in today's classrooms. In addition to the ideas and strategies that we have already mentioned for the teacher to be responsive to these sensorimotor issues, we would like to conclude this chapter by discussing our idea of the physically therapeutic classroom.

"Physical" Education: Not Only "P.E."

Pedagogies that are tuned into the sensorimotor needs of students from a wide range of contexts and cultures are also, of course, pedagogies that are the most holistically sensitive to the needs of *all* children. As William Schutz, one of the leaders of the Human Potential Movement in the 1970s, argued in his influential essay, "Education and the Body," almost three decades ago:

> As a person develops, if his tissues and organs are all used in the various ways in which they are capable of being used, he develops to his full potential. Of course, no one does. Three factors prevent it: physical trauma, emotional trauma, and limited use. (1976, p. 105)

Everyone can benefit from education that is physically therapeutic. What is more, with the wildfire growth of new technologies such as cell phones, laptops, iPods, beepers, and so on, all students—even those who live in poverty cultures—are surrounded by such an ongoing storm of electronic stimuli that they are all at risk of losing touch with themselves as physical beings, children of nature, creatures whose highest cognitive, ethical, and spiritual capabilities are inseparably bound to their biological functioning. As Sardello and Sanders remind us in "Care of the Senses: A Neglected Dimension of Education":

> One essential task for educators is to recognize that the senses, and therefore perceptions and experiences, are disrupted and will continue to be disrupted by the stimulated world of technology, science, and economic pursuit. Balance in and of the senses, and the subsequent freedom of thought and actions, can be consciously sought and taught, but it cannot occur naturally. As more people live in areas of high population and as technical devices of every sort intervene in our sensory contact with the world, we will need to become trained in the art of living in our senses. . . .

What better way to train ourselves and our students "in the art of living in our senses" than to explore and share our differential cultural rhythms in the classroom—many of which are still healthily in touch with essential, even eternal, natural rhythms? Multicultural pedagogies can thus serve as a humane means of resisting the global obsession with technologies—using those technologies, of course, when it is productive to do so, but also knowing when to "switch them off" when they are beginning to encroach upon one's sensorimotor health and thus dull not only the physical but also the emotional and moral senses.

Foshay's (2000) seven dimensions of physical education can be employed in both public and private classrooms at all levels from kindergarten through graduate work. Nor need these activities be limited merely to P.E. classes— although it is true that physical education is a very suitable venue for such things. For example, "Movement Education," an alternative approach to traditional physical education classes, attempts to "cut the win/lose knot while systematically teaching [students] the basic movement skills that are needed in sports and life" (Leonard, as cited in Foshay, 2000).

We as teachers have used such things with our students in sites as varied as third grade classes and graduate seminars (Mayes, 1998). According to Foshay:

> Seven aspects of the physical self should be sought out if one intends to find opportunities to increase students' awareness of their physical selves: 1. physical

growth—changes in the body that accompany increasing age; 2. health—prevention of physical disorders; 3. body image—awareness of the bodily organs and functions, awareness of one's appearance; 4. movement—including sports and dance; 5. body language—nonverbal expressiveness; 6. metaphors deriving from primarily physical experience; 7. image schemata, including path, cycle, blockage, and so forth.

Research in Gardner's *Multiple Intelligences* (Kornhaber, 2004) has provided a rich fund of information and techniques about how to stimulate and expand the student's "kinesthetic," "naturalistic," and "artistic" capacities with physically rich activities at all grade levels and in every academic field from history to chemistry. Indeed, an impressive body of research has shown beyond any possibility of doubt that there is a close connection between the student's holistic attunement with and development of her body, on one hand, and her academic performance, on the other hand.

There are few things that will ultimately make our children *less intelligent* than the misguided and (we believe) even immoral approach to education that views teaching and learning as a mechanical, standardized process. This "vision" of education as a form of "robotics" is not only encouraged but required by "reform" documents such as *No Child Left Behind,* for the effect of those reforms is to tie students down to their chairs for excessive lengths of time in order to memorize disconnected bits of information that they must reproduce by rote on standardized tests. This is not education. It is a form of dulling the mind, heart, and body. Its effect is to turn children into nonresistant "workers" in the new transnational corporate machine.

This is not to say that standardized tests do not have a place in education—but they should have a limited one, as merely one among many kinds of *diagnostic assessments* that are used in order to help the child rise to her full, holistic potential. They should *not* be used as the *only summative assessment* on the basis of which rewards or punishments are doled out from some unseen corporate hand, depending upon how slavishly the teacher and students forced themselves to conform to physically, emotionally, and cognitively meaningless tasks so that they could score well on "the test."

An education that is responsive to the student as a multisensory, culturally embedded being, one who may have suffered for personal or political reasons a variety of physically encoded traumas in her life, can have the following healing effects:

A connectedness with the world of nature and the physical universe; physical health, a love and appreciation for the body and good maintenance; good capacity for expression through the body, through voice, gesture, and facial movements; the development of physical skills and the capacity to do things well with the hands; a greater capacity for enjoyment and enhanced sensory awareness, thus eliminating boredom; good respect and care for object; a positive self-image with the confidence that accompanies it; a capacity to liberate energy that is encapsulated in the body through past emotional traumas and experiences, so that psychological problems are not retained in the body; and the ability to experience higher states of consciousness through the body and to feel the body as the home of the Self. (Whitmore, 1986, p. 42–43)

The Holistic Education Movement has produced many texts that address both the theoretical and practical sides of the sensorimotor domain of education. The reader might wish to begin with such standard works as the following: *Transpersonal Education: A Curriculum for Feeling and Being* (Hendricks & Fadiman, 1976), *Psychosynthesis in Education: A Guide to the Joy of Learning* (Whitmore, 1986), and *Transpersonal Psychology in Education* (Roberts & Clark, 1975).

THE RICH SENSORIMOTOR CLASSROOM

We have seen in this chapter how a holistic multicultural pedagogy at the sensorimotor level fosters a classroom environment that: (1) honors the sensory learning preferences of different groups of students—and thus also teaches all students how to learn with all of their senses; (2) enfolds different cultures' senses of timing into classroom talk and activity—and thus also shows students how to live more richly in various kinds of creative time, not just corporate time; and (3) allows some degree of psychosomatic healing to take place in students with a wide range of embodied traumas—and thus has a healing effect on all students.

4

The Psychosocial Domain

Education is more than just the transmission of information or the cultivation of cognitive skills. It is also an extremely complex psychoemotional and social process.

In this chapter, we first examine the psychoemotional—or "psychodynamic"—nature of teaching and learning, discussing how the cognitive and affective domains are inextricably linked in educational processes. For, learning is "neither 'cognitive' nor 'affective' but a compound of both" (Barford, 2002, p. 57).

We then move on to a discussion of how the emotional nature of teaching and learning is very much a cultural issue because: (1) our emotions are shaped, and in some respects even "created," by the cultures we come from; and (2) we are emotionally committed to the "causes" of our culture-of-origin. Thus, just as our teaching and learning are inseparable from our emotions, our emotions are inseparable from our cultures. Education is a thoroughly psychosocial phenomenon.

Following that is a theoretical and practical exploration of some of the most important pedagogical consequences of the psychodynamic and sociocultural nature of education. We then conclude with an explanation of what we call "the therapeutic classroom" as a way of responding most sensitively to the psychodynamic and sociocultural problems and potentials that each student brings to a classroom.

Throughout, we will be stressing the main theme of this book—namely, that sensitivity to diverse ways of being, feeling, expressing and doing benefits not only children from minority cultures but children from all cultures in a classroom.

COGNITION AND EMOTION

One of the most powerful characteristics of a holistic approach to teaching and learning is that it affirms the importance of the teacher's and student's *emotions* in the classroom, stressing the need to nurture those emotions. As important as facts, theories, and cognitive skills undoubtedly are in education, they are simply not *all* that there is to education.

Imagine two students, A and B. Student A leaves a classroom at the end of the day having received both the explicit and implicit message from the teacher that he is a good learner—or at least *potentially* a good learner. Student B leaves the same classroom at the end of the day having received both the explicit and implicit message from the same teacher that he is neither a good learner nor really has the potential to be one. It is not as if both students will then say to themselves on the way home, "Oh, well. I'm a good (or bad) learner. How interesting. Now, I'll move on to other matters in my day which are completely unrelated to my hours in class and my image of myself as a learner—and will be completely unaffected by any of it."

Obviously, each student's day, week, term, and even his entire *life* may be dramatically affected by how he saw himself as a learner on just that one day—not to mention the effects of seeing himself in such a way for an entire term or an entire school career. Emotionally, professionally, politically, ethically and spiritually, how others have judged him as a learner—especially teachers and classmates—will contribute to his overall feelings of either hopefulness and empowerment or despair and weakness in many aspects of his life.

This simple example illustrates how *learning involves and affects us at all levels of our being.* As Salzberger-Wittenberg (1983) has said, teaching and learning are deeply "emotional experiences." Any wise and humane pedagogy must attend to this crucially important fact. Pedagogies that do not do so run the risk of being unethical. They also run the practical risk of simply being ineffective since students learn best when they are emotionally engaged and feel supported and affirmed (Brophy, 1997).

This commonsensical point continually seems to elude the proponents of standardized instruction and testing. In the name of "efficiency," standardization insensitively reduces students to mere objects of someone else's political or economic agendas. Categorizing the student with a number, standardization communicates to a student that he is of little value because his number is low or that he is of great value because his number is high—both of which are emotionally, intellectually, politically and ethically toxic messages for a person to internalize. This is why psychoanalysts who are interested in education and educational theorists who are interested in psychoanalysis have, over the last eighty years, stressed the point that education is *both* an emotional *and* a cognitive process. Our emotions and cognitions are so intertwined that it is usually impossible to separate the two.

Even scientists, who are supposed to embody the so-called virtue of "dispassionate objectivity," are often deeply invested emotionally and professionally (and sometimes even "invested" financially) in certain theories and techniques. What kinds of questions are considered "important" and "valid," what kinds of evidence will be admitted as "legitimate," and what kinds of conclusions are "acceptable" because they do not challenge the basic (and sometimes unconscious!) commitments of the scientist—all of this is often a matter of the scientist's deep emotional needs and cultural preferences. By definition, *no one* is dispassionate about issues, topics, or fields that really *matter* to them. There is probably no important *intellectual* issue of any importance that does not grip people psychodynamically and culturally.

The psychoanalytic educational theorist Greenspan goes so far as to insist that "from prenatal life and the early postnatal period, emotional, social, and 'cognitive' learning must be viewed as occurring together," making it is only reasonable to suppose that the most effective forms of education in the classroom should also "support all these domains of 'intelligence'" (1989, p. 239). Another psychoanalytically inclined educator, comparing the ideal classroom to a supportive family environment, similarly asserts that just as "there is no artificial separation of the emotional and the intellectual in how children learn in their home settings, neither should there be in the classroom" (Kirman, 1977, p. vi).

In short, cognition is not clinical and *"cold."* It is personal and *"hot"* (Pintrich, Marx, & Boyle, 1993). Several decades of research have demonstrated beyond the possibility of controversy that students will learn more quickly, internalize more deeply, and employ knowledge more creatively if they are learning it for reasons that are personally meaningful and pleasurable to them ("intrinsic motivation") than if they are learning that knowledge simply to gain artificial rewards or avoid externally applied punishment ("extrinsic motivation") (Brophy, 1997).

"Hot" Cognition

The idea of hot cognition comes from recent research in learning theory that examines the issue of how and why a student's ideas about something either do or do not change in the course of instruction. This field of study is called "conceptual change theory."

The classical, "cold"-cognition view of conceptual change was outlined in a famous essay by Posner (1982). There, he claimed that there is a similarity in how students and scientists change how they think about something. In both cases, he asserted, the individual's "knowledge claims" and "beliefs" will change to deal with "anomalies" and "contradictory evidence" that a previous paradigm could not handle. In this model of conceptual change as a coldly objective process, Posner claimed that a student would change his idea about something if: (1) he was dissatisfied with an existing conception because it failed to account for new evidence; (2) he found the new conception that the teacher offered intelligible; (3) he found the new conception plausible; and 4) further experience proved the new conception to be fruitful. To promote learning, therefore, the teacher should look to the scientific method as his model.

This model overlooked one important fact. Children are not scientists. Indeed, as we have seen, not even *scientists* are scientists if by that term we mean a person who is completely uninfluenced by emotions in the questions he chooses to examine, the evidence he chooses to see or ignore, the personal advantages in certain lines of research and certain findings, and the cultural and political uses to which he plans to put his information and ideas. Donning a lab coat should not mean becoming dead to one's emotions. When it does, the results are almost always horrifying as history has amply shown in the last century.

As the conceptual change theorists Vosniadou and Brewer (1987) point out, conceptual change in students—or anyone else for that matter—is typically neither as logical nor total as Posner believed. It is entirely possible (and in fact usually turns out to be the case) that when a student's concepts do change, they usually (1) are issue-specific, not system-wide, and (2) range from "weak" to "radical." In other words, a person can more or less change a belief about something with regard to a certain issue but—in an act of perfect self-contradiction—blithely apply that same previous belief to another issue. For instance, after a class in sociology, an undergraduate, who had previously held racist views across the board, might now agree that all children should receive equal educational opportunity because there is no fundamental difference between people. At the same time, he would not want any of his children to choose an African American spouse!

As Vosniadou and Brewer have also noted, even when a person's views *do* change radically, it is not just cool reason that effects the transformation, and sometimes it is not reason at all that does the trick. Rather, it is symbols, metaphors, and passionate appeals—the poetic, emotional language of the unconscious—that often prove most effective in effecting conceptual change. As the psychoanalytically oriented educational theorist Bernstein (1989) reminds us, we are motivated primarily by feelings, not concepts. What is more, a student may *understand* a new paradigm and its superiority to one that he presently holds but continues to cling to and defends the old one despite the teacher's most insistent and tactful urgings. Generally, it is emotional and cultural commitments that underlie this enormously strong resistance. Cognition is *hot* because it is fired by psychic energy and deeply held cultural beliefs (Pintrich, Marx, & Boyle, 1993).

Erickson (2001) has suggested that there may even be a physiological basis to hot cognition:

> Contemporary neuroscience shows that when we engage in routine activities not only are the neural networks activated that involve prior cognitive learning (i.e., neural connections to the cerebral cortex), but also that neural connections to our emotional states at the time of our initial learning are also activated (i.e., neural connections to the limbic system). . . . Through continued participation in daily life we thus acquire culture models for its conduct that involve feeling in our knowing. (p. 37).

Dole and Sinatra (1994) have therefore suggested that honoring and sensitively managing a child's "hot cognitions"—his strongly held emotional and cultural commitments—is an indispensable factor in creating deep and lasting conceptual change, and that *not* doing so leads at best only to temporary and patchy conceptual change in students. What this means in simple terms for the teacher is that the more he takes into account the emotional needs and nature of his students (*he* learning from them), the greater the success he will have in helping them entertain new ideas (*they* learning from him).

This is similar to a phenomenon that we noted in chapter two. In looking at Krashen's idea of the Affective Filter in second-language acquisition, we saw that if the teacher honors and fosters the student's native language (L1), this will lead to quicker, deeper, and more durable learning of the new language for the student (L2); for, the student knows that, in the course of being taught the L2, the emotional and cultural commitments involved in his L1 have also been respected. This is an important pedagogical principle to keep in mind in general when the teacher wishes to offer the student some new information, theory, or perspective that challenges the student's existing psychosocial commitments. If the teacher honors those commitments to the maximum degree that is appropriate, it will cause the student to be *more* receptive to the new ideas. On the other hand, if the teacher rudely challenges and flatly dismisses the student's psychosocial commitments, then the student either will refuse to consider new "evidence," or will pretend to change but will not really do so, or will misconstrue that evidence as further support of what he already believed (Garner, 1990).

All children, of course, come to the classroom with a wide range of emotional predispositions and cultural perspectives that occasionally run quite

counter to what the teacher is trying to teach. By being sensitive to those predispositions and perspectives, the teacher accomplishes two things with *all* of
his students—*whether they are from a cultural minority group or a culturally
dominant group*. First, the teacher's sensitivity and tact will create a safe
space for the student so that he feels secure enough to perhaps begin to look
at his deeply held beliefs in a more "critical" fashion (especially if the teacher
can model this himself by being open to alternative student perspectives and
to new ways of seeing, doing, and teaching). Second, having looked more
closely at his own beliefs, the student's commitment to those beliefs will be
more "considered" and productive—whether he has now changed, discarded,
or reaffirmed those previous beliefs upon critical analysis.

Again we see that a pedagogy that is both holistic and multicultural simply
makes good sense for *all* students, encouraging each student to develop himself in the important "imaginal domain" of the "subjective curriculum" (Barford, 2002, p. 57). This is that exciting zone of teaching and learning "where
objective ideas and subjective emotions are joined together" in a way that allows educational processes to be both cognitively strong and emotionally rich
(Barford, 2002, p. 57). The most engaging teaching and the most enduring
learning tend to take place here. "Educational experiences which foster the
subjective curriculum are likely to be most effective in promoting learning"
(Field, 1989, p. 52). This is just good common sense. We all learn best from
teachers whom we consider emotionally engaging and sensitive, and we all
tend to resist teachers (no matter how wonderful their ideas) who put us off
emotionally—not to mention those who are emotionally hurtful to us.

Clearly, the "official curriculum" in a classroom—the texts and the syllabus
—is only part of the curricular story. There is also the all-important "subjective curriculum," which is "the invention of both teacher and students. [The
teacher and student] project distillates of [their] own inner perceptions and
experiences, past and present, onto the subject under study, be in mathemat-
ics, reading, history, or literature" (Cohler, 1989, p. 52) with the result that
"no two children in the same classroom are having the same experience" because each one has his own "subjective curriculum" that exists in his "imaginal domain" (Blos, 1940, p. 492).

Simply being aware that such subjective curricula exist in himself and each
of his students—even if he does not know the specific subjective details and
nuances of each student's subjective curriculum—helps the teacher to: (1) understand that there is more to education than "just the facts," (2) create classroom environments where people feel safe enough to challenge some of their
deepest assumptions, (3) avoid unproductive classroom confrontations that
arise out of gross emotional insensitivity to students' beliefs and needs; and
(4) foster discussions and create activities that allow students to explore not

only their own but also each other's emotional responses to *an "official curriculum" that may need to be challenged because it is emotionally sterile and culturally insensitive*. These are not small accomplishments for a teacher, and they are most likely to occur when a teacher is teaching in a manner that is holistically sensitive to the psychosocial aspects of teaching and learning.

Armed with the kind of knowledge that we are offering in this book, a teacher will be more able and more likely to occasionally "hit the pause button" in his classroom when there seems to be some sort of emotional tension or interpersonal confrontation brewing and ask himself, "What might *really* be causing this trouble?" For example, a student's aggressive behavior during a morning reading lesson may really be caused by the fact that the child did not eat breakfast, had to work late into the night, or came home to find his father abusing his mother. Thus, something as elemental as hunger or as traumatic as spousal abuse may lie behind the child's behavior. A student may be clowning around during a math lesson and getting the teacher and fellow students off track because he is secretly intimidated by the subject matter. In the heat of the classroom confrontation, such determining factors too easily get overlooked.

However, if the teacher can "push the pause button" within himself (even for a moment), take a deep breath, and try to look behind the behavior to its cause, or if he can at least simply remember that there *is* a cause that often involves deeper issues than just this mere classroom difficulty, then he will benefit in various ways.

First, he will be less prone to take the student's behavior a personally wounding way to himself, knowing that it is not necessarily his inadequacy as a teacher but something else that may be upsetting the student. Second, he will be more skillful at handling the problem precisely because he is not taking it in such an emotionally threatening way. Third, he may even on some occasions be able to sense or infer what the child's problem is, whether there is something he can appropriately and productively do to help in his role as a teacher, or whether this is perhaps a problem that requires the student to receive professional therapeutic help out of the classroom.

The Psychoanalytic Contribution to Understanding the Emotion-Learning Connection

Psychoanalysts interested in education and educational theorists interested in psychoanalysis have had the most, and the most enlightening, things to say over the last eight decades on the subject of the relationship between emotions and learning. Therefore, in the following section, let us look at some of the major statements that they have made along these lines over the last half century in order to offer concrete examples of the relationship between cognition and emotion—regarding both academic *under*performance and the less widely acknowledged problem of *over* performance.

First, however, we should emphasize again that the tie between emotion and cognition is not something that exists only in children who are having special problems at school. For, *learning*—which often entails changing some deeply cherished beliefs and making mistakes in the process—*is an inherently risky business!* Who has not experienced the feeling of being lost or confused in a classroom at the beginning of a term? Who has not known the dull fear in the pit of the stomach as the term begins when one feels that other students are better prepared for what is to come than oneself? Who has not, at least once in his lifetime, spent the first hour or day in a new learning situation tied up in knots because he does not know what, exactly, will be expected of him or his classmates—whether it will be reasonable or excessive? And who has not, along with his classmates, spent some anxious moments scrutinizing the new teacher with an almost clinical eye to try to get a feel of who this person is, whether he is open and generous and will make the classroom experience an enjoyable one, or whether he is on some sort of power-trip that is destined to turn the whole term into a living hell?

The psychodynamics of learning exist in all students, not just those who are, for individual or cultural reasons, experiencing a certain "problem." Education is inherently problematic—as anything inevitably is which involves human beings and the potential for change. We would go so far as to claim that education that does not see itself as problematic is not really education but is simply technical training or an attempt at political indoctrination.

A Few Examples from Psychoanalytic Research into Under- and Overperformance

Almost sixty years ago, Redl and Wattenberg (1951) called educators' attention to the "neurotic 'mechanisms' that 'inhibit learning' in children" (p. 51–70). Examples of these "mechanisms" of learning inhibition would be such things as a child who has trouble studying about a famous person's mother because of a troubled relationship with his own mother, or a girl who refused to read about the sexual exploitation of black female slaves in the American South because she is being sexually abused at home. Indeed, "a whole subject may have special and disabling emotional meaning" (p. 196).

Another example of a "neurotic mechanism inhibiting learning" might be a child who—artistically gifted but only average at math and science—has received the relentless message from his father that a person is only *really* intelligent if he is good at math and science. This boy will soon approach math and science with so much anxiety and guilt that he will only be able to perform beneath the average level that he is really capable of.

Pearson (1954), another psychoanalyst who wrote a great deal about the psychodynamics of education, employed classical Freudian terminology to discuss two types of learning problems. The first one is a conflict between the student's ego (i.e., the practical part of the psyche that deals with daily reality) and his superego (i.e., the conscience). The second one is a conflict between the ego and the id (or the student's animalistic drives and desires).

An example of an ego-superego conflict would be a child whose perfectionist parents expect so much of him academically that he develops severe performance anxiety and cannot perform well, or even perform at all. An example of an ego-id conflict would be a child who, feeling murderous rage against an emotionally distant father, has negative feelings about his male teacher, on whom he has projected his anger against his father. In both cases, what might seem like a merely cognitive problem of academic underperformance would, upon closer examination, turn out not to be a cognitive issue in the student at all but rather something relating to his personal psychodynamics.

The origin of these kinds of problems sometimes goes back as far as the child's earliest experience of its mother and breast-feeding (Ekstein 1969). After all, do we not often speak of learning in eating terms? One *devours* a book, *consumes* information, *chews on* new ideas, tries to get *the flavor* of an argument that somebody has *brewed or cooked up*, takes time to *digest* facts or concepts, and sometimes is even required to *regurgitate* knowledge on tests. Surely these colloquial parallelisms are not accidental but reflect a psychosomatic tie between *taking in* abstract pieces of knowledge cognitively and taking in nutrients physically.

Considering how much a baby learns of its world in its first feeding encounters with its mother—whether the world is safe, full, and soothing or whether it is unpredictable, unsatisfying, and cold—one can appreciate Ekstein's initially surprising but ultimately plausible suggestion that:

> the first curriculum struggle ever developed does not take place in school but rather ensues between mother and infant as she is nursing her baby. The full breast is the first curriculum the baby must empty and digest in order to meet the goal and requirement of satiation. (1969, p. 49).

Regarding another developmental issue, if toilet training is not handled well—if, for instance, the parent is impatient with the child, severe in handling him, and openly disgusted with the whole process in general—the child "learns" that he is also disgusting and that his products—"what comes out of him" (first physically, then conceptually)—are bad, inadequate, and a cause for shame. The classroom consequences of this may include underperformance and blocked creativity despite inborn talents (Kirman, 1977).

Developmental damage to the child at any stage may impede that "courage to try" and "courage to learn" which are vital to intellectual growth (Cohler, 1989, p. 49, 53). "No matter how great the opportunity, motivation, or innate capacity, no learning will occur unless the individual finds within himself the courage to try" (Bernstein, 1989, p. 143). The child who has trouble putting together a project for a science fair may be scientifically gifted but developmentally wounded. This theme, so prominent in psychoanalytic pedagogical literature from its earliest days on into the 1970s, continued to be stressed and explored later on, perhaps in the greatest detail in Field et al.'s (1989) classic text in psychoanalytic pedagogy, *Psychoanalytic Perspectives on Learning*.

In that book, the critical point was made that *not only did a child's development affect his experience of schooling, but his experience of schooling would also affect his subsequent development.* A person's experience of school—his triumphs and tragedies there, his loves and alienations, hopes and disappointments—are prominent strands in the tapestry of his life narrative. A rich, vibrant, and humane store of experiences regarding one's school years goes a long way in promoting mental health, whereas an opposite set of bad school experiences may continue to peal like a dire bell throughout the student's life, damaging his "learning ego" (Anthony 1989, p. 108).

Oskar Pfister (1922), who had been a schoolteacher before becoming a psychoanalyst in the early twentieth century, gave various examples of student behaviors that should have alerted him to psychodynamic problems during his teaching years but didn't at the time. Some of them, he now felt, would have been relatively obvious if he had had even rudimentary psychoanalytic knowledge: the presence of dark and troubling themes in a student's compositions, a student developing tics during a certain kind of activity or discussion, "flat affect" (or dull emotional responses) in the presence of some teachers but not others, and so on.

Caroline Zachry (1929), another teacher who was deeply involved in psychoanalysis, dealt with the problem of *neurotic overperformance* in students. Here the problem is not cognitive deficiency but, instead, a lopsided focus on "cognitive excellence" in order to "mask" deep emotional problems. She tells of a Jewish girl named Esther who lost herself in schoolwork in order to try to forget the painful fact that she was shunned by her gentile peers. For Esther this strategy of academic overperformance in order to hide from psychological pain ultimately resulted in a complete nervous breakdown.

Like Pfister and Zachry before her, Melanie Klein (1975 [1932], p. 67, 90), one of the most famous child analysts of the twentieth century, reported many cases of students whose problem was that they were "perfect"—a fact, she believed, that signaled the possible presence of some form of concealment, compensation, or compulsion in the child. Klein wrote about one of her young patients who was an obsessively good student but showed virtually no emotions.

Redl and Wattenberg (1951) analyzed the case of a girl who had trouble working out a puzzle containing the words "sick," "heart," and "well" because of her anxiety about her mother's coronary condition. Pearson (1954) discussed a boy whose number phobia stemmed from his association of that number with a traumatic event, and a girl whose problems with long division were ultimately traceable to a separation anxiety. Peller (1978 [1958]) illustrated how excessive praise of a little boy's paintings when he was two-years old had so stressed the child that by the time he began school he was unable to paint at all despite (or rather, because of) his innate talent.

In the 1960s, various psychoanalysts and educational theorists were interested in how *to channel students' fantasies and feelings* into the classroom in educationally enlivening ways. Thus Hill (1969), in a very practical essay, gave many concrete examples of how to enlist the student's unconscious into the study of subjects ranging from art to geography, civics to history, and physical education to creative writing. Jones (1968, p. 244) pointed out that such psychoanalytic skills are not just icing on the cake but are indispensable in teaching the humanities or social sciences, where the issues touch upon the deepest layers of self and society. "Any lesson in the humanities or social studies which confronts children with the truth of its subject matter—be it family life among the Eskimos, the invention of the steam engine, the Boston Tea Party, the death of Abraham Lincoln, or what have you—will naturally provide effective stimulation of their emotions and fantasies" (1968, p. 244).

To return to the issue of high levels of scholastic performance as potentially problematic: it is important to acknowledge that some teachers may understandably find it difficult *ever* to see scholastic excellence as a problem. This is perhaps especially true today, as neoconservative as well as neoliberal federal agendas for educational reform, from *A Nation at Risk* to *No Child Left Behind,* have stressed "excellence" on standardized instruments of assessment as the *only* legitimate educational goal. This makes it doubly crucial that we attend to the warning that psychoanalytic pedagogy has vociferously raised throughout its history: prizing only cognitive excellence in a child at the expense of attending to his emotional life not only *reinforces* existing neuroses but can *create* them.

It is therefore not an exaggeration to say that the corporate, standardized curriculum, breeding psychological illness in children, is *pathogenic.* The authors of this text believe that *instituting policies and engaging in practices that are psychologically damaging to children is immoral,* which is what makes high-stakes testing such a "high-stakes" issue.

Some of the earliest and best statements along these lines in the psychoanalytic literature are found in Melanie Klein's writings. Speaking of what she called a healthy "instinct for knowledge," Klein (1975 [1932], p. 103) proclaimed that the fundamental educational question from a psychoanalytic point of view is how to promote "a relatively undisturbed development" of that instinct, which will ideally "turn freely in a number of different directions, yet without having that character of compulsion which is typical of an obsessional neurosis."

About twenty years later, Redl and Wattenberg (1951) cautioned that a certain kind of obsessive conformism, which slavishly submits to every teacher and every rule, is not evidence of healthy social adaptation but is, instead, a red flag signaling that the child's behavior, at school and at home, is probably the result of fear. Fear is an emotion that furthers totalitarian purposes, not the democratic ones which, as Dewey (1916) said, should be a primary purpose of schools to promote.

As the psychoanalysts have pointed out throughout the twentieth century, curricula that inspire anxiety and blind obedience in students kill the confident free-thinking that citizens must possess in order to maintain a true democracy (Castoriadis, 1991). Hence, "when a boy or girl shows signs of being unusually anxious to please, we should realize we have a delicate problem on our hands, instead of feeling flattered" (Castoriadis, 1991, p. 204). This child, seeing himself as a scholastic object to be manipulated by others, engages in learning only in order to confirm his servitude, not to win a principled intellectual and moral freedom. This confounds the whole purpose of the educational enterprise. "In a sense, each bit of good work [such students] do is a gift, or more accurately a bribe. Their actions carry this meaning, 'See, I've done what you wanted; I've proved that your wish is my command. Now, reward me by taking me under your wing. Lift me to joy by saying you like me'" (Redl and Watternberg, 1951, p. 203). Teachers must be vigilant in recognizing and helping these unfortunate children, "whose defensive specialty is that of excessive intellectualization" (Jones, 1968, p. 230), "the frequently defensive use of the purely intellectual act" (Piers and Piers, 1989, p. 202).

Such pronouncements as these reflect the ideas of one of the twentieth century's most prominent neo-Freudians, Heinz Kohut (1978), that overintellectualization (and perfectionism in general) is often a sign of an excessive need to be loved as compensation for a lack of adequate and appropriate love and validation in a person's infancy. Such intellectualism and overperformance to win a parent's or teacher's love stems from and reinforces what the great child psychiatrist Winnicott (1992) has called the "false self." Similarly, Fairbairn (1992) asserted that many people construct elaborate intellectual structures as a psychotic defense mechanism against authentic engagement with life—the famous "bookworm" syndrome (1992, p. 15–20).

The most humane, creative, and democratic forms of schooling occur when educational processes foster a synthesis of cognition and emotion. Rigidly standardized approaches, on the other hand, with their system of unhealthy rewards and harsh punishments, breed the problems and others, too.

CULTURE AND EMOTION

We generally think of our emotions as things that are uniquely *our own* as individuals—as "things" that just exist "inside" of us—in a "private" world. However, our emotions are also cultural and public—stemming from the "cultural vocabulary of emotions" that our cultures provide us with from birth as well as from the fact that we are emotionally invested in the "cause" of our cultures. Let us examine this idea and then some of the pedagogical consequences that follow from it.

The Cultural Construction of Emotions

A Spaniard may see the killing of a ferocious bull in a ring by an elegantly clad toreador quite differently than a North American might. Whereas the Spanish spectator perceives grace, nobility, and courage in the spectacle— and even feels a sense of social and spiritual bonding with his fellow spectators—the North American might be registering only a scene of absurd exposure to danger and senseless slaughter. What accounts for the fact that the Spaniard is exhilarated and uplifted by the very same event that outrages and depresses an American?

The answer lies in the way that each observer has *learned to feel about the scene in accordance with the values of his society*. Exhilaration and depression are obviously universal human emotions, innate. Both the Spaniard and the American feel them. However, what *stimulates* those emotions in a certain person is often influenced by his culture's deeply held ethical values and spiritual commitments (Berger, 1967; Berger & Luckmann, 1967). How an individual's emotions play out in response to situations that he confronts is, therefore, often *socially constructed*—at least to some degree.

In other words, two different people may respond to the situation in different ways as a result of their different cultural styles, which involve a subtle intermixture of cognitive and affective factors. According to Shade (1989):

> The responses involved in making adaptation to the environment involves: the cognitive appraisal or interpretation of the information gleaned in the environment or situation; the affective processing or reappraisal of the situation based upon the person's dominant needs, values, and emotions; and the

decision-making or adaptation process in which the individual selects the strategy or action which they believe to be most appropriate. Each person or group proceeds through these steps based upon their own affective state, personal agenda, resources, options, and constraints available to them and the previous experience and understanding of the situation. . . . Consequently, each individual or commune of individuals develops a unique way of coping with life which becomes their cultural style. (p. 9–10)

As in chapter one, we would like to stress again, however, that we do not believe that the cultural dimension of emotions implies moral relativism—the view that, simply because certain behaviors and emotions are "normal" in a (sub)culture to which one belongs, that they are necessarily acceptable and good. On the contrary, we maintain that there are certain acts that run so counter to any fundamental sense of human decency that they *must* inspire the emotions of revulsion and resistance in ethically sane people. When they do not inspire such moral outrage in a person or culture, we may conclude that the person or culture is *immoral*—at least regarding that practice.

Millions of Germans during the Second World War, for instance, held the culturally constructed belief that the grotesque extermination of Jews, Catholics, homosexuals, and Gypsies was permissible for political reasons. Far from revulsion or resistance, some of these Germans apparently felt a "culturally constructed" sense of pride and approval about their government's monstrous policies and practices. This socially constructed set of emotions was evil. The fact that it was a "socially constructed emotional norm" at that time in Germany did not make the emotions or practices any less evil. Indeed, it made them more so.

Of course, the concentration camps in the Second World War provide a glaringly obvious example of a cultural norm that we may (indeed *must*) judge as morally unacceptable. But many other (sub)cultural practices are not so clear. The difficulty in ethically evaluating them lies in deciding whether they rest upon views that in one's best judgment are: (1) *ethically universal*, (2) *culturally unique* but capable of being *celebrated* because they are fundamentally moral and enrich one's view of the world; (3) *culturally unique* but morally questionable yet still *tolerable* in a pluralistic democracy, where we must get along with each other despite differences in opinions and practices; and (4) *unacceptable* because they so violate one's sense of morality and social functionality that accepting them would represent an *intolerable* violation of one's most deeply held ethical commitments and would endanger social cohesion.

Smaller but still important examples of this are prevalent in multicultural classrooms and need to be addressed effectively in order for the class to be able to move forward interpersonally and academically. For instance, a non-

Muslim American female teacher teaching traditional Muslim boys might find herself confronted by cultural attitudes and practices toward women that are different from her own cultural norms. Such a teacher may find herself confused or angry at certain of the beliefs and practices regarding gender roles held by the Muslim boy and his family (Sabbah, 2005). The teacher's responses would be quite understandable, but attending to the psychoocial domain of teaching would allow this teacher to more readily "hit the pause button" and think through her own responses in order to figure out effective "compromise" ways to proceed in the classroom that honor both the student's and teacher's culturally constructed view of "womanhood."

Confronting these difficult questions both in and out of the classroom is the moral task of every mature individual—and one that is becoming ever more complex and necessary in a world that is increasingly being defined by the fact of cultural diversity. Resolving these complex moral dilemmas is clearly beyond the scope of this book. Indeed, it may well be beyond the scope of *any* book. What this book *does* offer is theoretical models and practical suggestions for teaching and learning in ways that promote the maximum degree of mutual respect and mutual enrichment in the classroom in this Twenty-first-Century Age of Multiculturalism (Fay, 2000).

Emotion, Culture, and the Self

The social psychologist Hewitt (1984) uses the terms "emotion work" and "feeling rules" to signify the psychosocial shaping of a child so that he learns which emotions he should feel in which situations (p. 161–162). According to Hewitt, this learning occurs in three interrelated ways.

First, our emotions "arise naturally in our efforts to complete individual and social acts." This means simply that when we are doing something, either alone or with others, the action is usually accompanied by some type and degree of emotion. What we do, think, and feel are interrelated. We are not robots, however much behaviorist psychology and corporate education might wish to convince us that we are!

Second, says Hewitt, our emotions are "an experience of self." What Hewitt is claiming is that *we know who we are by how we feel* about things and situations, yet how we feel about things and situations is often a matter of how our culture has taught us we *should* feel. In this manner, a person's "experience" of his "self"—his sense of "identity," his degree of "self-esteem," his beliefs about "who he is"—is an emotional fact that is affected by his culture's norms.

Ideally, of course, a person wants to feel and act in a way that he believes to be culturally and morally congruent. Indeed, conveying to others in our (sub)culture that we *are* socioethically "solid" is a major goal of much of our communicating. According to the narrative theorist Charlotte Linde (1993), who has studied the implicit messages that lie below the surface of everyday conversations, the *subtext* of many of our daily communications with others is essentially as follows: "I was in (or am in, or will be in) a certain situation involving another person or persons. In this situation, such and such events took place. In response to those events, I felt the following things and acted in the following way. These actions and feelings of mine, which I am expressing in this narration to you, my audience, affirm the explicit and implicit norms of our culture. *Therefore, I am a 'good' person!*"

We talk in order to assure ourselves and others of the validity of our reference groups and of our place in them. In this way, we confirm our identity and enhance our self-esteem. If a person feels—or is *made to feel* by others—that his culture is inferior or that his place in it is unimportant, then he will almost certainly experience a *crisis of identity* and *low self-esteem.* This fact has serious educational implications that we will examine presently.

In other words, a person finds a major portion of his identity by how well he "fits in with" others in the culture and subcultures with which he identifies —his *reference groups,* so called because he defines and evaluates himself in reference to their standards. According to the psychiatrist Alfred Adler (1930), this "social feeling" is a prime motivator of our behavior. We spend a good deal of our day involved in what Goffman (1997, p. 109) has dubbed "impression management" and "face work"—those dialogues with others as well as our internal talk with a "Generalized Other" in which we engage to assure ourselves and others that we "get the rules," are "living by them," and are "good" people.

Impression management and face work are not, in themselves, bad things. In fact, they are very necessary things in the smooth operation of any (sub)culture. Problems arise only if a person comes to conclude that one of his cultural beliefs or practices is morally unacceptable or psychologically painful for some other reason in some other context that is also important to him. Then he must face the agonizing decision of whether to *conform* to his native but now problematic cultural norm or *resist* it, even *reject* it, and thereby risk being ostracized from his culture, in order to gain acceptance into the new group. Violating one's cultural norms is no small step to take, and it often exacts a heavy emotional toll, for *not* meeting one's cultural standards and expectations often engenders intense feelings of anxiety and depression (Bandura, 1986).

The example given previously in this chapter about young traditional Muslim boys being schooled in the United States exemplifies a situation in which a student must decide whether to conform to a cultural norm that is viewed as problematic by another culture. Does the boy change his idea of gender roles in order to fit into his new school community even though doing so seriously offends his mother and father? Other students from other cultures face such decisions many times throughout the day in the typical public school classroom.

These can obviously be painful choices—choices which, because of the psychological energy they require and because of the social consequences they entail, often impact a student's school performance. Thus, it behooves teachers to be aware of these struggles and their academic consequences. This is another opportunity for a teacher to "hit the pause button" when evaluating students. Attention to these psychosocial dimensions of multicultural students' school experience can enable the teacher to help students face these issues and be better prepared to engage in the academic curriculum.

Third, Hewitt points out that our emotions "are a regular part of the role-making process" (1984, p. 70). By this, Hewitt means that an individual's sense of identity and feelings of self-esteem largely grow out of *what roles* he plays in his culture and *how well* he feels that he plays them. What is a role? It is "a place to stand as one participates in social acts. It provides the perspective from which one acts. . . . "What is more, "the roles of others, through our own acts of imagination, provide perspectives from which we view both their conduct and our own." Our emotion-laden evaluations of ourselves and others reflects how we: (1) *judge others* on the basis of how well *we* feel they are playing *their* roles and (2) *judge ourselves* on the basis of how we feel that *they* feel we are playing *our* roles (Hewitt, 1984, p. 61).

To make the relationship between roles, identity, and emotion even more complex, bear in mind that every individual plays a wide variety of roles in just one day—not to mention a lifetime! Getting her children off to school in the morning, a woman assumes the role of a "mother"; during the day as she sits at her desk, she is a a "financial advisor"; in the lunchroom, she then becomes a "friend" as she chats with some close acquaintances—until, that is, the CEO shows up to get some lunch and then she becomes an "employee" under his watchful eye. On the way home, she stops to shop and becomes a "customer." Later that night, after the children are in bed and she and her husband are snuggling on the couch, she becomes a "confidant," "therapist," and "lover."

Each of these roles entails: (1) certain emotions to be felt and expressed at different levels of intensity and openness depending upon the situation; (2) various types of body language and degrees of physical closeness; (3) certain words, expressions, and even grammatical forms that one will use depending upon the person with whom one is talking; and even (4) different visions of one's place and purpose in the universe. The psychologist Paolo Ferrucci has suggested the breathtaking emotional complexity inherent in our many roles in declaring that "each of us is a crowd!" (1982, p. 47). And all of this just in the course of sixteen hours in one day! Over a lifetime, the interaction of culture, role, identity, and emotion grows colossally complex and consequential for almost every individual.

Multicultural students are often required to play so many different roles during the day that it might well boggle the mind of a person from a dominant culture to consider. The multiple roles played by multicultural students in one day potentially involve at least three types of language—the language spoken at home, the language spoken by teachers and administrators, and the language spoken by peers. Being able to perform in different languages and dialects on demand is called "code switching." Moreover, multicultural students must learn how to meet the cultural expectations of both the home and outside world—a cognitive, affective, and social feat of no small magnitude, requiring great emotional maturity. Educators who are aware of these complex and impressive psychosocial abilities in their multicultural students will be more ready and able to harness these strengths in classroom work.

Contrary to the popular understanding of a role, it is not a prescribed list of behaviors but rather a "repertoire of possibilities" upon which one can draw as he finds himself "positioned" in various situations throughout the day and throughout his life. Thus, our roles make it possible for us to navigate the world with relative efficiency because they offer "predictive and sense-making capacities" which do not envisage every possibility but which *do* make it unlikely that much will happen that is not expectable (Hewitt, 1984, p. 62). Roles provide "typifications" that help us know what to expect *from* and feel *about* ourselves and others in certain situations (Schutz, 1976, p. 119).

When a person is thrown into a social situation in which his role is either unclear to him or awkward for him because it varies so much from his cultural norms, then he may feel considerable anguish and be unable or unwilling to perform—an important fact to consider, as we shall see, when trying to understand the experiences of children from minority cultures in classrooms where the rules and roles of the typical American classroom may differ greatly from the rules and roles that they knew and were expected to conform to in their native cultures.

PSYCHE, CULTURE, AND CLASSROOM

At the beginning of this chapter, we examined how teaching and learning are not only cognitive but psychodynamic processes. After that, we saw that our emotions are shaped in profound and complex ways by our cultures. Clearly, *education*, far from being an emotionally or culturally neutral process, *is inextricably tied into the student's emotions, which, in turn, are inextricably bound to his culture.* We now turn to some of the most important pedagogical implications of this fact.

Cultural Discontinuity in Teacher-Student Roles

The first socioemotional factor to consider in the classroom is the degree of "fit" between the student's culturally conditioned view of what a student should be and the teacher's culturally conditioned view of what a student should be. This is a question of the degree of congruity—or "cultural continuity"—between the teacher's and student's understanding of a student's *role* in the classroom. A high degree of continuity between the teacher's and student's view of the role of a student will make that student's life all that much easier in the classroom. A high degree of discontinuity can cause problems for the student that may be misinterpreted by the teacher as cognitive deficiency or lack of respect whereas, in fact, it is simply a matter of cultural difference.

In many Asian countries, for instance, a college student is generally expected to be silent, listen to the teacher with great care and obedience, make close notes of all that the teacher has said, memorize that information, and then reproduce it by rote on a test. The teacher's role is *authoritarian* and the student's role is *passive*. Conversely, in many American college classrooms, the student is expected to listen to the teacher as a knowledgeable figure, one who is to be respected of course, but one who can—and even should—be probingly questioned by the student if the student thinks that the teacher is making a mistake, has been unclear, or has not said enough on a topic. Tests are often seen as an occasion for the student to show not only that he has read the material, listened to lectures, and understood them, but also that he is dynamic and inquisitive enough to pose novel and interesting questions and suggest unique solutions in his answer.

The American teacher's role is *authoritative*, and the student's role is *active*. In the Asian classroom, the student gains approval and self-esteem by filling a passive role. In the American classroom, the student gains approval and self-esteem by playing an active role.

In an American classroom, an Asian student might be constantly prodded and pushed by his teacher to be more involved in discussions and more self-assertive in activities. This might well make the Asian student feel that he is being pushed so far out of the "comfort-zone" of his "role" as a "student" that he cannot perform academically. This, in turn, might lead to an even more general state of emotional distress, involving issues of self-esteem that would not be limited to the classroom but might well "bleed over" into other areas of his life.

One of the authors of this book, Cliff Mayes, taught in Japanese universities for almost a decade. He discovered that if the teacher is an American and brings American role expectations to that classroom (as American teachers often do in foreign settings), there will almost certainly be cultural discontinuity between what the teacher expects of a student (active participation) and what the students expect of themselves (silent obedience). This also entails a cultural tension between the teacher's understanding of his role (an informed and amiable facilitator of conversation and inquiry) and the student's understanding of the teacher's role (as a taskmaster and the infallible source of all valid knowledge on a subject).

Where both the teacher and the student are confused and anxious because they are uncertain of their own and each other's roles, we may well expect for problems to arise (Pratt, Kelly, & Wong, 1999). It is quite common for a beginning American teacher in a Japanese university to be seen by students as "too easy," "not serious about his subject," "just there to play games and have fun with students," and "not really interested in his students because he doesn't care enough about them to be strict." On the other hand, it is not uncommon for a beginning American teacher in the same setting to see his students as "mindless," "robotic," "uncreative," "dull," and "lacking in any kind of intellectual curiosity." In such a situation, both the teacher and his students wind up feeling resentful and inadequate. Self-esteem for all involved can plummet to some dangerously low levels unless the teacher and students explore ways to understand, negotiate, and creatively work with these differences.

We want to suggest that they *can* achieve these more positive consequences by engaging in what the sociologists Berger and Luckmann (1967) call *cool alternation*, an idea which we will explore in depth below (p. 172). Teachers can also be more explicit and "up-front" with students about what he and they can do to learn what to expect of each other and how to help each other in the classroom (Tinney, Morgan, & Rogers, 2006).

How students are grouped together can also have emotional repercussions for students, affecting their academic performance. For instance, Hawaiian students work most comfortably in mixed-gender groups of four or five students while Navajos perform best working either alone or in same sex groups of two or three students (Tharp, 1989). Thus, for example, pair work involving a Navajo boy and girl would probably be awkward and unproductive, as would extended individual desk work for a Hawaiian student. The teacher should honor these organizational patterns in the single-minority classroom and accommodate them *as much as possible* in the multicultural classroom.

Cool Alternation

Cool alternation means scrutinizing and trying on new roles in a given situation, but doing so in small increments and with open and frequent discussions among all the participants about the process. In this way, no one is pushed too far or too fast out of their cultural comfort zones. Cool alternation is an example of what sociologists call "secondary socialization" (i.e., learning about one's new roles in new cultural contexts) without "desocialization" or "deracination" (i.e., being forced to renounce one's own culture and its roles in order to unquestioningly, totally, and immediately fit into the new culture). Cool alternation is the best way to help students adapt to a new classroom culture, for it allows them to learn the "cultural vocabulary" of the new school without negating their natal culture.

In the above example, Cliff, who had a tendency as a novice teacher to be too lenient with students, discovered the value of toughening up a bit—setting rigorous standards for students and not accepting any flimsy excuses for not meeting those standards. On the other side of the table, his students learned, slowly but surely, the importance of venturing an opinion in class now and again—even if that opinion might not reflect or reinforce the teacher's opinions! Everyone benefited from this culturally accommodating pedagogy—which, far from being merely a "compromise position," gave birth to something new and better, more exciting and rich, in the diverse culture of that American/Japanese classroom than a "merely" American or "merely" Japanese approach would have yielded. Teacher and students both "coolly alternated," tried on new classroom roles, and wound up being better teachers and learners because of it.

Cool alternation, when handled sensitively by the teacher and in dialogue with the whole class, can be an exciting way of gently inviting not only students from a minority culture but also the students from the dominant culture, students from other minority cultures, and the teacher himself, to examine their own and others' roles with more critical insight, emotional openness, and cultural generosity. The increased knowledge regarding self and others in the classroom affords everyone more flexible, varied, and creative views about how to carry on the business of teaching and learning. In practical terms, this type of psychosocial awareness in the classroom allows everyone, teacher and students, to just plain get down to work on academics more quickly as opposed to spending most of the class period lost and frustrated in unnecessary emotional and cultural confusion and conflict.

The culture of the classroom, becoming more "pedagogically diverse," also becomes more comfortable (because everyone's "style" is being honored and included) while also becoming more challenging (because one must try to empathetically look at other ways of doing and being—and even try them on from time to time!). The growth that we have seen take place in both teachers and students when they "coolly alternate" by experimenting with new ways of acting and interacting in the classroom testifies to the power of a holistic multicultural pedagogy to enrich and enliven the lives of both teachers and students.

Ways in Which Teachers and Students can Help Each Other Understand and Adapt to New Role Expectations and Rhetorical Styles

Cool alternation is one way in which teachers and students can examine roles with more openness and emotional safety. Additional ideas for helping teachers and students avoid misunderstandings were given by Tinney, Morgan, and Rogers (2006). They provided pedagogical suggestions to teachers who are working with students from other cultures. They also suggested ways that teachers can get students to begin to examine their own cultural assumptions and be receptive to new points of view. These suggestions are not limited to role expectations but also include how to approach the accompanying rhetoric, vocabulary, and learning strategies that might otherwise cause confusion.

In terms of pedagogical suggestions for the teacher himself, Tinney et al. noted that he should: (1) be aware of individual student backgrounds, learning about their culture in a way that helps *him* help *them* to be better learners; (2) take the time needed to assess students' needs and understanding because often students *claim* they understand something only to avoid embarrassment; they need extra help to learn to feel comfortable asking questions and responding in class; (3) set the example for his students of being open, patient, and interested regarding people of other nationalities or cultures; (4) stretch but not overwhelm his students; (5) teach them learning strategies to use not only in his class but to transfer to all their classes; (6) recognize individual differences *within* a culture; for, particular members of a culture may adhere to or enact the norms of their primary culture(s) in different ways and to different degrees; (7) with the exception perhaps of a course meant to teach computer or technology skills, keep the technology needs of the students as simple as possible, remembering that students from different cultures tend to come to the classroom with a wide range of technology experience; indeed, some already feel so overwhelmed by cultural and linguistic difficulties that they may be put over the edge by even minor technological challenges. Tinney et al. pointed out that students of other nationalities are often overlooked or not called on in class or teachers have lower expectations of them. They encouraged teachers to remember that when an ethnic minority student is having problems, language and culture may well be the issue, not "intelligence."

The level of English capability of international students poses a real challenge for teachers. Because our ability to communicate through the use of language does so much to shape others' expectations of us, Tinney et al. offer some specific advice for how teachers can approach these issues: (1) do not judge students based on their English level capability because often their ability to speak English has as much or more to do with their social skills and personality than their intellect; (2) consider which difficult words and phrases in your discipline you can make more explicit and/or show with more examples in important contexts; (3) explain difficult vocabulary and technical terms in your field (give helpful definitions and tell them when people use those terms so they can get a better feel for the correct nuances); (4) as much as possible, make connections between course content and real life (relate materials to multiple social and cultural situations and consider inviting students to experience your community of practice); (5) read aloud in class and explain especially complex text by showing examples; (6) go beyond the spoken word to encourage understanding (use charts, pictures, videos, role-playing, real objects, and stories in all the formats that make sense for your content); (7) teach the lesson "backwards" (start with mini-lessons to connect with prior knowledge and background information); (8) use supplementary materials to connect with various learning styles, preferences, and cultural expectations; (9) encourage students from the same countries or islands to not work together in the same project or groups so they use English on team projects and learn about other cultures and methods; (10) give students advanced notice of written or oral reports, with topics and due dates; and (11) clearly identify your expectations. Doing all of these things will help increase comprehensible input.

Another way to help students is to give them suggestions of how they can help you. Tinney, Morgan, and Rogers (2006) give some examples of suggestions for students that will help them make the most out of a challenging experience: (1) realize they are joining a separate academic discourse community of practice for each course they are taking (biology, sociology, accounting, or history); (2) notice each professor's individual discourse style and work with the professor's quirks; (3) try out some new discourse practices, like finding the ten most important words or concepts one must know for each lesson; (4) choose to have an adventure as they discover new learning habits and adapt to other discourse styles (taking small steps until they get comfortable enough to ask questions and express their opinions; (5) face their fears with the help of others (join study groups, get a study buddy, take a study skills class or workshop, join other social groups and get others' views, seek ESL help, use the advice from people in an English language center or in a writing center, talk to teachers about accommodations that are reasonable for their style or ability level, etc.); (6) get straight to the point in class discussions and in creating written work; (7) know that teachers usually define success in terms of effort and completion of individual goals; (8) participate actively in class discussions (speak up and give their opinions!); (9) when in doubt, ask students and teachers for their preferred method of communication; (10) learn at least the basics of the educational cultural assumptions and expectations for the country in which the instructor originates. These suggestions are intended to help students make more sense of both the communicative intent (the purpose of a message) as well as the context (the key to interpreting communicative intent) in a classroom where role expectations can initially be very different from what they are used to.

Examples of Some Culturally Conditioned Interactional Differences in the Classroom

Grossman (1995) has summarized some of the major cultural role and relational differences that tend to exist in the classroom.

For instance, he concluded that white students, middle-class students, and Native American students tend to feel most comfortable with the teacher playing the role of an authoritative facilitator. This tends *not* to be the case with Hispanic, Asian American, and Polynesian American students, who will come to a classroom expecting to find a more authoritarian type of teacher. It may take the latter group of students a while, Grossman notes, to get used to authoritative teaching, which the authors of this text believe is generally the best kind because of its blending of high degrees of both care and demand.

Another set of opposites in teachers' roles are the poles on the continuum that run from the teacher-as-emotionally-aloof to the teacher-as-emotionally-close. Hispanic, Native American, and African American students tend to favor an emotionally close teacher. Asian Americans and some white students, on the other hand, prefer that a teacher not try to get too close. As teachers who favor the emotionally close style of teaching, we have seen how, on one hand, students from more emotionally aloof preference groups have come to appreciate a closer degree of intimacy with their teachers—at least occasionally—so long as the teacher does not try to get too close too fast. What is more, *we as teachers* have learned from those same students the value of a certain degree of distance from our students from time to time.

Like many American teachers, we sometimes try too hard to be our students' "friends." Sometimes this works and is appropriate, but sometimes it is pedagogically inefficient and emotionally depleting for us as teachers to also be "buddies" to our students. Indeed, in such cases a teacher may be trying to win the student's love more than actually *teach* him something. In teaching students from more emotionally aloof groups, then, we have learned this invaluable pedagogical lesson. In this case, our students have been *our teachers* in helping us learn more about how best to interact with *all* our students for their good as well as our own—intellectually and emotionally.

Another set of "role-poles" in students has to do with interactive versus noninteractive learning. Some students seem to feel most comfortable when they are allowed to learn material more or less on their own while others find interactive environments to be more agreeable and supportive. Generally speaking, females tend to be more interactive learners than males, who tend to be more noninteractive—a very broad generalization, to be sure, but one that seems to be roughly true across ethnic and socioeconomic groups—with the interesting, and somewhat puzzling, exception of African American females (Belenkey et al., 1986; Chodorow, 1978; Gilligan, 1982).

Another interesting finding made by Grossman was that many non-European students such as South, Central, and North American Hispanics; Native Americans; Filipinos; and Southeast Asian students tend to be more interactive, frequently seeking feedback from teachers. In the typical U.S. public school classroom (where the general U.S. cultural norm of "rugged individualism" causes great value to be placed on independence and self-assertion) students who often seek out the teacher's opinions and praise may be incorrectly judged as emotionally overdependent, intellectually timid, and academically weak. In fact, it is simply that they just have another way of learning.

In a classroom where both types of learning are fostered, all students may learn the important lesson that there are some types of intellectual activities that lend themselves most productively to individual analysis and articulation and others to group effort and exploration. Learning about both of these styles of inquiry and action can enrich the "learning-strategy" repertoire of all students—helping them avoid the extremes of either self-absorption or conformism. Another strong selling point for having a diverse teaching and learning repertoire is that in a classroom or school, educators will rarely find only one cultural group represented. More than likely, the school and classrooms will be filled with various groups—a large percentage of the class being made up of one cultural group and the rest a mixture.

When students' different cultural norms regarding their roles in the classroom are honored, where those different norms can come into contact with each other and occasionally even be discussed openly, and where all students are invited to coolly alternate and meld role possibilities within themselves, the result is likely to be a learning environment that is rich, creative, and multifaceted—instead of one that gets stuck in only one way of doing things.

Socioeconomic Factors in Minority Students' Emotional Blocks to Learning

School is often a particularly emotional (and frightening) place for students who are already living under considerable stress outside of the classroom because of socioeconomic difficulties. In a sense, these students' emotional "resistances" are "lowered," exacerbating their "susceptibility" to the range of emotional "viruses" that, as we have seen, can impede any child's ability or willingness to learn in the inherently emotion-laden processes of education.

Since students from ethnic minorities represent such a disproportionately high percentage of children in the lower socioeconomic regions of society—for example, almost 55 percent of black children in the United States live below the poverty line—poverty is also a cultural issue in the United States (Anyon, 2001). Accordingly, we should not be surprised to discover that students from cultural minorities often evidence some of the most painful and complex forms of psychodynamic disturbances in the classroom, which, of course, get in the way of them rising to their full potential academically and socially (Littner, 1989).

This lowered level of performance may then be misinterpreted by a teacher as evidence of the child's "cognitive deficiency" and "low I.Q." if he is not aware of the psychosocial dilemmas and dynamics that are compromising this student's academic performance. This evaluation of the child's "shortcomings" then serves to damage the child's self-esteem even further, which, in turn, creates even more anxiety and academic performance. And on and on the vicious cycle goes until, as is presently the case in the United States, 35 percent of African American students, 45 percent of Hispanic American students, and 60 percent of Native American students do not even graduate from high school (Spring, 2006).

The poverty environments in which so many children now live—with one in five children growing up beneath the poverty line in the United States—will, year after relentless year of struggling to exist in such exhausting and often dangerous circumstances, produce a wide range of emotions in the child that he will then bring to the classroom. "Among these are self-hatred, over-identification with those in power, anxiety, hostility, [and] aggression" (Shade, 1989, p. 19). A child whose entire life has been lived on the ragged and perilous socioeconomic edges of our socioeconomically unjust society—where the top 5 percent of the population owns around two-thirds of the wealth—may bring with him to the classroom the understandable sense of alienation and anger that has quite naturally arisen in him in response to his marginalized circumstances in general.

One of the authors of this book, Fidel Montero, has had his own experiences along these lines. He reports that his own sense of subordination was inculcated in him in many ways, some overt and some covert, in U.S. society when he first crossed the U.S.-Mexican border with his family as a child. The message that he was to play a subordinate role in society was made even clearer to him in school when the children of wealthy farmers were consistently given preferential treatment over him and other immigrant children of laborers.

It is not surprising, therefore, indeed it is to be expected that, given the emotional riskiness of learning in general, a minority student may well feel a wide range of frightened, angry, and self-destructive emotions with special—and especially self-destructive—intensity in a classroom environment that is not sensitive to his unique needs. What is more, given the fact that 85 percent of teachers are white and middle class, it is understandable that a student might, at least at the beginning of a school year, project his feelings about the dominant white, middle-class culture onto his teacher (Anyon, 2001).

Exacerbating this problem is the fact that lower-SES community members and parents are often not involved in the schooling process—not because of lack of concern for their children but because they may feel inadequate, embarrassed, or even resentful in the presence of well educated, middle class, and usually white teachers in schools that are filled with a dazzling, daunting array of expensive electronic equipment, thick texts, and shiny whiteboards with words, symbols, and numbers written on them that these parents cannot decipher.

For instance, there is a large body of research showing that conventional school-home connections such as parent-teacher conferences are often unsuccessful with Latino parents because of parents' demanding and inconvenient work schedules (which not infrequently require each parent to work two jobs to make ends meet), language barriers, or different cultural understandings of parents' role in schools (Riordan, 2000).

The fact has also emerged from these studies that when teachers and parents of upper-SES children converse during parent-teacher conferences, the discussion tends to center around the student's academic performance and collegiate future with the parent taking the lead in the conversations. However, when the conversation is between teachers and lower-SES parents, the teachers tend to do most of the talking and what they talk about is mostly the student's "behavior in class"—his obedience to the rules. When schools and parents do not communicate effectively, the parents have a difficult time providing a supportive academic environment at home (Gonzalez, 2001).

For instance, in meetings with parents, especially immigrant ones who do not even know what questions are appropriate to ask about their children's performance in the school, school personnel will sometimes focus on the negative, cut the conversations short, and not initiate conversations. This deprives poverty-stricken, cultural minority students from that essential base of academic and emotional support that their more privileged peers enjoy in abundance and as a matter of course (Riordan, 2000).

Exacerbating this socioeconomic dilemma is the feeling among many lower-SES students after they have reached a certain age (often in their teens but sometimes much earlier) that the system that is promising them a brighter socioeconomic future—one in which they can live a life like the people whom they see every day on TV—may, in fact, be lying to them (Kozol, 1991; Ogbu, 1987). As much as we as teachers want to encourage such children (and we should, indeed, do so!), it is sometimes difficult to argue with these students that they are totally wrong in their "political analyses" and their feelings of betrayal and despair.

Indeed, it is hard to tell an adolescent from a poverty environment that, if he just works hard enough, his chances of breaking out of the culture of poverty into which he was born are excellent! He may find this hard to believe—and understandably so—after twelve years of a vastly inferior and underfunded education; after summers of working at car washes and burger joints (if he can find a job at all) while wealthier students are spending their carefree summers involved in intellectually enriching activities at home or culturally enriching trips to other nations or even other continents that serve to consolidate and build upon what they learned during the previous academic year; after being surrounded by gangs as *his* social networks while more privileged students are able to network with important professionals and other interesting people with whom their parents socialize and do business; after having heard from his parents and grandparents how the inferior education that they received made little, if any, positive difference in their lives while more privileged students have rich family narratives of academic success at prestigious schools to draw upon; and after a lifetime of living in the aesthetically bleak, emotionally depleting, physically dangerous, and economically perilous inner cities or isolated rural communities and not the well manicured and architecturally delightful suburban neighborhoods of their wealthier peers with their "gated communities."

This is a subject that the educational anthropologist John Ogbu (1987) has addressed in his "Perceived Relative Deprivation" model of minority student academic failure. So far in this book we have taken a cultural discontinuity perspective, which, as we have seen, successfully accounts for a wide variety of academic problems as a bad fit between a student's culture and the classroom culture. According to Ogbu, however, in order to fully understand differential academic performance among minority groups, it is not enough to use merely a cultural discontinuity model; we must also distinguish between the two different types of minority groups in the United States—"immigrant minorities" and "caste-like minorities."

An *immigrant minority* is one such as the Punjabis in Gibson's (1988) famous study, *Accommodation without Assimilation*. Looking at these Hindu students in a central California high school, who had just recently arrived in America, Gibson discovered that they have a positive and coherent view of their own culture, a close connection with their culture's language, and an optimistic perception of their chances to advance in the American labor market, which, compared to the labor market back home, is excellent. Hence, they are motivated to succeed in school.

Caste-like minorities, on the other hand, such as the Mexican American students in Gibson's study, who were born in the United States and whose ancestors have been victims of many generations of systematic discrimination, may have a damaged view of themselves culturally, have probably experienced contempt for their culture's language among teachers in the schools, and are typically pessimistic about the labor market.

Hence, a job at McDonald's may seem a real step up to a student from central Pakistan (who *perceives* that work as an *advantage relative* to where he came from, for he makes more in an hour at McDonald's than he could in a week in a factory in his native land). However, for the Mexican American student—who, like his Anglo peers, has been brought up watching the same television programs and hearing the same high-flown rhetoric about "The American Dream"—a job at McDonald's may seem less like a boon than a bane which he and people in his family neighborhood are destined to suffer. He *perceives* a *disadvantage relative* to the promises about equal opportunity that are constantly being made in the news, on the campaign stump, and in his classrooms. Hence, the ghetto American Latino may, quite understandably, feel that there is little reason to succeed in school if all it will lead to is low-paying, low-prestige employment (MacLeod, 1987).

In short, says Ogbu, minority academic success is largely a function of how intact a student's culture is and how optimistic or pessimistic he is about finding good work after finishing a degree—whether school and the work it leads to represent to the student a perceived relative advantage or perceived relative disadvantage.

To be sure, teachers who work in impoverished school environments must do all that they can to help students escape such conditions. The so-called "poverty pedagogies" (Lieberman, 2003) offer many ideological models and pedagogical strategies for doing so. As different as these approaches to teaching students from poverty cultures are, they all assert that teachers must approach these students with great sensitivity to the cultural and economic circumstances in which these students have developed—honoring those students' fear, anger, and despair but helping them harness and transform those emotions into concerted, practical, and hopeful "strategies" for using what resources *do* exist and for finding ways to claim *other resources* so that education may help them escape the socioeconomic prison into which they were born.

However, teachers must also be aware of the emotional attachment that some students have to their cultural background no matter how difficult the socioeconomic circumstances in that culture were. One of the authors of this book, Ramona Cutri, grew up in relative poverty. Though she now has upper-middle-class socioeconomic status, she still finds herself emotionally attached to certain elements of her poverty background. In this sense the socioeconomic "prison" of her youth abides in her memory not only as a prison but also as the site of many emotionally and spiritually rich experiences. Of course, no one wants to be poor. It is not enjoyable growing up financially deprived. However, poverty is the "culture" that some people "know." Poverty is where the people that you love are—or used to be. One fears that in leaving the poverty environment, one is also being forced to give up the people one loves, and that one's memories (good and bad) will become vaguer and vaguer and finally die as one climbs up the socioeconomic ladder. This nostalgia and anxiety may militate against students pursuing higher educational and professional dreams.

Teachers aware of these psychosocial dynamics are in a better position to help students realize that they do not have to give up their loved ones, memories, or the lessons that poverty has taught them. Students can have the opportunity to take all of these things with them as they advance beyond the confines of a life of poverty. And in so doing, they also have the marvelous opportunity to make conditions better for others like them.

Of course, schools cannot do it all. As Bullough (2001) has forcefully argued, any attempt to address the issues of children in poverty in the United States today must do so in a "wider context" than just that of the classroom. We need to immediately put in place a dynamic array of medical, nutritional, therapeutic, and vocational services for these children—and, indeed, for all children. But, as Bullough also argues, teachers *can* make a vital contribution.

As Jencks (1992) has also demonstrated, education can provide up to one-third of the "force" necessary to help a student break out of the deadening orbits of the culture of poverty. And teachers can accomplish this noble work all the more effectively—both in terms of their pedagogical successes with their students and their political influence as informed citizens awakening other citizens to this national scandal—the more they are sensitive to and able to work with the complex emotions that have arisen from their students' experiences as members of minority, disempowered cultures.

Trauma in Recent Arrivals to the United States

Many of these same psychological, political, and pedagogical insights and practices can be marshaled to help other minority students—those from immigrant groups—who are making up an increasingly large sector of the public school population. Many of these students are also suffering from sociopolitically related traumas (such as "ethnic cleansing") that are, in many respects, quite similar to those of native-born American minority students. As Collier (1995) reminds us:

> Among our new arrivals to the U.S. are undocumented as well as legal refugees seeking refuge from war, political oppression, or severe economic conditions. These students bring to our classes special social, emotional, and academic needs, often having experienced interrupted schooling in their home countries. Students escaping war may exhibit symptoms of post-traumatic stress disorder, such as depression, withdrawal, hyperactivity, aggression, and intense anxiety in response to situations that recall traumatic events in their lives (Collier, 1995)

Cool Alternation—or Resistance!

Cool alternation exemplifies what Gibson (1988) has claimed is the best approach to helping minority students deal with the transition into a new culture: *accommodation without assimilation.*

Cool alternation *accommodates* the student's natal culture because it gives him the time and space to learn, in an emotionally comfortable way, how to navigate through the new culture in a manner that *he* perceives to serve his psychosocial needs best. It does *not* force him to *assimilate,* which means more or less turning one's back on one's natal culture and rapidly accepting the new one in virtually every respect. Forced assimilation is not only morally wrong and psychologically damaging; it is simply unworkable, as the tragic educational experience of so many Native Americans throughout the nineteenth century and even into the twentieth century demonstrated.

Wrested away from their families, clans, tribes, and lands to go to white schools, often thousands of miles from home in unfamiliar urban surroundings, Native American students were punished for speaking their own languages, were required to wear torturously confining European clothing, and were compelled to listen in silent and shamed obedience to the negative interpretation of their cultures by the teachers and texts. Not surprisingly, some of these students ran away from the schools. Others "bought into" the oppressive curriculum—or at least, pretended to do so—which, of course, led to feelings of self-hatred and smoldering anger against their oppressors. It was, as Adams (1995) has so poignantly put it, "education for extinction," its purpose being to take the "Indian" out of the Native American and turn him into a "white man in red skin."

Such forms of "education" are tantamount to "deracination," for their intent is ultimately to eliminate the student's natal culture—or at least to eliminate his allegiance to it (Spring, 2006). This, of course, often implies nothing less than turning one's back on (or at least taking a negative view of) one's own past, one's own traditions and religious commitments, one's own language, and (most painfully of all) one's own family. And as Berger and Luckmann (1967) have demonstrated, when a person is *forced* to reject his natal culture in favor of a dominant one, it can result in the collapse of his sense of psychological and social reality. He is left feeling inauthentic, unhealthy, dishonest, afraid, and alienated equally from the old culture he has rejected and the new one he is trying to join (although he can never completely do so) at the price of his past. Deracination is a form of psychosocial homicide.

Fidel Montero reports that in high school, he confronted this dilemma in his attempt to balance his love of sports with his desire to keep his childhood friends from the work camp in which he grew up. His friends from the work camp were all lower-SES Mexicans and were not involved in extracurricular activities. During his high school years, he often felt, while practicing with his team on the football field, that he was betraying his cultural roots by spending so much time in the "non-Mexican" activity (as he viewed it at the time) of football.

These traumas, which are a daily occurrence in the lives of many minority students, can be avoided by the accommodative process of cool alternation, which, if nurtured by the teacher and school, can go a long way in helping a student learn how to negotiate the dominant culture, and even incorporate certain elements of it into his own psyche and worldview if he wishes to, all the while maintaining what is so foundationally important to him in his natal culture. It represents the balance that Nieto (2002) calls for between "critical consciousness" and "strategic accommodation" in a student's view of his new culture.

When schools do not allow students the option of cool alternation but force them to adopt ideas and practices that run completely contrary to those of their natal cultures, students often undermine the teacher and the school by refusing to perform well. This refusal may take the form of something as simple as not raising one's hand to answer a question in class or something as dramatic as dropping out of school—although, in such cases, it is probably more appropriate to say that the student has been *pushed out* of school by a set of curricular assumptions and instructional practices that the student perceives as being fundamentally threatening to his identity as a member of his and his parents' culture. Typically, it takes the intermediate form of simply doing poorly academically, being disengaged or troublesome in class, and not taking part in the extracurricular life of the school.

According to Giroux's (1983) "Resistance Theory," such a student's academic failure is not a result of his "lack of intelligence" but rather of his anger —both conscious and unconscious—at an educational system whose hidden agenda is to erase his culture. The student's resistance, far from being due to a deficient intelligence, actually stems from his highly intelligent recognition of the unspoken philosophical and political assumptions embedded in what is taught and how it is taught in the classroom—the "hidden curriculum" (Eisner & Vallance, 1985). Resistance is a strategically "creative maladjustment" (Kohl, in Nieto, 2002, p. 59) to a "reality-threatening" situation (Berger & Luckmann, 1967).

For instance, Wax, Wax, & Dumont (1964), in their study of Native American Oglala students on a reservation, showed how these students began to sense after the fourth or fifth grades that their white teachers viewed Oglala culture as an impoverished one. The message that the students were finally able to piece together at around ten years old was that they were seen by teachers as laboring under a "cultural deficit"—indeed, that the teachers felt that the students lived in a "cultural vacuum" (p. 73). To preserve their sense of cultural identity and integrity, these students naturally began, both individually and in peer groups, to stonewall the teachers' obvious agenda of "educating" them into the "correct" Caucasian way of doing and seeing things.

More recently, Deyhle, in a highly illuminating set of analyses, dealt with related phenomena of resistance in her studies of the Navajos and Utes (1986), showing how a "break-dancing" subculture—which displaced and subverted the official curriculum and culture of the school as a social "institution"—arose among the students on reservation schools. In this subculture, a person's excellence at break dancing meant acceptance and prestige by a peer group. Doing well in school, however, led to his being shunned by those same peers. It is often through peer pressure that students are enlisted by other students into the political subculture of resistance at a school, for adolescence is a time of life when the opinions of one's peers—one's primary reference group in adolescence—are particularly influential regarding one's vision of oneself and one's worth (Conger & Galambos, 1997).

Intragroup Variability

Before concluding this section, it is necessary to discuss the idea of intragroup variability. This refers to the fact that, although there are often good pedagogical reasons to think of students in terms of large ethnic groups—such as "Hispanic" or "Asian"—as we have done throughout this study, we should always be aware that there can be considerable subcultural variation within such groups.

Matute-Bianchi (1986), for instance, identified five subgroups among students of Mexican descent in her study of a California high school. Each subgroup identified itself differently in ethnic terms and showed different behavior patterns. Moreover, each group had different attitudes to schooling in Anglo society: for some of those groups, schooling in an Anglo society did not pose a cultural threat; for others it did. Furthermore, intragroup variation among Hispanics is often a function of country of origin, with Cubans and Central Americans doing best in school and Mexican immigrants doing worst.

Along similar lines, Gibson (1988) has warned that a single view of "Asians" encourages "neglect of the serious problems many people of Asian descent continue to face in this country" (p. 7). A newly arrived Vietnamese student and a fourth-generation Japanese American student, although both ethnically Asian, will probably have radically different experiences of, say, a tenth-grade history class. And the fact that a Hmong student speaks a language that has no written form will certainly be an important consideration in teaching that child how to read English.

In general, intragroup variability is a function of the following factors: (1) contrasting physical conditions experienced by the student in the country of origin, (2) whether the student comes from a rural or urban environment in his country of origin, (3) how long his family has been in the United States, and (4) the extent to which the student accepts and is proud of his ethnicity—the more ethnically secure students generally doing the best in school. For, schools that take a positive view of a cultural minority student's native language and culture—and thus encourage that positive view in the student himself—have much greater success in teaching English to that student than schools which send him the explicit and implicit message that his native language and culture are inferior.

The ABCs of Psychosocial Awareness in Teachers

Hopefully it is clear by now how vitally important it is that teachers be aware that a minority student's poor academic performance may be emotionally caused, not cognitively—rooted in the student's sense of himself as a member of a particular culture in general and as a member of a subculture of peers within that culture. Teachers who are aware of this fact are more likely to respond with more tact and compassion in their interactions with these students.

In this approach to the multicultural classroom, the various socioeconomic cultures represented by the students in the classroom are honored. The job of the teacher is to operate as a kind of cultural broker, who helps negotiate the interaction among cultures in the classroom so that each culture can learn from and be edified by all of the others (Castaneda, 1995). He does this in what he teaches and how he teaches it, allowing, to the greatest degree possible, different voices to be heard and different perspectives to be entertained in classroom discussions on topics ranging from westward expansion in U.S. history to the characterization of racial minorities in Shakespeare's plays, to the theory of the Big Bang in astrophysics.

We have also seen that the best pedagogical approach to dealing with cultural resistance in the classroom is to allow as wide-ranging a view of the topics under discussion as possible and doing so in a way that accommodates various learning styles. This is a pedagogy that, in its stress upon multiple perspectives and varied pedagogical modalities, is both holistic, multiculturally sensitive, and of potential benefit to all students in the classroom.

Clearly, not all culture-specific emotions and behaviors are to be celebrated and incorporated into the culture of the classroom. Some subcultures—for instance, inner-city ghetto cultures as they presently exist with their rampant crime, many out-of-wedlock births, and widespread drug usage—do have real, systemic problems that must be frankly acknowledged and addressed (Wilson, 1987). It is simply not acceptable to "celebrate" such a situation as merely another form of "subcultural diversity," for the situation is psychologically and socioeconomically perilous not only for those who are forced to live in it but for a society that cannot bear the price—either financially, politically, or morally—of this state of affairs, where so few people have so much and so many people have so little. However, these are cultural problems that the classroom teacher can best do his part in helping to address if he approaches them with maximum cultural sensitivity in both what he teaches and how he teaches it.

THE THERAPEUTIC CLASSROOM

Throughout this chapter we have offered various suggestions to aid teachers in increasing their awareness of and effectiveness in responding to cultural diversity in their classrooms. We have stressed throughout that they should try to embrace diversity in the classroom so as to allow the maximum degree of accommodation of various cultural and subcultural perspectives—as much, that is, as is practicable given the demographic and institutional realities of the public school classroom, which will almost always tend to favor the dominant cultural group at a school site (Ballantine, 1997).

We would like to expand on these ideas by looking at the classroom as a therapeutic site—a place where the teacher can promote nurturance and healing in students in addition to fostering their academic skills. In saying this, we are not claiming that the teacher is, in fact, a therapist. Clearly he is not, and it would be both inappropriate and potentially dangerous for him to believe that he is somehow empowered to "do therapy" with his students. However, in being as emotionally attuned to and supportive of his students as he can be in his role as a teacher, *he may often fulfill a therapeutic function.* As Basch (1989) has noted, this delicate calibration of the teacher to his students' psychodynamic processes is essential to any really humane pedagogy, given the complex psychosocial elements at play in most educational situations:

> Like it or not, the teacher, if he or she is to be successful, must function as a psychotherapist, not in the formal sense of conducting therapy sessions with the students, but in the practical sense of being alert and responsive to the psychological needs that students evince both by what they do and what they do not do. (p. 772)

The teacher does not have to have training as a therapist in order to be a therapeutic teacher. All it really takes is compassion, cultural sensitivity, and a desire to create a learning environment in which all students can learn not only from the teacher but from each other. Goodwill and common sense—coupled with the kinds of ideas and approaches that we have suggested in this book—will go a very long way indeed in helping a person become a highly effective therapeutic teacher. It is not necessary "to unravel a person's past history in order to understand him. If we are observant, we can gain insight into his assumptions and beliefs from his behavior and reactions to ourselves and others in the here and now" (Salzberger-Wittenberg, 1983, p. 36).

In becoming a therapeutic teacher, the teacher is not only responding to the needs of students who are experiencing elevated levels of stress in the classroom for sociopolitical reasons. *He is practicing a pedagogy of nurturance and care that is of great benefit to all of his students* (Noddings, 1984). He is also fulfilling the moral call of the Jewish philosopher Martin Buber to all teachers that they try to establish a pedagogically loving relationship with their students—what he called an *I-Thou relationship*—and that they avoid treating students as empty, anonymous objects into whom they are simply pouring official "information" and "knowledge" without much regard (or even *any* regard) for who the students are as individuals and members of a culture (Buber, 1985; Freire, 2001).

The authors of this text passionately believe that *a holistic multicultural pedagogy is an ethical pedagogy of love*. And, although it may seem a paradox, a pedagogy of love is also, ultimately, the most efficient type of teaching, for it helps teachers and school leaders most gracefully negotiate those complex psychosocial issues which, left unaddressed, undermine good teaching of sound academic content.

The Culturally Therapeutic Classroom

According to the educational anthropologists George and Louise Spindler (1992), the classroom can become a site of "cultural therapy." By this phrase they meant that many classroom topics and activities can be an occasion and opportunity for all students—those from dominant as well as minority cultures—to examine their own and each others' cultural assumptions and insights regarding their approach to that topic or activity.

According to Gay (2000, p. 216), this cultural therapy brings "one's own culture, in its manifold forms—assumptions, goals, values, beliefs, and communicative modes—to a level of awareness" that allows a student to see the potential strengths and limitations in his own and others' culturally conditioned views about a subject under analysis in the classroom. In this way, the student learns more about himself and his culture, his peers and their cultures, and in the balance gains access to a wide and enriching variety of perspectives that he and his classmates would not otherwise have.

Teachers and students thus become what Heath (1983) has called "practical ethnographers" and "ethnographic detectives" who are constantly exploring each others' worldviews. They can learn to turn an analytic eye on their own culture to uncover its practices, strengths, and challenges. This is an excellent way of avoiding what too often happens when teachers and students do *not* turn an investigative eye to their own or others' cultures: they may consciously and unconsciously impose their own cultural assumptions on each other in ways that lead to isolation, anger, and limited vision.

In passing, we would like to emphasize yet again that we are *not* calling for teachers to bring their chemistry or reading lesson to a dead stop and become ethnographic detectives—and *only* that—on the spot. What we are trying to offer are perspectives, approaches, and facts that will help the teacher devise ways, in the midst of their very busy days, to incorporate reflecting on their worldviews while simultaneously teaching and learning the academic curriculum. Here again, the "pause button" metaphor comes in handy.

The important metaphor of hitting the "pause button" allows reflectivity to happen in the midst of classroom and school life. As educators become more aware of the holistic approach to multicultural education, they will find that they can reach with increasing ease into their mental "grab bag" to pull out whatever models or information that will help them be better and happier teachers in multicultural settings. We cannot overemphasize the importance of this simple act of the teacher's pausing and reflecting occasionally in the midst of the hubbub of the classroom in order to find greater joy and fruitfulness in his work.

To be more adept at being practical ethnographers and at teaching their students how to become ethnographic detectives, teachers can do such things as learn about: (1) some of the rules and roles of interaction in their students' cultures, (2) a minority culture's phonological patterns in order to help students with their phonological difficulties, (3) differential eating protocols, (4) patterns of play and politeness among their students' cultures, and (5) the student's home life in order to link school to home in classroom activities and thereby draw minority parents into classroom projects. Additionally, teachers can use "texts" generated by students as classroom material for all of the students to study, thereby fostering both intercultural awareness and a "meta-language" that members of the class can use to discuss their differences.

For example, in both spoken and written form, students from all different cultures can tell stories or write poems that everyone in the class listens to or reads. They then analyze the "texts" together in order to examine different cultural styles and perspectives. In this process, students:

> meet very different notions of truth, style, and language appropriate to a "story" from those they have known at home. They must learn a different taxonomy and new definitions of stories. They must come to recognize when a story is expected to be true, when to stick to the facts and when to use their imaginations. (Heath, 1983, p. 294)

Heath shows in detail how successful such storytelling can be in forging a language community at school. This is a large step in the direction of creating a democratic synthesis of cultural and conversational styles in a classroom—one that honors and enlarges all students' worldviews.

As Grossman (1995) has pointed out, there are essentially four basic ways that a student from a minority culture can deal with the fact of cultural differences in a classroom.

The first two ways are not functional: (1) the student can maintain the values, beliefs, and practices of his native culture in order to completely reject the mainstream, (2) he can reject the values, beliefs, and practices of native culture and completely accept the mainstream. In the first case, the student allows himself to remain in a socioeconomic straitjacket, completely disempowered because he has refused to learn how to deal with—and even learn from—the dominant culture so as to increase his own and his culture's socioeconomic influence in the society in which he must, after all, exist. In the second case, the student, by abandoning his culture, opens himself up to feelings of self-hatred and resentment towards the politically dominant culture for which he has committed psychosocial suicide by turning his back on his parents, his people, and his history.

The beauty and power of Heath's model is that it allows students from both dominant and minority cultures to adopt the next two, and infinitely healthier, options that Grossman has defined, in which a student can: (3) accept both cultures and "code switch" between them depending on the particular situation he finds himself in and his needs and goals, or (4) synthesize both cultures into a new cultural form that comes more and more to influence his worldview. In becoming ethnographic detectives, teachers and students grow closer to each other and thereby learn from each other while maintaining a healthy degree of psychosocial independence from each other, too. This strength in diversity is, we believe, the promise of cultural pluralism, and it is a promise that can be realized every day in the ordinary democratic setting of the public school classroom.

The Personally Therapeutic Classroom

The idea of a personally therapeutic classroom rests on two pillars. The first is the enhancement of a student's self-esteem, his "learning ego"—so necessary for him to have satisfying and productive educational experiences. The second is the creation of a classroom that is "a holding environment."

Self-Esteem: A Prerequisite for Deep and Durable Learning

As we have seen throughout this book, a student with high self-esteem as a learner is a student who has that "courage to try" and "courage to learn" that are prerequisites of deep and durable learning (Brophy, 1997; Conger & Galambos, 1997). As we have also seen, however, many students, for personal and cultural reasons, find the classroom threatening. They come to the classroom with a damaged "learning ego" (Anthony, 1989). The teacher can do a great deal to alleviate these fears and help all students transcend them cognitively and emotionally by creating nurturing environments—what the child psychoanalyst Winnicott called "holding environments."

Creating a Holding Environment in the Classroom

Winnicott (1992, p. 259) saw the roots of psychological health or illness in the infant's relationship with its mother. Ideally, the mother offers a good "holding environment" for the infant. This may actually involve the physical act of lovingly holding the infant. Yet, even when it does not, it *does* entail the mother providing the child with a physical and emotional context that is appropriate to its needs and beneficial to its growth—an environment, in short, that *holds* the child.

Yet—although it offers nurturance and safety for the child—a good holding environment is not one in which the child is protected from any and all tension and ambiguity. A good holding environment simply provides *enough* care, protection, and safeguards for the child so that, even if the child does fall or fail, the damage done will not be serious, and the child will always know that the mother is there to offer love and encouragement. Indeed, a good holding environment does not *avoid* tension. It simply makes sure that it occurs in a fundamentally safe and compassionate environment. In this way, the child develops the "courage to learn" and "courage to try."

The teacher provides a "holding environment" when he offers a safe space for his students to grow, just as the mother does for the developing infant. "Since our earliest learning arises in the intimate relationship of parent and child, each new course reawakens in students the need to have a target of idealization [i.e., the mother or teacher] and to have their efforts admired" (Elson, 1989, p. 789).

> Whether the course is biology, mathematics, sociology, or child care, the teacher provides a holding environment. . . . This holding environment is one in which the empathic understanding of the teacher creates the conditions which allow the student to reveal what he does not know. Seeing the student at his least effectual, and yet not breaking off contact or shaming him because of his limitations, becomes in itself a novel, healing experience for the student. (p. 801)

Holding environments provide the optimal conditions for the growth of all students in dealing with their psychosocial issues and cognitive tasks, providing a high degree of "care" as well as an appropriate degree of "demand." In almost every case, the best teaching is that which blends the teacher's high demands of his students coupled with his high care for them. This is called *authoritative teaching.*

Teaching that is high in demand but low in care is called *authoritarian teaching.* Teaching that is high in care but low in demand is called *permissive teaching.* Both authoritarian and permissive teaching are pedagogically unsound, for the former alienates students emotionally from the teacher while the latter does not stimulate students to perform to their maximum potential.

Authoritative teaching, however, has been amply demonstrated in instructional theory research to be the best form of teaching in most situations (Brophy, 1997)—not least of all classrooms with students from minority cultures, who, as the research literature unfortunately demonstrates, tend to experience authoritarian or permissive teaching more often than students from dominant cultures, contributing to lowered academic performance in minority culture students (Banks & Banks, 2001; Garcia, 2001; Ovando et al., 2006). Armed with common sense, compassion, and the ideas and strategies that this book has provided, the teacher can learn to create a holding environment in his class—one in which he teaches authoritatively—with high expectations of his students and genuine care for them. This is also the best style of parenting according to many developmental psychologists (Conger & Galambos, 1997; Dusek, 1994).

The teacher need not be perfect to foster his students' growth any more than a mother must be perfect to foster her child's growth. In fact, in Winnicott's view, it is not the perfect mother (whatever *that* might be) but the *good-enough mother* (as he calls her) who is best able to create a realistic and therefore viable holding environment for the child. Winnicott devised the phrase "good-enough mothering" to distinguish it from the so-called ideal of *perfect* mothering in which the mother must always be available to the infant, meeting its every need almost before it arises. Such a "perfect" mother would have to forego her own identity, needs, and boundaries and thus could not relate healthily to her infant. Such a mother would also not allow the infant to experience the tension and opposition that is necessary for it to confront—in healthy and monitored doses, of course—so that it can begin to realistically mature.

On the other hand, "good-enough mothering gives opportunity for the steady development of personal processes in the baby" (Winnicott, 1992, p. 456)—processes that will feed positively upon the mother's realistic humanity and not her neurotic perfectionism. Wool (1989, p. 750) has devised the notion of "the good-enough teacher" who creates an educational holding environment where the student can experiment in ways that offer both safety and a limited degree of risk without the teacher burning out because of the unrealistic need to be perfect. Although every teacher will develop his own style in being a good-enough teacher, we offer below some pedagogical points to consider in attaining this all-important pedagogical goal. We will do so by drawing from Brophy's (1997) excellent text in instructional theory and practice, *Motivating Students to Learn,* which any teacher, novice or veteran, would do well to study in depth. Here, we can only touch upon some of its highlights.

The notion of the "good enough teacher" can also help teachers avoid feeling guilty for "not doing enough." People generally become teachers because they love children and want to be instrumental in their growth. This noble motivation can too easily lead to a counterproductive sense of guilt, however, especially in first-year teachers.

New teachers leave the often idealistic haven of their teacher education programs to then be confronted with the hard realities of schools and classrooms (Artiles, Barreto, Peña, & McClafferty, 1998). First year teachers usually feel that they are scrambling through just to survive the daily tasks and situations they encounter. They often feel unable to implement all of the theories and strategies that they learned in their teacher education programs (Bullough, 1989). They then feel guilty and frustrated because they cannot "do it all." It is therefore quite liberating for teachers to realize that, in doing their best, they are generally being "good enough." This more realistic view of their work allows teachers to take a healthy sense of pride in their present successes as teachers, a mature view of their challenges, and a realistic appraisal of what they need to do to improve as they gain more classroom experience.

Elements of a Positive Pedagogy of Possibility

As just mentioned, a teacher can communicate low expectations to his students. When he does, students will generally oblige him by "living down" to his inferior expectations for them—their lesser performance then serving to confirm the teacher that he was correct in not expecting much from those students in the first place. This creates a vicious cycle that has often been observed in teacher-student relationships when the teacher is from a dominant culture and the student is from a minority one. However, it is part of a larger instructional phenomenon known as the "Pygmalion Effect." This refers to the fact that when teachers have high expectations of students, coupled with a high degree of care for them, they will perform much better than when the teacher has low expectations of them.

How does a teacher convey low expectations to a student? Some of the primary ways are: (1) using less wait time when they are trying to formulate a verbal response to a question, (2) giving answers to them, (3) criticizing them more often than favored students for wrong answers, (4) praising them less often than favored students for right answers, (5) not giving feedback, (6) calling on them less often than favored students, (7) asking them only easier questions than those posed to favored students, (8) not giving them the benefit of the doubt on tests but doing so with favored students, (9) being less friendly to them than to favored students, (10) giving shorter and less complete answers to their questions than those of favored students, (11) using their ideas less often than those of favored students, and (12) limiting them to an impoverished curriculum (Brophy, 1997). The authoritative teacher avoids such things, for they undermine a holding environment (Brophy, 1997).

It is also important for a teacher to be able to recognize the signs of the *lack* of the "courage to try" and the "courage to learn" that his students may bring with them to his classroom from the outset, whether that lack is primarily rooted in the child's conflicted individual psyche or marginal social circumstances. Butkowski and Willows (1980) have noted the following five signs of a damaged learning ego in a student—namely, when a student: (1) shows low initial expectancy for his success at the beginning of a task, (2) gives up quickly when a problem arises, (3) attributes failure to lack of his personal ability, not to controllable causes, (4) attributes success to external, uncontrollable causes, not to his own inherent potentials and abilities, and (5) responds to a problem with the prediction that he will only continue to fail in the future, no matter how hard he tries (in Brophy, 1997).

Wlodkowski (in Brophy, 1997) provides four suggestions for helping such students regain a healthy learning ego. The teacher should: (1) guarantee that students experience some successes regularly, (2) give recognition for real effort even if it does not necessarily result in stellar performance, (3) emphasize that it is the student's personal abilities and potentials that led to the success, not some external cause, and (4) use group processes so that students can help each other—each student assisting the other students in areas where he is strong and getting help from other students in areas where he is weak—so that they are all both teaching and learning from each other in what the Russian psychologist Lev Vygotsky (1986) called their mutual "Zone of Proximal Development."

In like manner, Grossman (1995) has proffered teachers a wide variety of pedagogical strategies for enhancing the student's sense of self-worth and efficacy. Grossman encourages the teacher to: (1) offer individualized instruction whenever possible, (2) help the student see the strengths that he brings to a task, (3) help the student be more accepting of his cultural style when it conflicts with mainstream expectations, (4) provide the student with opportunities to succeed in his strong areas, (5) encourage him to replace negative self-talk with positive self-talk, (6) break difficult tasks down into manageable steps, (7) demonstrate trust and faith in the student, (8) let students make choices about tasks and approaches when and as appropriate, (9) give dependent students help only when they truly need it, and (10) ask the student what he thinks about his work rather than the teacher always volunteering his own evaluation of it.

These suggestions are quite similar to those offered by Bandura (1986) in his ideas regarding how to enhance a student's "Self-Efficacy Perceptions" (Bandura, 1986). According to Bandura, a teacher can do this by: (1) helping the student set specific and difficult but attainable goals for himself, (2) modeling effective strategies for the student for solving the problem at hand, (3) providing the student with positive feedback and avoiding negative feedback, and (4) making statements to the student that help him see himself as a competent person who can make progress, even at a task that he may not be exceptionally good at (see also Shawaker & Dembo, 1996).

Many of these suggestions for practicing a positive pedagogy in the multicultural classroom are nicely captured in Ames's (in Brophy, 1997) easily remembered TARGET program, where each letter stands for an aspect of this pedagogy.

T stands for the fact that a teacher should select *tasks* that provide optimal challenge and excitement for students. **A** refers to *authority*. The teacher is in control but he negotiates ideas, tasks, standards, and prospects with students as much as is possible. **R** is *recognition*. Teachers should remember to give recognition to all students who progress, not just high achievers. Indeed, a child who is only performing at an "average" level with respect to a certain task may have had to exert a great deal more effort and integrity in reaching that level than a student who can excel with virtually no effort at all. With the letter **G**, Ames is talking about *grouping*—capitalizing on Vygotsky's idea of the Zone of Proximal Development to promote learning and empowerment in all students through cooperative learning situations that minimize competition. **E** is about *evaluation*. Use multiple criteria in evaluating students, not just one or a battery of standardized tests, and make the tests as individualized as possible, allowing students to draw upon various types of intelligences and talents in order to offer a holistic "portfolio" of their performance (Duschl & Gitomer, 1991). Finally, **T** stands for Ames's advice to use *time* creatively, not just rigidly in utter slavishness to the clock and a prearranged lesson plan, but to "go with the flow" when the class is on to an idea or activity that is generating palpable collective interest, even passion. Be flexible!

All of the above suggestions for conceptualizing and implementing a positive pedagogy of possibility for students will be enlivening and enriching for all students from all cultural groups—whether dominant or minority—helping them overcome whatever patterns of "learned helplessness" that they have fallen into for personal and/or social causes. As Carol Dweck (1999) has so wisely reminded all teachers, a pedagogy of possibility can work miracles in helping turn children's images of themselves from "helpless victims" into "capable learners," who: (1) do not become upset by failure, (2) do not talk about the failure as a failure but as an occasion to regroup and redouble effort, (3) learn to devise new self-instructions and strategies in the course of facing a problem, and (4) recall past successes whenever they run into a snag and use those memories to realistically anticipate the possibility of future successes.

This does not mean that all students should be led to believe that they can shine at all tasks. Creating such an expectation in a student would be pedagogically and emotionally disastrous, for *no one* is good at everything. Indeed, although authoritative teaching involves high care from the teacher, it also involves high demands by him, and no person can rise to every high demand in every subject and activity. We all have what the psychiatrist Carl Jung (1974) called our "inferior functions," those fields where, even with the most strenuous effort, we will probably never be much better than average. This is simply a fact of life for everyone.

Again, the idea of the holding environment helps us here. We know that a mother would do her child a great disservice by encouraging the child to believe that he could do anything he wanted to do with great competence and with success guaranteed. This would inevitably set the child up for failure, disillusionment, anger, and despair. Similarly, a teacher must sometimes help a student see that, although the student does very fine, even superb work, in one subject or activity, he may not ever be better than average or even below average in another subject or activity. Such compassionate realism is part of the teacher's role as an authoritative facilitator in the classroom as a holding environment.

This chapter has highlighted how the social, emotional, and cognitive domains are inextricably linked in educational processes. With this knowledge, educators can recognize that teaching and learning involves more than just the "facts." The reception of the facts always involves an emotional interpretation of them. Aware of this fundamental aspect of learning, teachers can then better "tease out" students' emotional responses from their cognitive understanding of the facts. This does not require that teachers stop their lessons to psychoanalyze their students, but it does call upon them to "hit the pause button" just long enough to consider students' responses and behaviors from a psychosocial perspective, and then proceed accordingly.

Teaching with the psychosocial dimensions of learning in mind helps the teacher teach with greater psychological and cultural sensitivity, inevitably helping the teacher to avoid many unnecessary confrontations with students. The ability to recognize the affective dimensions of teaching and learning allows teachers and administrators to avoid fruitless confrontations or to defuse them before they flare up and consume precious classroom time that could be devoted to more productive activities. Developing these types of skills not only helps the teacher and administrator to learn more about their students but also gives them opportunities to learn more about themselves. One thing they learn is how to be "a good enough teacher." This idea enables teachers to avoid falling into damaging cycles of guilt and frustration.

Sensitive to the culturally complex and psychodynamically complex nature of learning, equipped with the models and strategies of a culturally sensitive pedagogy such as those that we have laid out in this chapter, and guided by common sense and compassion, a teacher can create holistic multicultural environments and curricula that are vibrant, inclusive, and psychosocially empowering for *all* his students.

5

The Cognitive Domain

SCHEMA THEORY, CULTURE, AND PLURALISM

Learning is both cognitive and affective—involving "mind" and "heart." In the last chapter, we stressed the emotional side of learning. In this chapter, we turn our focus to its more cognitive side.

We begin by stating our assumption that at the organic level all "normal" brains function roughly in the same way within a broad range in terms of perceiving and conveying data. That data is then processed into information and stored; this "*information* processing approach" (Anderson, 2000) is common to all "normal" human cognition. A child born into Culture A would, we assume, think, speak and act like someone from Culture B if she had been taken from Culture A at birth and raised in Culture B (assuming, of course, that she did not experience prejudice from other members of Culture B during her development that would damage her understanding of herself and of her place and potentials in Culture B).

Just as every child in the cradle makes virtually every sound in every language until mother and others teach her through modeling and reinforcement, that "we" only use "these" sounds (the others then receding through disuse into the depths of unconscious oblivion), she learns in a similar, culturally conditioned fashion to select facts from the environment to interpret in certain ways and for certain purposes. These "ways" of selecting data, interpreting them, and putting them to personal and social use are what we call her culture's "cognitive schemas" (Anderson, 1977; Nickerson, 1985).

A simple example of this is a child from an American inner city who might look up in the sky and, seeing a bank of billowing clouds forming on the horizon, make nothing of it. A Native American child who was still close to her tribe's ancient traditions and still had access to its skills might look at the same sky and see a particular weather pattern forming—and might even be able to discern some spiritual significance in the cloud formation. Indeed, the inner-city child might not even particularly notice the same clouds in the same sky that would be deeply significant to the other child. This is because their differential cultural schemas had trained them not only to *see things differently* but also to *see different things!* On the other hand, the inner-city child, street-wise and cautious, seeing a group of people—and not clouds—forming at the end of the block, dressed in certain kinds of clothing and making certain types of movements, might well understand that a drug deal was going down whereas the Native American child, on the same street, would see nothing more than some people talking. As Shade (1989, p. 87) puts it, a culture's cognitive style "represents a superordinate construct which accounts for individual differences in a variety of cognitive, perceptual, and personality variables which influence the method of perceiving, organizing, and interpreting information." Not only lower order sensory-motor phenomena but higher-order reasoning processes are deeply affected by culturally shaped schemas.

The two children may be surrounded by the same scenes but are picking and choosing data, organizing those data in certain ways, and drawing (or not drawing) conclusions from that information because of their differential cultural schemas. Metaphorically, we can picture schemas as the differently colored lenses with different patterns on them that our cultures provide us to place over certain scenes in order to organize and make sense out of those scenes—in order to "reason" about them. It is not that the two children in our examples above do not know how to "reason." They each reason very well. It is simply that they do so in different ways from each other depending on their culture's different "hermeneutics"—or different "ways of seeing and interpreting things."

Moreover (and this is a crucial point!), every individual sees her world through her cultural schemas whether she comes from a dominant or minority culture. These schemas encourage her to select, choose, and interpret things in certain ways and not in others. *Everyone comes from a culture and every culture provides its members with schemas.* The child from a dominant culture does not necessarily reason any better (or worse) than the children from the minority cultures simply by virtue of the fact that she is from a politically dominant culture. All of the children may reason equally well—that is, they may all three be "hermeneutically" competent—although they reason differently from each other.

The existence of cultural schemas constitutes both a strength and a weakness for every individual. It is a strength because it delimits the otherwise chaotically overwhelming number of impressions, sensations, and ideas that would otherwise paralyze the person physically, emotionally, and intellectually with their sheer enormity. It is a weakness, on the other hand, precisely because it *does* delimit a person's world—causing her to take in and interpret some things in certain ways while excluding other things and other interpretations. As Kenneth Burke (1989) so wisely noted, "Every way of seeing is also a way of not seeing." Indeed, one of the great potentials of multicultural education is that it holds the wonderful promise of expanding each child's view of the universe through interaction with other views. And, as Dewey (1916) pointed out, this is the promise not only of inclusive education but of democracy in general, which insists upon the maximum possible *tolerance* and (in many cases) even the *celebration* of diversity so long as that diversity does not violate basic standards of goodness and practicality that every society must maintain in order to remain cohesive, strong, and humane.

The existence of various cultural schemas is, in itself, both universal and unproblematic. There are, however, two types of problems that *can* arise as a result of differences in (sub)cultural schemas. The first problem is quite general. It has to do with conflict when a (sub)cultural schema is seen by the dominant culture as so threatening to itself that that (sub)culture and its schemas are, literally, *in*tolerable to the dominant culture. As noted before, these questions, although certainly relevant to our inquiries in this book, tend to go beyond its scope into the broader realm of ethical and political philosophy (Rorty, 1999).

The second, more strictly "educational" problem falls precisely within the purview of this book, however. It has to do with the tensions that often arise in classrooms when the cultural schemas of certain minority students (on the basis of ethnic, socioeconomic, and gender differences) vary greatly from the cultural schemas of the dominant culture that defines the official curriculum and the standards of academic "success." When these conflicts arise, students with minority cultural schemas may do poorly in school—but not because they are in any sense less intelligent or have a less valid worldview but simply because they bring culturally conditioned cognitive schemas to the classroom that do not match the "official" standards and "discourses" (Foucault, 1980). When that happens, a student will be labeled as "cognitively deficient" when in fact she is merely "cognitively different."

Such mislabeling of a student is very damaging to the student from the minority culture, who, according to "Labeling Theory," may come to judge her own worth in terms of the negative labels that have been stuck upon her by other persons and institutions (Best, 2004). Such feelings of worthlessness have hurtful, even catastrophic effect, ranging from feelings of neurotic anxiety to the commission of criminal acts. Such invidious and destructive labeling is also subversive of the democratic educational dream of being mutually enriched by each other's perspectives. This "mutual enrichment" leads not only to deeper and more flexible forms of intelligence but also to more equitable and long-lasting forms of pluralistic democracy—a political necessity in our multicultural world if it is not to degenerate into politically unsustainable chaos of antagonistically screaming voices, on one hand, or the totalitarian imposition of just one group's worldview over all others', on the other hand.

CULTURALLY CONDITIONED SCHEMAS AND THE CULTURE OF THE CLASSROOM

By the time they reach the age to attend kindergarten and first grade, children already know a great deal. As mentioned in an earlier chapter, Heath (1983) has shown that kindergarteners already have quite definite—and culturally different—"literacy practices" in terms of the words that they have already learned to recognize, the uses to which they tend to put such book-based information, and the "authority" that printed material seems to have in their cultures. In general, "by five years of age, [children] already have internalized rules and procedures for acquiring knowledge and demonstrating their skills. These cognitive processing protocols are learned from their cultural socialization" (Gay, 2000, p. 150). Those sweet little children who file so innocently and energetically into class on the opening day of kindergarten or first grade are already amazingly "savvy" linguistically, textually, and hermeneutically (Halliday, 1975).

What is more, children are extremely sensitive from very early on to both explicit and implicit messages from the teacher about whether she finds their ways of being in and acting on the world acceptable or not. If the message being conveyed to students from a minority culture is, "Your (and your parents') way of interpreting the world is deficient, unhealthy, and therefore illegitimate," many of those students will understandably find ways to subvert—or at least detach themselves—from the life of the classroom. Obviously, very few teachers would consciously think such things and even fewer would be so insensitive as to say them. How, then, do these messages sometimes get formed and communicated by teachers?

Most teachers did well as students. Such positive school experiences probably contribute to many people's decisions to become teachers. It is quite natural for people who have been successful in conventional school settings to expect that others will—and even should—learn in ways similar to how they learned. Teachers from native-English-speaking, white, upper-middle-class backgrounds tend to learn in ways that match closely to how school is taught and how learning is demonstrated. When students from diverse backgrounds enter the classroom and "do school" in ways that differ to some degree from how school is done in the United States, educators can conclude that these students are not doing things correctly. These instances of cultural incongruence can be as simple as a child who is not used to sitting on the carpet for five minutes without getting fidgety—or a high school student who does not do her homework, explaining that doing homework is not important because she already has a job lined up and does not need to worry about school anymore. Another example is a parent who does not chat with the teacher when dropping her child off at school in the morning because she does not want to encroach on the teacher's authority and territory. To some teachers, these attitudes and behaviors may seem educationally counterproductive, even somewhat offensive, and this can result in a subtle shift in the teacher's attitude toward the student. Children and adolescents are very quick to perceive such shifts in a teacher's attitudes.

This does not mean that teachers must be hypervigilant in monitoring their every thought and attitude about their students. That would be exhausting for the teacher and unbeneficial for the student. However, teachers do need to maturely think through their assumptions about other cultural views of schooling that their students and their parents might hold. This does not mean that teachers have to agree with those other views, but it does mean that they can be more effective and satisfied in their work as teachers if they are aware of those views and accommodate them whenever it seems both good and practical to do so. The purpose of this book is to provide teachers with just those kinds of resources for reflectivity and action. "In experiments in which students were permitted to study in ways that were harmonious with their identified learning styles, academic achievement and retention have invariably improved" (Dunn, Dunn, & Price, 1977, in Shade, 1989, p. 174).

We have seen in the previous chapters on the physical and psychosocial domains of education that students whose cultures are being disprized in the classroom tend to either resist that type of education (and thus never learn the important "language of power" of the culturally dominant groups) or they uncritically "buy into it" (often at the expense of their sense of personal, familial, and social integrity). This is no less true of forms of education that are working to "erase" their cultural hermeneutics—their way of *reasoning* about the world. The best way to avoid these opposite—but equally damaging and disempowering—alternatives is to forge curricula and engage in pedagogical strategies which not only allow but encourage students—to the greatest degree practical—to retain and build upon their native ways while also learning about other ways. The teacher should attempt to be aware of these different sociocognitive styles. If she does, it will foster a "pluralistic classroom" in which those styles not only coexist with each other but actually enrich each other (Ferdman, 1990, p. 184).

This benefits all students by enlarging their "repertoire of cognitive strategies" in defining and dealing with problems. This makes them more flexible, creative, and dynamic *thinkers* and *actors* in a "global village"-world that is increasingly in need of people who can see and approach problems from multiple perspectives and in multiple ways (Friedman, 2000). It is to these different cognitive strategies and hermeneutic styles that we now turn. Knowing about them, and building them into what and how one teaches, is essential for the teacher who wishes to engage in "culturally responsive pedagogy" (Gay, 2000).

From the point of view of feminist pedagogy, it is important to make the classroom a "safe space" in which to nurture as many different styles of cognition as possible. This allows a multiplicity of perspectives leading to "mastery"—but not in the conventional sense of that term. Tetreault (2001, p. 164) explains:

> Mastery has traditionally meant the goal of an individual student's rational comprehension of the material on the teacher's and expert's terms. Women (and other marginalized groups) must often give up their voices when they seek mastery on the terms of the dominant culture. We found classrooms undergoing a shift away from unidimensional sources of expertise to a multiplicity of new information and insights. Students were no longer mastering a specific body of material nor were they emphasizing subjective experiences that risk excluding students from a wealth of knowledge. Rather, they were struggling through or integrating often widely various interpretations of texts, scientific research, and social problems. These teachers redefined mastery as interpretation, as increasingly sophisticated handling of the topics at hand, informed by but not limited to students' link to the material from their own experience.

Differential Sociocognitive Hermeneutics

Intelligence is not a single, absolute "entity" that a person has "inside her head" in some "amount"—an "amount" that can then be compared with the amount of the same "entity" that another person has in amount inside *her* head. Intelligence is not a "quotient," although that is, admittedly, the view of it that is erroneously taken by many people (not least of all many teachers and educational researchers) in their fixation upon the all-important "Intelligence Quotient"—or I.Q. That definition of intelligence, although popular, is not only limited; it is destructive when it is used as the only standard! It sends three dangerous messages to children when the I.Q.—the ultimate in standardized educational testing—is the be-all and end-all of teaching and learning.

First, it tells children that intelligence is something that they either have (and that they are thus "valuable" people) or do not have (and that they are thus "unimportant" people and will always be so). Second, it tells them that if they do not have this "entity" that some unseen person or agency has said is so important in sufficient quantities inside their heads, then whatever other skills, talents, dispositions, or visions they bring to the table are relatively worthless. And third, it tells them that if their I.Q. number is higher than someone else's, then they are, in some absolute sense, *better* than the other person; but, on the other hand, it also tells them that they are *worse* than someone else with a higher number. This most insidious of all forms of standardized education creates anxiety, depression, and unbridled competitiveness that do not make a person or a group of people smarter but, rather, "dumbs them down" to a perilously limited, one-size-fits-all standard of intelligence that not only inhumanely discourages other forms of creativity but officially kills creativity in the name of corporate efficiency. I.Q. tests do not really exist to measure intelligence in all of its glorious subtlety, complexity, and cultural and historical variety. Rather, "intelligence" is put in a straitjacket so that it will fit the "test." *The test does not exist for "intelligence." "Intelligence" exists for the test.*

A much broader and more exciting view of intelligence is as "the capacity to solve problems or to fashion products that are valued in one or more cultural settings" (Gardner & Hatch, 1989). As such, intelligence has quite legitimately meant—and will hopefully continue to mean—many different things to many different people across time and locale. For, when only one view of intelligence matters—and, as in the case of I.Q. tests, a very limited and specialized view of intelligence at that!—then we may well begin to fear that one group of people is subtly imposing its political views and purposes on everyone else in a way that empowers the group in control and disempowers those in other groups. When this is the case, then the signs of the times are pointing to the rise of a totalitarian form of government. The question of what constitutes "intelligence" is not just an educational one. It is heavily laden with political, ethical, and even spiritual implications. We do well to question the "experts" who tell us that intelligence is one, and *only* one, thing—and that they have the statistics to prove it, statistics which are usually the results of those very I.Q. tests themselves! These statistics are very often not a "scientific demonstration" of intelligence at all. Rather, they represent a "scientistic legitimation" of one group's view of intelligence over that of other groups.

To a medieval Christian monk, what counted as great knowledge was quite different than what constituted great knowledge to a South Pacific Islander chief several centuries ago, which in turn varied in many substantial ways from the view of "knowing" that a ninth century Japanese Zen monk would take. What constitutes great knowledge to a shaman in contemporary African culture—a first-world physician who travels to other realms of existence in order to bring about quite amazing and widely documented cures in his patients—is different than what constitutes great knowledge to a heart surgeon who successfully performs triple-bypass surgery. Which intelligence is "best"? The authors of this text believe that it all depends!

It depends on what worldview is "valued," what "products" are most useful, and what "solutions" are needed by different people in different "cultural settings" at different times. It requires no small degree of arrogance to assume that one's culture has a monopoly on that eternal mystery known as "human intelligence." We come much closer to the mystery when we explore and honor a great variety of intelligences. In the faith tradition of the authors of this book, it is believed that "whatever degree of intelligence a man [or woman] attains unto in this life will rise with him [or her] in the Resurrection" (Doctrine & Covenants of the Church of Jesus Christ of Latter-day Saints, 121:11). Surely, this does not just refer to a person's score on the Wechsler Adult Intelligence Scale or a college board exam sponsored by Educational Testing Services!

As is widely known, Gardner (1999) has hypothesized that the precious diamond of human intelligence has at least eight facets:

> *Linguistic* intelligence involves sensitivity to spoken and written language, the ability to learn languages, and the capacity to use language to accomplish certain goals. . . . *Logical-mathematical* intelligence consists of the capacity to analyze problems logically, carry out mathematical operations, and investigate issues scientifically. . . . *Musical* intelligence involves skill in the performance, composition, and appreciation of musical patterns. . . . *Bodily-kinesthetic* intelligence entails the potential of using one's whole body or parts of the body to solve problems. It is the ability to use mental abilities to coordinate bodily movements. . . . *Spatial* intelligence involves the potential to recognize and use the patterns of wide space and more confined areas. . . . *Interpersonal* intelligence is concerned with the capacity to understand the intentions, motivations and desires of other people. It allows people to work effectively with others. . . . *Intrapersonal* intelligence entails the capacity to understand oneself, to appreciate one's feelings, fears and motivations. . . . (Gardner, 1999, p. 113–131)

Recently, Gardner has added to this list "*Existential* intelligence," which is the ability to see oneself and others against the eternal backdrop of what the theologian Paul Tillich (1956) called those "ultimate concerns" that define the overarching purposes of our lives and give rise to the hope that there is, perhaps, something beyond this life in which we can dwell eternally. Religious visionaries are, by definition, high in Existential intelligence—although they may not be particularly good at balancing a quadratic equation. But then again, who cares how well the great Zen monk Dogen or the Spanish mystic St. John of the Cross knew algebra! This is not to say that mathematical intelligence is not important. It is very important. But it is no more important than the other intelligences that Gardner has defined for us.

Further, as Gardner has argued there are probably many other kinds of intelligence that future research and experience will uncover. He is the first to acknowledge that his categories are just one way of honoring the daunting complexity of human intelligence. In terms that Gardner has provided us with, the problem with standardized testing in general, and intelligence tests in particular, is that it tends to measure only linguistic and logico-mathematical abilities—and even *these* it measures in a very limited fashion. A great poet, for instance, might not score well on the linguistic section of the Wechsler intelligence test because that test awards only strictly limited, completely conventional, and militantly uncreative definitions of certain words. Indeed, for this reason, a great poet might well show up as being linguistically "challenged" on a Wechsler because of his radically unconventional use of words. And, even more tragically, a child with enormous poetic ability who took an I.Q. test and learned early on that she is "not good at" languages would probably internalize the official verdict that she is linguistically deficient—and we would lose a great poet, nipped in the bud. This happens thousands of times every day, we believe, in educational sites that—either by imposition or choice—define intelligence in simplistic, corporate terms.

Our mention of "retardation" is not just happenstance, by the way; for, what is considered "giftedness" and "retardation" is often a product of what certain groups of people value and what they consider as being "useless" or "ugly." Indeed, people from many spiritual traditions throughout history have insisted that what we consider very "useful" may in fact be extremely dangerous, what we consider "beautiful" may in fact be false, and what we discard as meaningless may, in Jesus's words (Matthew 13: 46), be "a pearl of great price" (Trent, 1994).

Discussing Mercer's study of the social construction of mental retardation, Banks and Banks (2001) correctly assert that "two people with the same biological characteristics may be considered persons with mental retardation in one system and not in another social system. A person may be considered a person with mental retardation at school but not at home." From this it follows that "people can change their role by changing their social group" (p. 18). Stephen Hawking, perhaps the greatest physicist since Newton, would (if sprawled on a couch while his complex wheelchair was being repaired for a moment) seem to the untrained eye to be just a mass of inarticulacy and immobile flesh. We must be very careful how we apply such terms as "disabled." The woman who is diagnosed as schizophrenic and heavily medicated in our business-oriented culture because she is hearing voices, might, in another culture, be honored as an oracle receiving vital messages for her people (Yogananda, 1946).

Let us now turn to the question of how "intelligence" is currently defined and promoted in most school classrooms—and what can be done to expand that definition so that many different types of intelligence are honored and all students learn new ways of seeing and being in the world.

STANDARD AND ALTERNATIVE RHETORICAL PATTERNS IN THE CLASSROOM

For students who are from non-English-speaking cultures, there are many assumptions about how to define, discuss, and resolve a problem in standard classroom interaction that might be quite new to them. Anyone who has ever taken a composition course in college will recognize these criteria as the guidelines in "English 101" for "How to Write an Expository Essay." Spronk (2004) has listed a few of these Anglo-centered standards that may strike learners from other linguistic and cultural traditions as alien. In Spronk's words, these features include:

1. linear logic, thinking in straight lines, rather than more lateral or spiral logics of other traditions;
2. an analytical approach that emphasizes dividing reality into its component parts, rather than more synthetic approaches that emphasize the whole over the parts;
3. an expository, declarative, and deductive rhetorical style that works from the "big picture" or thesis statement down through the supporting details or arguments, rather than an inductive style that requires learners to be more tentative, stating rationales and arguments before attempting a more generalized statement;
4. debate, discussion and original thinking, compared with academic traditions such as that which Robinson (1999) describes for Chinese learners, for whom three key rules are "memorize the lesson, practice the skill, and respect superiors";
5. the written over the spoken word. Despite the continuing dominance of the lecture as the teaching mode, learners in the West are assessed primarily on their ability to express themselves in written form. In contrast, most of the world's languages have only recently been written down, in the context of conquest and colonization, hence the cultures associated

primitive protosocieties—needed to be able to achieve a laser focus of mental and physical energy in order to be able to move and strike in deadly bursts of energy. Women, on the other hand, were always dealing with the nonstop buzz and whirr of activity around the home—children bustling within and without the home, animals meandering around the homestead, other mothers clamoring for attention or conversation, and food always cooking in the hearth or campfire. To manage such a scene entailed being able to spread one's attention in a constantly circulating, widely sweeping manner so as to keep everything in attention simultaneously and also to be able to "have a feel" for whether the scene is generally "in balance" or if something somewhere might have the potential to disrupt that balance (Stevens, 2000).

Another way of expressing this dichotomy is as "discrete-point/analytical" (field independent) versus "holistic/relational" (field dependent) (Hansen, 1979). This points to the tendency of field independent people to isolate the details and then "connect the dots" to create patterns out of them in a step-by-step, rule-governed manner. At the opposite extreme, field dependent people "get a feel for" or "a sense of" the entire situation in one intuitive, emotionally rich flash—in the context of which they then begin to examine specific details in relation to that whole picture. Field independent people work from facts to patterns. Field dependent people work from patterns to facts. Or, as More (1989) has put it:

> One perspective of cognitive processing is on a *global/analytic continuum.* Global processing emphasizes the whole and the relationships between its parts (e.g., whole language, sight word vocabulary building.) Analytic processing emphasizes processing individual parts and gradually building the whole in a *carefully controlled sequence* (e.g., phonics, sounding out words). Other terms for global are simultaneous, holistic, relational. Analytic processing is usually sequential and ordered. (p. 154, emphasis added)

Regardless of the terms that one uses to describe this fundamental difference in "cognitive processing," it is certainly the case that it is a serious educational issue because *standard American schooling*—with its focus on the memorization of details and the formulation of abstract analyses—*favors field independent cognition.* However, women, people from a wide range of various minority cultures, and lower SES individuals tend to favor field dependent cognition (Shade, 1989). Students who prefer field independent cognition tend to do much better in standard classrooms—not because they are more intelligent necessarily but because their way of solving problems matches the "official way" of doing these things in the culture of most public school classrooms. In short, it is a question not of intelligence but of "cultural (dis)continuity."

Tharp (1989) uses the descriptor "verbal/analytical," which denotes the field independent orientation of most classrooms, and the descriptor "visual/holistic," which indicates the predispositions of some minority groups to prefer using the entire physical setting and their intuitions and emotions to approach cognitive tasks. He has shown how the typical field independent forms of curriculum and instruction—with their focus upon fact and theory—put students from field dependent cultures—with their inclination to use their "inner senses" and interpersonal relationships—at risk of failing academically. Is this because students from field independent cultures are superior to people from field dependent cultures? We believe that one could reach that conclusion only if it were clear that field independence is somehow innately superior to field dependence. But this is clearly not the case. Each field style has its particular strengths and weaknesses. They are simply different. And what is more, the most dynamic and creative thinking generally uses both modes. There is a time for measured, systematic analysis. There is also a time for emotional subtlety and flashes of intuition. Analysis without emotional and intuitive depth runs the risk of being *personally* insensitive and *ethically* irrelevant, even dangerous. Emotion and insight without analysis run the risk of becoming *irrational,* excessively *subjective,* and *morally relativistic.* Thus, Tharp suggests that the teacher learn to value and synthesize both styles in the classroom to: (1) honor different cultural styles, and (2) help all students become better thinkers by having access to both styles, even though most individuals will continue to prefer one of the two styles (Jung, 1974).

Gay (2000) has written about the differences between the detailed/analytic style of conventional classrooms and the more global/inductive style of students of color:

> The most common practice among teachers is to ask convergent (single-answer) questions and use deductive approaches to solving problems. Emphasis is given to details, to building the whole from parts, to moving from the specific to the general. Discourse tends to be didactic, involving one student with the teacher at a time. In comparison, students of color who are strongly affiliated with their traditional culture tend to be more inductive, interactive, and communal in task performance. Their preference for inductive problem solving is expressed as reasoning from the whole to parts, from the general to the specific. The focus is on the "big picture," the pattern, the principle. (p. 93)

How can a teacher know which field style a particular student or group of students favors? The following checklist might come in handy.

Field dependent persons and groups tend to:

1. rely on the surrounding perceptual field,
2. experience their environment in a relatively global fashion by conforming to the effects of the prevailing field or context,

3. depend on authority,
4. search for facial cues in those around them as a source of information,
5. be strongly interested in people,
6. get closer to the person with whom they are interacting; have a sensitivity to others that helps them to acquire social skills, and
7. prefer occupations which require involvement with others.

Field independent persons or groups tend to:

1. perceive objects as separate from the field,
2. be able to abstract an item from the surrounding field and solve problems that are presented and reorganized in different contexts,
3. experience an independence from authority which leads them to depend on their own standards and values,
4. be oriented toward active striving,
5. appear cold and distant,
6. be socially detached but have analytical skills, and
7. prefer occupations that allow them to work by themselves. (Spodek & Saracho, 1981, p. 154)

Another useful guide has been formulated for the teacher by Grossman (1995), who has discovered the following differentiating characteristics between field independent and field dependent individuals, who, respectively: (1) rely on internal clues or external information, (2) prefer solitary study—or group activity, (3) are indifferent to opinions of others—or sensitive to them, (4) prefer to be physically close to the teacher and other students—or distant from them, (5) prefer competition—or cooperation, and (6) prefer abstract theoretical fields like physics—or fields in the humanities and social sciences.

There is an interesting linguistic dimension to this as well that recalls our previous discussion of the Sapir-Whorf Hypothesis, which holds that a culture's worldview is actually *caused* by its different linguistic patterns and possibilities. Although that theory in its strong form has been discredited at this point, it is still generally acknowledged that there is some kind of relationship between a culture's language and its worldview. Pai and Adler (2001) nicely capture this complex point when they write:

languages are capable of expressing thoughts and feelings that the society considers appropriate. Hence, no language or language group should be regarded as inherently superior to any other. But this does not imply that all languages are equally functional; some may be better equipped to express logical and analytical thoughts, whereas others might be better suited to communicating more global or aesthetic thoughts and feelings. (p. 9)

This, by the way, offers another compelling reason to make public education as thoroughly multilingual and multicultural as possible; for, by doing so we not only teach children *to communicate with many different peoples* but also *to think in many different ways.* This reinforces the ongoing theme of this book: Good multicultural education is simply good education. A complete and balanced education must be multicultural.

GENDER, ETHNICITY, AND COGNITIVE STYLE

Of all the areas of multicultural education, nothing has been studied as deeply or systematically as the question of the relationship between ethnicity/gender and cognitive style. Let us look at some of the findings in that large body of literature that are most relevant to classroom teachers. In doing so, we will focus on women and African Americans (the most highly studied groups) and Native Americans (the least studied group) in order to give the reader a sense of the scope of the different cognitive-style preferences various minority groups tend to favor.

Gender

According to Tetreault (2001), a leading voice in feminist pedagogy,

> a gender-balanced perspective, one that is rooted in feminist scholarship, takes into account the experiences, perspectives, and voices of women as well as men. It examines the similarities and differences between women and men and also considers how gender interacts with such factors as ethnicity, race, culture, and class. (p. 153)

Tetreault believes that the history of the curriculum in the United States has passed through five major stages. Stage 1 was the "male-defined curriculum" in which it was overwhelmingly men's ideas and ways of knowing that constituted the official curriculum. Stage 2, the "contribution curriculum," allowed a few women's ideas and products into the curriculum, but they were very limited and conformed to the strict "field independent" cognitive style that was considered the only "legitimate" way of knowing. Stage 3 introduced the "bifocal curriculum," which, while still privileging "men's ways of knowing," nevertheless gave increasing attention to ideas and products that resulted from "women's ways of knowing" (Belenkey et al., 1986). Stage 4, the so-called "women's curriculum," lay at the heart of the growing "Women's Studies" movement. The fifth, final, and, in Tetreault's view, best curriculum is the one that is currently in the making. It is a "gender-balanced curriculum" which gives equal weight to male and female perspectives and attempts to synthesize them in creative ways.

An example of the "gender-balanced" curriculum is offered by Naomi Ruth Remen (1999), a physician and medical educator, who argues for the integration of holistic, alternative medical ideas in conventional medical-school curricula, in addition to courses that help medical students explore the deeper emotional and spiritual dynamics of their sense of calling as healers so that they can be more nurturing with their patients and happier and healthier in their work. This approach allows women and more nurturing perspectives to enter and change institutions that have heretofore been dominated by men and traditional male points of view. Certainly, there are few educational sites that have been such well-guarded bastions of male privilege as medical schools. Remen's alternative, which balances the male-analytical and female-relational perspectives, shows how everyone, not just women, benefits from a gender-balanced curriculum.

Gendered Language

The intuitive, relational, and holistic ways of seeing and being that characterize what Belenkey has called "women's ways of knowing" manifest themselves in uses of language that are more common among women than men. This is of enormous educational significance since so much of what happens in most classrooms involves speaking and listening. Following are some of the most prominent linguistic features of "female discourse patterns."

Crawford (as cited in Tetreault, 2001) isolated nine speech traits in female discourse that seem to be admirably suited to caregiving, homemaking, and the intuitive exploration of situations. They are mild forms of expletives (i.e., "My gosh!" instead of "Damn it!"); descriptors that express the speaker's emotional reactions but do not attempt to "photographically" portray the situation, person, or thing that the person is reacting *to* (this reflects the often subjective, impressionistic nature of female discourse); tag comments that are midway between questions and statements (indicated by a lilting rise of the voice at the end of the statement); exaggerated expressiveness ("That movie was so, *so* hilarious!"), super-polite forms (so that the speaker does not offend a listener, who might otherwise respond in a disruptive or aggressive manner and thus upset the harmonious flow of interpersonal relationships); hedges or qualifiers ("I'd like to go to that kind of weird foreign movie that's playing downtown, but, you know, only if it seems interesting to you, too!"); hypercorrect grammar (which is an indication that the speaker has been "well groomed" and is "modest"); and little use of humor (since it may put another person at a disadvantage or be misconstrued as racy or cutting).

As Gay (2000) has said in her summary of research into discourse patterns of American females, they tend to:

> use more affiliative, accommodative, and socially bonded language mecha-
> nisms, while males are more directive, managing, controlling, task-focused and
> action-oriented in their discourse styles. Girls speak more politely and tenta-
> tively, use less forceful words, are less confrontational, and are less intrusive
> when they enter into conversations. By comparison, boys interrupt more; use
> more commands, threats, and boasts of authority; and give information more of-
> ten. . . . Because of these gender patterns, Maccoby (1988) concludes that
> "speech serves more egoistic functions among boys and more socially binding
> functions among girls. . . . " (p. 105–106)

Some other characteristics of European American female discourse often include a woman: (1) being the "audience," listening to information that is be-ing given by male speakers; (2) not highlighting her own expertise in a field because doing so might engender a competitive spirit among the conversants, who (especially if they are males) might feel threatened by the female's higher level of "qualification" and "certification"; (3) engaging in conversa-tions in order to provide and receive emotional nurturance with others and so-lidify interpersonal bonds—rather than talking in order to establish one's higher position in a "pecking order"; and (4) avoiding conflict and con-frontation (Gay, 2000, p. 92). As the sociolinguist Deborah Tannen has noted, European females' discourse patterns often evidence the choral "cooperative overlapping" of voices, which is an indication that they are engaged in "rap-port talk"—that is, conversation whose primary purpose is creating and strengthening close emotional bonds. Girls' speech patterns, therefore, tend toward "*implicit avoidance*" while boys' conversations often have to do with *direct confrontation* (Gay, 2000, p. 107).

These gendered discourse patterns can have dramatic educational conse-quences. Why? Because the discourse of most classrooms explicitly stresses and openly rewards self-assertion, individual demonstration of knowledge and expertise, fierce competitiveness, the production and analysis of abstract knowledge, and—above all else—high test scores on standardized instru-ments of assessment that are administered in emotionally sterile and interper-sonally alienating environments. Simply by virtue of the fact that one uses a more feminine set of discourse patterns (whether one is female or male!) au-tomatically puts one at a disadvantage on the gladiatorial battleground of the high-stakes classroom. Because a student speaks in more intuitive, poetic ways in order to attain more relational, holistic goals, she may very well be rated "cognitively inferior" by her teacher or on the test—whereas, in fact, she is not at all inferior but quite competent, processing and communicating ideas that are not only as good as other ways but—given certain tasks, such as the analysis of poetry, the creation of community, or humanely interpreting and applying scientific data—are superior to other approaches.

Creating classroom environments in which the male/analytical/discrete-point way of knowing is balanced with the female/intuitive/global way of knowing allows not only men and women to have equal say but also permits male students to explore the more "feminine" side of their psyches while allowing female students to explore the more "masculine" side of theirs (Jung, 1959). This leads to forms of thinking, speaking, and writing that are both theoretically sound and emotionally rich—surely a highly desirable educational and social goal.

Some African American Cognitive Preference

Central to African American conversational and cognitive patterns are the dynamics of "Call-and-Response" interactions between the speaker and her listeners, which, with its roots in African culture, Gay (2000) has described as follows:

> African Americans "gain the floor" or get participatory entrance into conversations through personal assertiveness, the strength of the impulse to be involved, and the persuasive power of the point they wish to make, rather than waiting for an "authority" to grant permission. They tend to invest their participation with personality power, actions and emotions. Consequently, African Americans are often described as verbal performers whose speech behaviors are fueled by personal advocacy, emotionalism, fluidity, and creative variety. (p. 91–92)

African American cognition and discourse, therefore, tends to put a premium on "personal investment in ideas" much more than on that "impersonal objectivity" which—incorrectly assumed to be "the best" way of thinking and speaking—is the one that is rewarded and cultivated in standard classroom activities and discussions" (Gay, 2000, p. 100). Thus, African Americans—who in this respect are quite similar in their cognitive and discourse patterns to Latino Americans—tend to be more "contextual," wanting to approach tasks and problems in groups, with lots of colorful "stage-setting" involved. (Gay, 2000, pp. 93–94ff).

The reader may be reminded of "Rap" and "Hip Hop" music in the following description of African American discourse:

> African American conversational discourse uses repetition for emphasis and to create a cadence in speech delivery that approximates other aspects of cultural

expressiveness such as dramatic flair, powerful imagery, persuasive effect, and polyrhythmic pattern. . . . Some individuals are very adept at "playing on" and "playing with" words, thereby creating a "polyrhythmic character" to their speaking. It is conveyed through the use of non-parallel structures, juxtaposition of complementary opposites, inclusion of a multiplicity of "voices," manipulation of word meanings, poetic tonality, creative use of word patterns, and an overall playfulness in word usage. (Gay, 2000, p. 101)

A teacher who wishes to accommodate both the standard worldview of the dominant white culture(s) and the minority worldview of black culture needs to understand that for many African American children:

communication and participation involve the whole self in a simultaneous interaction of intellect, intuition, and sensuality. Since communication and participation are central to learning, it appears that children coming to school with the black worldview learn best in settings encouraging a simultaneous response of thought, feeling, and movement. Silence and "sitting still" are often a sign that the black child is bored. (Shade, 1989, p. 80)

Conversely, children raised according to the norms of the mainstream culture have become adept at "compartmentalizing" aspects of their existence with the result that:

intellectual, emotional, and physical responses are easily separated. Messages become distinct from people in the form of memos, and ideas are analyzed in their written form only. . . . Children of this worldview can be comfortable in the classroom role of passive recipient. They can learn to be "rational" and to remove emotions and feelings from decisions. Many are unable to concentrate in a more active "noisy" environment. (Shade, 1989, p. 80–81)

Another difference between the dominant white discourse in the classroom and the minority black discourse is that the former places the highest value on the written word while the latter stems from a moral oral tradition of recording and transmitting knowledge. "Traditional Africa boasted of elaborate communication systems using drums, singing, and dance rituals. From the time blacks first arrived in this country, music and the spoken word have been at the heart of the black experience" (Shade, 1989, p. 81). Their oral/aural tradition thrives among many African Americans today. Recognizing this difference, a teacher can magnify her ability to help her students grasp even traditional material:

A geography teacher in California discovered that her students, mostly black or Latino males labeled remedial, scored considerably higher on tests when she read the questions provided in written form. Another teacher, working with black and Latino eighth graders in Texas, found that their comprehension of a U.S. history text was better if they listened to a tape of the text while reading it. Her Anglo pupils preferred to read without hearing the tape. (Shade, 1989, p. 81)

Richly poetic, deeply intuitive, and emotionally galvanizing, African American discourse is beautifully designed to attain the goal of all artistic expression—"to express the inexpressible intuitively" (Gay, 2000, p. 102). What is more, it is a way of thinking and communicating that reflects the Afro-centered childrearing preference of promoting "shared function groups, which "promote a cooperative approach to learning [in which the participants] are more likely to engage in relational rather than analytical thinking styles" (Shade, 1989, p. 21). Yet, in spite of the fact that they are so aesthetically compelling and interpersonally vibrant, African American styles of cognition and expression are often dishonored, and their use is even punished in classrooms where the emphasis must always be on empirical facts, individual competition, and depersonalized theoretical knowledge. Certainly there is room for empirical facts *and* passionate emotions, elegant theories *and* poetic subtlety in the education of any child. A holistic multicultural pedagogy honors the possibility of such synergy between science and spirit within the individual and among the various groups that make up the contemporary American classroom.

Native Americans: The Forgotten Educational Minority

Although the differential cognitive styles of African Americans and females have received great attention in the research into culture and education, less attention has been paid to Hispanic students and Asian students. But Native American students are virtually "invisible" in this body of research (Kaulback, 1989). This is extremely unfortunate; for, educational approaches which honor the Native American student's culturally specific ways of learning, on one hand, while simultaneously helping her learn about the types of knowledge and forms of expression valued in the standard classroom, on the other hand, have proven to be successful in helping Native American students succeed in school while maintaining their cultural integrity (Macias, 1987).

Unlike childrearing practices in much of white, middle-class culture, Native American childrearing practices do not rely on a great deal of talking, and they almost never resort to open scolding of a child, which is considered to be hurtful and unproductive. Children are encouraged to observe, explore, practice, and participate in the adult world from very early on. Indeed, "childhood is a

time for figuring out the world and for giving a full rein to curiosity by experimenting and testing, by questioning the old and trying to invent the new." *The
child, in a sense, learns to discipline herself* by discovering what it means
(with a high degree of independence but always, of course, under the watchful
guidance of the surrounding adults) to fully become a member of the culture
into which she was born.

The locus of discipline is internal, the ways of teaching are often silent and
subtle, and the child's budding sense of self-control is intimately involved
with her growing identity as a member of her society. Hence, to "Indian people, discipline doesn't mean something as simple and narrow as obedience. It
is a process powerfully connected to an Indian child's emergence of self-
discipline." In a manner that is sensitively timed to natural developmental
rhythms and honors individual agency and potential, Native American children organically *emerge into* a recognition of "a number of important values.
These include such things as generosity and sharing, cooperation and group
harmony, placidity and patience," more fluid conceptions of time, and less
grasping values regarding ownership and property than characterize the avari-
cious materialism of much of the current American culture. These are profound ethical lessons that are intuitively apprehended and concretely enacted
by the Native American child "in an informal manner and unconsciously applied" (Kaulback, 1989, p. 35). Globally intuitive, emotionally delicate, and
profoundly respectful of others, the Native American way is a beautiful man-
ifestation of the field-sensitive mode of cognition.

However, in a classroom environment where argumentative discourse, constant asking and answering of questions, and explicit direction-giving fill the
air in a dizzying stream of unrelenting words, Native American children may
well "find themselves in a culturally incoherent situation with an effect ap-
proximating culture shock" (Kaulback, 1989, p. 34). A teacher who is unaware of the Native American preference for quiet observation, steady practice, and then unselfishly competent performance may very incorrectly and
damagingly judge the Native American student "unresponsive," "dull," "stub-
born," and "resistant." It therefore behooves the teacher to be aware of both
the strengths and challenges that a Native American student may bring with
her to the classroom. Among these are the facts that Native American students
tend to: (1) be highly skilled in managing visual, imaginal, and spatial information and tasks; (2) do very well in tasks that holistically include all aspects
of the student's being, not just verbal ability, in which they tend not to perform as well as children from highly verbal, white American culture(s); (3)
prefer to work in small groups that allow considerable freedom of physical
movement and plenty of time to observe and practice skills in a deliberate, reflective manner; (4) prefer to move from the practical to the theoretical, not

from the theoretical to the practical as tends to be the case in many standard classrooms (Kaulback, 1989, p. 38–39).

Pepper (1989, p. 40) has offered the following set of twenty practical guidelines for teaching in Native American schools. Although what he presents is geared toward teaching where all the students are Native Americans, it nevertheless offers criteria for making teaching culturally responsive in mixed-ethnicity settings. In Pepper's words, the teacher of Native American students should:

1. use cooperative learning groups rather than traditional grouping;
2. provide a high percentage of group projects and a low percentage of oral questions and answers;
3. incorporate manipulative devices and activities which allow a student to "feel and touch";
4. provide a variety of informal classroom settings with freedom of movement—studying on the floor, sitting at a table or desks arranged in small groups, etc.;
5. present the whole picture of things before isolating skills into small segments;
6. provide activities which are experience based;
7. provide a high rate of encouragement;
8. provide mobility through scheduled activities;
9. provide values clarification activities;
10. use peer tutoring and cross-age teaching;
11. provide artwork illustrating people and animals; cartoons, wood carving, model building, miniature displays, map-making;
12. use role-playing and creative dramatics;
13. organize learning center materials to address the needs of all learners in the classroom;
14. encourage opinionated expression of viewpoints in social studies and other subjects where controversy can be found;
15. present new and difficult material in a visual/spatial mode rather than a verbal mode;
16. use metaphors, images, analogies, and symbols rather than dictionary type definitions;
17. use parades and productions;
18. use brainstorming and open-ended activities;
19. schedule sports and play days;
20. use instructional games and student-designed games.

Pepper also recommends using Native American learning styles in presenting lessons in classrooms made up of Native American children, using those styles 65 percent to 75 percent of the time. The other 25 percent to 35 percent of the time should employ non-Native American learning styles. In this way, the Indian student will learn effectively, maintain her traditional ways, and become adept at negotiating the discourses of power in the larger U.S. society.

Using various learning modalities also addresses the fact that teachers less and less frequently have classes with just one kind of student. If the teacher is teaching on a reservation or in an all black neighborhood, there will be a large degree of homogeneity, of course. But many urban classrooms, and an increasing number of rural and suburban classrooms, are ethnically diverse. There may, for instance, be a relatively high percentage of Latino students attending a school in an area that is predominately Korean and Korean American—or, to take another example, a white upper-middle-class neighborhood may experience an influx of Middle Eastern students.

There seem to be some important implications regarding reading that grow out of the research into Native American cognitive styles. Focusing on the holistic, visual orientation of many Native American students, Shears (cited in Kaulback, 1989) has speculated that:

> if we can [infer] that visual methods of instruction promise the most success in Native education, then we must question the effectiveness of phonetic based reading programs, both in English and in the child's Native language. Perhaps a more visual approach to reading (i.e., Language Experience, Whole Word Method) would be more appropriate. Indeed, one researcher, in comparing visual and auditory methods of teaching reading to Native children, noted that the low-readiness group of children responded best to the visual method (Shears, 1970). (p. 147)

With its reverence for balance, respect for the individual's autonomy and innate capabilities, emphasis upon careful observation and precise performance, delicate attunement to the needs of others in a group, cultivation of intuition and concrete artistic expression, and immense practicality, the Native American ways of teaching and learning not only can but should play an important role in any classroom. When they do, then all students will be deepened and brought into greater harmony with themselves, others, and nature by engaging and internalizing this venerable and humane vision of education.

Culture and Testing—and the Culture of Testing

Mainstream U.S. society is increasingly one of credentials. A person is judged, and her horizons of social possibility are broader or narrower, depending on the degrees she holds and the letters after her name. This ethos of "credentialism" pervades contemporary society for two interrelated reasons, according to the sociologist Anthony Giddens (1990).

The first has to do with the initially Western and now global glorification of scientific "expertise." An "expert" is one who, having "mastered" an "official body of knowledge" about something, is empowered, through the degree that she receives to certify her mastery, to enter the ranks of authorities in that field. Once in that elite group, she may play a role in deciding what other kinds of "knowledge" will be declared "legitimate." She may also now serve as a gatekeeper in determining—again through testing—who else will be allowed into this privileged group of "experts."

The second has to do with the radical uncertainty of daily life in the ideologically and technically complex world in which we all live in the twenty-first century. People feel that it is only experts who can provide answers to questions—many of them life-and-death questions—that affect them at every level of their being on a constant basis. The questions can range from the most concrete to the most abstract, but contemporary people feel (and in many cases are quite *right* to feel) that only the "expert" can answer the question, provide the product, or issue the warning that will give us the correct and safe view of things and how to proceed. "Shall I take this pill or that?" "Which automobile has the highest crash-safety rating?" "Does this new type of housing insulation really cause cancer?" "What prompted the civil war in that small country halfway around the world, and is the outcome of that war somehow so vital to our national security that we must send our young people there to fight and die in it?" "Is stem cell research an attempt to play God or a scientifically justifiable procedure to find cures to various diseases?" "Is a fetus alive in a human sense at the sixth month of gestation or not?" "Are we really just primates that have evolved to a certain level of intelligence or unique creations of a Deity who shaped us for special purposes?"

People today feel they must rely on individuals with the appropriate letters after their names to answer these questions for society. Furthermore, given the complexity of things these days, one individual can only be an expert in a small subdivision of a particular field of knowledge—which seems to grow geometrically with each passing hour so that a certain bit of knowledge is obsolete almost the minute after it is gained. Thus, even an "expert" must rely on other "experts" in other aspects of her life. As Giddens (2002) puts it, in a "runaway world" of such unfathomable complexity, it is difficult to feel that one can "trust" anyone else to make consequential decisions unless that person has the appropriate "credentials" to vouchsafe her "expertise."

The educational consequences of this world-historical development are enormous and cannot be discussed here except to mention that it underlies the increasing pressure on schools—generally becoming most intense around the secondary school years but now even going back as far as the elementary school years—to "guarantee expertise" (or at least the student's future potential to show some level of expertise in some socially useful skill) through the reliance upon standardized testing about official bodies of knowledge.

There is no doubt that there is a place for credentials and expertise. Before one gets on an airplane or allows herself to have her skull opened up for brain surgery, it is nice to know that the person in control has been officially qualified by a credible professional agency to fly a plane or wield a scalpel! However, when *all*—or, at least, *most*—education is seen as merely a preparation to perform some sort of technical or managerial skill in the new transnational, capitalist, electronic world order (where all that ultimately matters is the cultivation and management of new "markets" for the consumption of increasingly glitzy products of dubious democratic and moral value) then we have reason to fear that education is becoming less a means of political and moral enlightenment and more a tool of subtle totalitarian control.

This problem becomes even more egregious when we consider that, in our "culture of testing," there are certain minority cultural groups whose cognitive styles ill prepare them to score well on the tests that they are bound to face in most classrooms. Decades of research have shown quite conclusively that the very structure of such tests guarantees that certain groups of students—whose upbringing and academic training has prepared them to do well on these tests—will tend to score high, while other groups of students—whose upbringing and academic training has not prepared them to do well on these tests—will tend to score low (Willis, 1977; Oakes, 2000). A disproportionate number of African American and Mexican American students are labeled as "mentally retarded" because intelligence tests, far from being culturally neutral, "reflect the abilities and skills valued by the [white, Anglo Saxon, middle-class] American core culture" (Mercer, in Banks & Banks, 2001, p. 13).

These tests put primary emphasis on certain highly valued conversational strategies, grammatical forms, and vocabulary items which students from minority cultures do not have access to, or do not have access to in the same degree as students from the majority cultures, who have been brought up speaking that particular "code" of English (Bernstein, 2000). The test, therefore, does not measure the student's "intelligence" so much as it measures the kind of language that she has been brought up speaking (Riordan, 2000). "Most African American and Latino students are socialized within microcultures that differ in significant ways from the U.S. core culture. These students often have not had an equal opportunity to learn the knowledge and skills that are measured in mental ability tests" (Banks & Banks, 2001, p. 13). The test does not exist to measure intelligence so much as it exists to officially decide which forms of "intelligence" should be assigned to which social category—

along, of course, with that category's corresponding degree of financial and social rewards, or lack thereof.

Hence, intelligence tests—and indeed all forms of standardized testing—if not used sparingly, judiciously, and as a way of *helping students improve* ("diagnostic assessment")—becomes a means of sociopolitical control ("high stakes rewards testing"), "sorting" some classes and cultures of students into higher stations in life and some into lower ones (Spring, 1976). This accounts for the scandalous fact that the single biggest predictor of how a student will do on an American college entrance exam is her parents' socioeconomic status (Morrow & Torres, 1995).

Great progress has been made in eliminating gender bias from these tests. However, socioeconomic bias continues to riddle these tests (Grossman, 1995). Indeed, many immigrant and refugee students have never even *been* tested before and so inevitably do poorly on standardized assessments, even if they *can* speak English well (which is not typically the case). Three pedagogical strategies exist in order to help minority cultures regarding testing.

The first is to offer them special instruction in standardized test-taking strategies. Five to fourteen hours of instruction along these lines, spread out over five to seven weeks seems to be the best way to schedule such instruction, which teaches the student important things about time management, creative guessing, the types of questions that will be asked, the types of protocols that can be used to solve certain problems, and physical and emotional strategies for being optimally prepared for the test.

The second pedagogical strategy for helping make assessment a productive and encouraging experience for students—not an anxiety-ridden and damaging one—is to use many different forms of assessment to help a student see her strengths and areas for improvement (Duschl & Gitomer, 1991). Here we need to make explicit an implicit distinction that we have already employed—the difference between *testing* and *assessment. Assessment* means gathering information about the student's understanding and/or performance so that the teacher can be even more sensitive and effective in aiding that student in her holistic development. This type of information gathering is markedly different than *testing* with its harsh punishments or seductive rewards for the student depending on how well the student has been able to demonstrate— usually in one anxiety-ridden sitting—that she has "learned" (which usually means "memorized") something. Assessment is concerned with "learning," of course, but in ways that are conceptually deep, emotionally rich, politically astute, and therefore durable and fruitful. This is learning that matters because it is meaningful and lasts. What a student learns to take a standardized test will generally be forgotten soon after the test is over and the grade has been given.

In portfolio assessment (one of the best forms of authentic assessment) the student "performs" her understanding of a topic or task in various ways and using various intelligences. These can include everything from a traditional written report, to an artistic creation, physical demonstration, or emotional evocation—all of which evidence not only her mastery of something but her many-faceted understanding of it. *This form of assessment is good not only for students from socioeconomic minorities but for all students!* It teaches a student that any question has many different aspects, that it may resonate at many different levels of her being, that it may have various "solutions" with different consequences stemming from each solution, and that she can (depending upon how she decides to approach the problem) use it either as an occasion to hone one of her competencies or improve in one of her weaknesses. High-stakes, standardized testing "neuroticizes" the child. Holistic, creative testing empowers her. Good multicultural education is good education.

In addition to "portfolio assessment" another example of alternative assessment was given by Rogers (2006) in his examination of an innovative biology teacher who, recognizing a difficulty that minority students were having, discovered a solution that turned out to benefit all students.

This particular biology professor had been teaching clearly things like "A is inside B", but she looked and noticed she had students who would write on lab notes things like "B is inside A". She wondered how they could get it so backward. She figured out, which was very clever of her, that *the students who were having the most difficulty with that were students whose first language was a language where word order was not important because word endings signified relationships.* Whereas in English word order is important, in other languages word order itself is not necessarily important, you can mix and match or whatever, and it doesn't matter because whatever the ending is on the word makes it accusative or dative or whatever. Many students think in their first language and then translate it, and of course they can't translate it word by word, so then you get this kind of a thing. . . . As it turns out, there are distinct types of languages: analytic languages (which rely on word order), and synthetic languages (which use prefixes and suffixes to signify relationships). . . . This teacher found a creative solution to this problem, by introducing a way of taking notes and conducting exams with more drawing and labeling of diagrams. To her surprise, not only did the international students do better, but so did the local ones (although they fought against the idea at first). (2006, p. 162)

Once again it is evident that sensitivity to linguistic and cultural differences helps teachers become better at reaching all students and that good multicultural education is simply good education.

The third pedagogical strategy comes from Ovando (2001), who points out that a good place to start constructing pedagogies that will help students perform their best on a wide range of tests and assessments is the same as good teaching and authentic assessment in general. This entails: "(1) posing problems of emerging relevance to learners; (2) structuring learning around 'big ideas' or primary concepts; (3) seeking and valuing students' points of view; (4) adapting curriculum to address students' suppositions; and (5) assessing student learning in the context of teaching" (p. 281). Furthermore, as Slavin (1990), a major researcher in cooperative-learning forms of teaching, has shown, cooperative-learning environments are very effective in multicultural classrooms, especially with field-sensitive children, such as Native American, Latino American, and African American, all of whom tend to be group-oriented (Banks & Banks, 2001, p. 12).

What is *intelligence*? What does it mean "to think" about something, "to know" it—perhaps even well enough "to teach" it? These are supremely difficult questions to answer. In fact, they may be impossible to answer; for, the question of what counts as knowledge is really the question that lies at the heart of the human mystery: What is true, how can I come to understand it, and what are the best ways to act in the light of that truth? The question of cognition is not simply a technical one—an exercise in cut-and-dried, statistical parameters. The question of what is real and important—and how to know it and teach it—is, in the words of the poet T.S. Eliot, "the overwhelming question" of human life, involving the individual's innate characteristics, professional goals, cultural backgrounds, ethical standards, and spiritual hopes. In the words of another poet, William Wordsworth, we "murder to dissect" intelligence if we see it merely as an "entity" to be sterilely defined and clinically quantified.

In this chapter, we have looked at the mystery of intelligence through the lens of culture, one of several of the major lenses that can be used to view intelligence. We have seen that what constitutes knowledge and the proper uses to which it should be put often has a cultural dimension—and sometimes an extremely strong one. When only one cultural way of knowing and expressing that knowledge is allowed in a classroom, and when there is only one way to assess if learning has taken place, then other ways of being, seeing, and acting get unfairly marginalized, even violently erased. This is obviously damaging to those students who are thrown to the edges of things where they are not allowed to explore or develop their potentials. But it is damaging to *all* students, for it deprives them of the emotional and moral richness of deep communication with people from other knowledge traditions. This can serve only to limit everyone's options and abilities in knowing things about this enigmatic universe and our place in it. Indeed, the dictatorship of standardized, corporate "education" does not lead to education at all—but to *antieducation*, discouraging people from developing the best *within themselves* as individuals and *among themselves* as brothers and sisters on this planet.

The most democratically empowering, emotionally satisfying, cognitively complex, morally enriching, and globally cohesive ways to discover and create knowledge arise in educational settings that are holistically multicultural.

6

The Ethicospiritual Domain

In this chapter, we will tie together many of the themes that we have discussed throughout the book by looking at the experience of one teacher at a particular middle school in a Rocky Mountain state. We will call the school "Madison Middle School." We will gain insight into this first-year Latino teacher—whom we will call "Carlos"—through examining extracts from a journal that he kept during that first year as a novice teacher of color.

Carlos's journal is fascinating because he not only writes about his personal experience of many of the issues that we have discussed throughout this book but also because he reflects on them in ethical and spiritual terms, not only instructional and political ones. Carlos's journal embodies both his strong political commitments as a young Chicano and also his religious commitments as a devout member of his church.

Considering that deeper ethical and spiritual commitments probably play a significant role in many teachers' sense of "calling" (Serow, Eaker, & Ciechalski, 1992; Mayes, Blackwell Mayes, & Williams, 2004), Carlos's experiences offer an example for teachers to consider in reflecting on their multicultural teaching in not only political terms but also spiritual ones (Bullough, Patterson, & Mayes, 2002; Clift, Houston, & Pugach, 1990; Joseph & Burnaford, 1994; Valli, 1990). For, a truly holistic approach to multicultural issues could hardly ignore the ethical and spiritual domain.

Of course, the question of the expression and cultivation of a student's spiritual commitments in the public school classroom is complex and contentious (Mayes & Ferrin, 2001) and well beyond the scope of this book. However, teachers are quite free to reflect privately or together on their teaching in whatever ways and terms are most useful to them—including spiritual and religious ones—so long as such things do not occur in the classroom. Indeed, as Mayes (2003) has argued, for many teachers (such as the authors of this book, for whom their teaching in multicultural contexts both stems from and enriches their spiritual lives), it would be impossible to deeply and productively reflect on their classroom practices *without* considering the ethical and spiritual nature of their work (Cutri & Ferrin, 1999; Mayes & Ferrin, 2001; Miller & Seeler, 1985).

In each section of our presentation and analysis of Carlos's journal, therefore, we begin by talking about the themes in the research literature that relate to one of Carlos's experiences, move on to that experience in Carlos's journal entry itself, and conclude with what we believe to be a few of the ethical and spiritual implications of that particular issue.

In doing this, we certainly do not mean to privilege Carlos's religious commitments (as a member of the Church of Jesus Christ of Latter-day Saints, or "Mormon"). We simply offer Carlos's experiences as an example of how one teacher from a particular faith-community viewed his multicultural teaching in terms that were ethically and religiously meaningful to him. Our only purpose in doing so is to help other teachers reflect on their multicultural teaching in ways that are equally relevant to them in light of their own ethical and spiritual commitments. In short, Carlos's experiences and our analyses of them are *a* way to reflect spiritually on one's practice, but they are far from *the only* way to do so. If this chapter can offer some guideposts for teachers to begin to define new ways to reflect on their practice in not only political and pedagogical but also in their own ethical and spiritual terms, then we will be well pleased!

In beginning our discussion of spirituality, want to make it clear that we do not consider all formal religious practice as necessarily spiritual. Much (indeed, too much) of the practice of institutional religion is a matter of cultural conformity or social expediency. We all have known people like the man in the story who *prays* on his knees every Sunday—and then *preys* on his neighbors the other six days of the week! Nor do we believe that one must necessarily have an institutional religious allegiance in order to be vitally involved in the pursuit of spirituality—whatever that might mean to a particular person.

For the purposes of this essay, we want to define the phrase "spiritual commitment" in functional terms in the following manner. Spirituality in organized and/or personal forms involves an emotionally and ethically authentic pursuit of a higher reality, which, although transcending this world, must result in compassion and service to others in this world if it is to be genuine. Or, as one of the most famous lines from the authors' religious tradition puts it, "When ye are in the service of your fellow beings, ye are only in the service of your God" (Mosiah 2: 17).

Several excellent examples of the kind of spiritual reflectivity for which we are advocating have been offered by Jewish educational scholars over the last decade or so. Like us, these scholars, drawing from their faith-community, have argued that *critical reflectivity*, which aims at sensitizing the teacher to the political implications and applications of his practice, will often be incomplete if it omits "spiritual reflectivity" (Mayes, 2001a, 2001b). Hence, Wexler (1996), Purpel, and Shapiro (1995) contend that educational research and discourse must incorporate spiritual matters. For as gladly as materialist political philosophies would wish to ignore spiritual considerations in pedagogy, it simply cannot be denied that one's understanding of and relationship with the transcendent frequently underlies an individual's political vision and action.

The lives (and deaths) of such figures as Mahatma Gandhi, Reverend Martin Luther King, and Archbishop Oscar Romero demonstrate with power and authority that political action is most passionate and productive when it is born of a spiritual vision. Spirituality is the basis of "justice-making" (Lepage, 1991, p. 73), as Liberation Theology—which sees the empowerment of marginalized people as a spiritual duty—vividly shows (Schipani, 1988). In our view, "spirituality" devoid of political dimensions or consequence is vacuous.

ISSUES, EXPERIENCES, AND REFLECTIONS ON A LATINO TEACHER'S EXPERIENCES IN A MULTICULTURAL SETTING

The Pygmalion Effect

A teacher's expectations of a student often have a marked effect on that student's performance. High expectations of students correlate significantly with high student performance as do low expectations with low performance (Brophy, 1997). Called the Pygmalion Effect, this is a problem generally in the schools but is especially pronounced regarding students of color, for whom certain white teachers have reduced expectations (Riordan, 2000). In the following passage from his journal, we see Carlos struggling with this as the school year nears its end.

May 6, 2002

Many of my students are busy preparing for their transition to Lakeview High School [fictitious name of a mainstream high school in the area] *while others are preparing to attend Washington High School* [fictitious name of a low-prestige high school in the area, often seen as a "dumping ground" for low-performing students]. *Those preparing to attend Washington fulfill a stereotype that many teachers have. A large percentage at Washington are*

Hispanic, and most come from low-income families. If they wind up attending Washington, it is because they have failed to meet Madison's academic standards or have been involved in truancy issues.

My concern regarding these students attending the remedial high school is twofold. First, I question how many of the students attending Washington will complete the graduation requirements. Second, I question why some of the students feel more comfortable attending Washington rather than Lakeview. The latter became apparent as I spoke today to one of my Hispanic students preparing to graduate from eighth grade.

Sonia Delgado is a mature eighth grader, popular among her peers, outspoken, and very likeable. In the conversation I had with her, she expressed her desire to attend Washington High School rather than making the normal transition into Lakeview High. When I questioned her reasoning, she justified her decision by telling me that at Washington, she would feel more comfortable in smaller classrooms and also be secure around peers already attending Madison Middle School. From what I have observed of Sonia and gathered in conversations with her, it seems that some of her teachers have not expected as much from her as I know she is capable of giving.

Her reasoning is disturbing because attending a remedial school will not give her the same preparation for college as a regular high school will. She will be surrounded by peers with lower aspirations and goals. As her teacher, I see the potential Sonia possesses. Her articulation of arguments is strong. She comprehends foreign notions, infers, and is able to contribute to classroom discussions. Yet, in the time I had her in my class, I did not once meet her parents. I consider Sonia a borderline student. If she decides to attend a remedial school, she might be setting patterns in her life that will lead her to other places rather than college. Currently, Sonia is failing most of her classes.

Sonia typifies many of the Hispanic students in our junior high school. I can name ten students with similar cultural, social, and academic backgrounds. Most are likely to end up at a remedial school, and most will not attend college. What are we doing in our junior high schools to discourage our Hispanic students from entering a mainstream high school and enrolling in a college prep plan? We have to find ways to encourage them not to lower their standards by attending a remedial school if they are capable of more.

Avoiding the Pygmalion Effect

Carlos's reflections prompt consideration of how teachers can look beyond traditional attitudes and approaches regarding language-minority students. Exploring the ethical dimensions of multicultural education may provide some direction. In our view, the ethical commitment to the *equitable* treatment of all students, in contrast to the merely *equal* treatment of all students, provides a key to overcoming the Pygmalion Effect. The *equal* treatment of all students—an impersonal approach in which all students are simply treated in the same way—is sometimes seen as a way to combat the Pygmalion Effect because of its attempt to treat all students uniformly regardless of any gender, racial, ethnic, or socioeconomic markers. Certainly, this was the approach that characterized the "liberal" pedagogies of the 1960s (Ravitch, 1983).

However, we believe that *equal* treatment is fair only in a rough, legalistic sense. By its very nature, however, it is insensitive to the wide range of psychological, cultural, political, and spiritual elements that uniquely constitute each student. On the other hand, the *equitable* treatment of each student as a unique spiritual being in the process of eternal development is a powerful antidote to the depersonalization of *equality-based* perspectives that lump students together categorically. Equitability, as distinct from equality, stresses that students will often require different, individually tailored forms of teaching—not necessarily "equal" ones—depending upon their unique needs and goals. As Mayes, Blackwell Mayes, and Sagmiller (2003) have found, when a teacher views the student as a unique spiritual being with eternal possibilities, that teacher's commitment to the *equitable* treatment of each student is often reinforced and enhanced.

Of course, one sometimes—although still too rarely!—sees such an individually sensitive approach in various new pedagogies. Too often, however, they are based on the utilitarian motivation of creating an "excellent" educational system that will produce more effective economic warriors in the transnational corporate capitalist economy (Mayes, 2003, 2005a). By this view, the political economy of a postmodern, information-based democracy such as the United States both shapes and relies upon such an educational system (Cutri & Ferrin, 1999). If certain skills and behaviors are not in place, it is argued, the society will not be sufficiently robust socioeconomically to prevail in the new "global economy." Furthermore, because linguistic diversity is a powerful geopolitical asset in creating and controlling markets, we should cultivate that diversity.

This argument illustrates Gelberg's (1997) assertion that post-industrial capitalism has co-opted certain student-centered approaches for its own political purposes. Gelberg argues that many of the "new student-centered" approaches to instruction are not new at all but are pedagogically based in progressive social reconstructionism. What *is* new about these pedagogies is that—unlike in Dewey's, Ruggs's, and Counts's vision of pedagogical innovation in the service of political and economic democracy (Cremin, 1964)—the new pedagogies are rooted in the agenda of transnational corporate business, an agenda that actually runs quite counter to the Deweyan vision of social reconstruction (Dewey, 1916).

We do not believe that such motivations for responding to linguistic and cultural diversity in our students are morally authentic or educationally sound. Further, such utilitarian approaches are highly unstable since policymakers will be committed to a certain educational approach only as long as it maximizes the "bottom-line." When it no longer does so, it will quickly be abandoned in favor of one that does, leaving language-minority students once more in the lurch.

Carlos's religious convictions, however, contain a basis for grounding a pedagogy of *equity* in his ontological commitments. Specifically, Carlos's religious beliefs include a doctrine called *eternal progression* (*The Doctrine and Covenants of the Church of Jesus Christ of Latter-day Saints* 132: 22). According to this doctrine, each individual is a radically unique soul engaged in a process of eternal evolution toward a divine status. One can hardly imagine a pedagogy more consistent with this idea than one stressing *equitable* treatment of each student because of his unique and unbounded potential.

We want to stress again that we are using Carlos's religious commitments simply as one way of illustrating how this particular teacher's spiritual commitments might connect with his reflectivity and classroom practice as a teacher. However, it is easy to see how a wide variety of other sorts of spiritual commitments—both formal and informal—would also be consistent with a pedagogy of equity. Our point is simply this: whatever the teacher's spiritual commitments, a pedagogy that is based in them will tend to be more deeply rooted, durable, and effective in responding in a *sustained* way to the needs of *every* learner in a pluralistic democracy.

Authoritative Teaching

The literature in instructional theory as well as adolescent psychology generally affirms that the best way to help both students and teachers avoid the debilitating consequences of the Pygmalion Effect is to teach *all* students in an "authoritative" manner, for adolescents tend to respond best to a teaching style that is high in both "care" and "demand" (Brophy, 1997). That is to say, students do not respond well to teachers who demand a great deal but do not seem to care about them—the "authoritarian" style of teaching. Nor do they respect the opposite type of teachers who might seem to care about them but do not expect much from them—the "permissive" style of teaching. Rather, they respond best to the high-care/high-demand style of "authoritative" teachers.

This is a multicultural issue because it seems that not a few teachers take either an authoritarian or a permissive approach to students of color as a means of either rigidly controlling or anxiously appeasing them (Pai & Adler, 2001). Students of color, however, need an "authoritative" approach no less than other students do (and arguably even more so). Thus, Carlos notes the following in a journal entry.

November 29, 2002

The term is quickly coming to an end. It is sad to review grades with many of my Hispanic students. In many cases, their grades are very low. Many of them struggle to pass a few classes and then fail the rest.

Today I asked Ricardo Valencia who his favorite teacher has been in the last few months. He thought about it for some time, and then he mentioned Mr. Dailey. Several of his buddies agreed that Mr. Dailey is a very good teacher. I asked them what they felt made Mr. Dailey a good teacher. They said, "He's not too mean, but he is strict." They continued by telling me that they understand his classes and his assignments. Often I have seen them working on homework for his class.

Ricardo also mentioned that he knows what is expected of him every day he walks into class. I was very impressed by Mr. Dailey's ability to reach these students. When I asked the students about their other teachers, they used words not appropriate to repeat. In short, today I learned that the Hispanic students will respond to teachers, not because of racial or cultural identity alone but rather to teachers who understand and treat them with high expectations.

The Authoritative "Spirit"

The high-care/high-demand qualities of authoritative teaching correspond to two components of Cutri and Ferrin's (1999) definition of spirituality in educational settings: (1) a compassionate desire to connect with other people and oneself in a way that promotes an individual and collective sense of a mission for the greater good, and (2) a holistic consideration of a student in all of his multifaceted complexity—physically, cognitively, affectively, socially, culturally, and spiritually. As Noddings (1995) has made clear in her notion of "ontological care," the desire to connect with others and self in complex patterns of interaction and intersubjectivity creates a pedagogy that is *both* demanding *and* nurturing.

Such instructional approaches not only recognize but thrive upon both the similarities and differences among students from diverse cultural and linguistic backgrounds—and what is more, they do so because of the belief that we can all teach and learn from each other in intellectually rigorous ways in our personal, political, and spiritual journeys. Such a consideration and commitment not only acknowledges a connectedness between one's own actions and what one receives from the world, but also a selfless concern for others' well being in the context of high-expectation intellectual exploration.

Intragroup Variability and Entry Conditions

When teachers and administrators see students of color, they may be tempted to see them as being members of a single, homogenous group, not understanding that there is great variability among subgroups within that student's racial/ethnic group. Thus, for instance, the perspectives and needs of a student from a middle-class family from Venezuela may differ in important respects from those of a student from a migrant farm-working family from Mexico. However, the teacher may simply see both of them simply as "Hispanic students"—whatever that term may mean to him—without seeing the significant differences between them and the role those differences may play in the two students' differential performance in the classroom (Ogbu, 1987; Valencia, 1991).

Four of the most important variations within groups relate to: (a) how long the student has been in the United States at the time of first enrollment in the public schools, b) how old the student is at the time of enrollment, (c) what grade level the student is first placed in at the time of enrollment, and (d) the student's level of English proficiency upon initial enrollment (Gibson, 1988; Valencia, 1991). Students who have been in the United States only a short time, who are adolescents, who have limited English proficiency, and who first enroll at the middle or secondary levels typically face the greatest challenges. Below, we see Carlos encountering such a student and beginning to ask himself how he and his school can better respond to the needs of such students in the future.

November 26, 2002

Walking through the main office today on my way home, I saw that the principal was in need of some translation help. He was in the middle of a parent conference with a Hispanic parent and his son. When I offered my assistance, the principal quickly accepted and the discussion continued. The tone of the conversation was very stern. The boy under the magnifying glass was Ramon Flores.

Ramon has been getting into a great deal of trouble since he has enrolled in our middle school. This time he had been fighting with other boys who appeared to be teasing him. In days past, he has been kicked out of English class for not participating. The principal is very disappointed with Ramon, and his patience is running low. Today he told Ramon he can no longer participate in any after-school classes until after the new school year. During our conference with the parent, Ramon's dad was very quiet. He recognizes that his son is causing a lot of trouble and that Ramon is going down a dead-end path.

As I have gotten to know Ramon, I'm the first to recognize he's no angel. He curses, is cocky, does not show respect, and the list goes on. However, it's necessary to see both sides of the story. Today after digging deeper into his past and talking to his father, I discovered a completely new side to Ramon. Ramon has only been in the United States for a year and a half. Ramon's reading and writing skills are very low, at second or third grade level. His father told me that, even in Spanish class, Ramon struggles to structure simple sentences. Another discovery I made was that Ramon lives alone with his father. For some reason Ramon's mother is not around. Thus, many of Ramon's emotional needs are not met at home. His father is a mechanic, but his lack of schooling is very apparent.

As I began to discover Ramon's past, his present situation started to make more sense. At our school, Ramon is not involved in any of the reading programs tailored to help students with reading deficiencies. He has just been kicked out of the after-school program. The administrator was surprised to discover Ramon has only been in the states for a year and half and will now look into providing some of the services Ramon desperately needs.

As I drove home, disturbed at what I just witnessed, many questions flooded my mind. I wonder how Ramon fell through the cracks? How did we not know about his lack of literacy skills prior to his enrollment? Have we labeled Ramon as a troublemaker because of his appearance and behavior before giving him a fair opportunity to excel? Did we provide a mentor for him? Did I reach out to him? The questions regarding his situation will continue to be around for some time. The bigger question is what will we do with the next Ramon Flores that comes into our school?

(In the next brief passage, we see that Ramon unfortunately is continuing to fall through the cracks of a system that is unprepared to deal with his needs as an older, late-arriving, limited-English-proficiency student. His future is not bright.)

Today while spending the day at [a nearby recreation facility], *I ran into Ramon Flores. Ramon was surprised to see me but was very polite as he filled me in on what has happened to him in the last few months. Since he was kicked out of Madison, Ramon was enrolled at another middle school in the area. However, his stay at the school was not very long. Soon after his arrival, he continued to get into trouble and was quickly kicked out of that school. He completed the year at a third middle school in a different city but is uncertain about the next school year.*

The "Double Hermeneutic" at Madison Middle School

Carlos's impassioned query about how Ramon was allowed to fall through the cracks institutionally raises important personal, professional, and ethical questions for a teacher like Carlos striving to respond to his students in the most ethically responsible ways. He wonders how much one teacher, especially a first-year ethnic-minority teacher at a predominately white school, can change the system. It would be easy for a teacher to despair in such circumstances.

Giddens's "double-hermeneutic" theory (1990, 1991), however, says that an individual is not a mere victim of the institution. The individual is indeed influenced by the system, but he also has power to influence the system in turn. In other words, the system "interprets" the individual (hence the term "hermeneutic"), but the individual also "interprets" the system in a recursive process of mutual influence.

Carlos's presence as a teacher at the predominately white middle school has already influenced the institutional makeup of that school—most obviously because he is one brown teacher's face in an otherwise all-white sea of teachers' faces. But even more significantly, as is clear in other passages from Carlos's journal, the institution's dynamics *have* already changed to some extent through the relationships he has with other staff members as well as the Latino students. Indeed, this study will probably be read by the administrator and other teachers at Carlos's school and will thus influence that school's culture in yet another way.

In brief, one of the institution's *own* is an *insider* with the Latino student population. This is cause for optimism in Carlos—particularly in light of his strong religious belief that we are, with God, cocreators of history in a macrocosmic sense. Here, Carlos can perhaps be helped to envision himself as a cocreator of history in a microcosmic sense at his school. Nevertheless, the paradox of Carlos's positioning in the culture of Madison Middle School remains—namely that, just as he is both an outsider and insider in the staff culture of the school, he is also both an outsider and insider in the Latino culture of the school. We see this in the next section.

Academic Success as Cultural Betrayal

Beginning in the 1960s and growing rapidly since the 1970s, there has been a growing body of literature documenting the fact that minority students who fail academically often do so because academic success might open them up to the charge (usually by their peers) that they are betraying their racial, cultural, or socioeconomic group by trying to fit into middle-class, White culture (Gibson, 1988; Riordan, 2000; Willis, 1977). An academically successful African American student, for instance, might be accused by his black peers of being an "Oreo" (i.e., black on the outside but white on the inside) just as a successful Native American student may be called an "apple" by his Native American peers (i.e., red on the outside but white on the inside).

In being categorized as "El Prep" (or "The Preppie") by some of his Hispanic students, Carlos is subtly stereotyped by them as being a Hispanic who has sacrificed some of his "Chicano" identity in order to succeed in the white world. This is especially problematic not only because of its troubling effect on Carlos but also because it highlights these students' belief that academic success is somehow inconsistent with cultural identity and solidarity.

January 25, 2002

A new semester, new classes, and some new students. My relationship with the Latino students continues to grow. Many stop by between classes just to say hello. Some students ask their teachers for permission to come into my classroom during their advisory period. I'm teaching some of these students how to play chess. Others already know how, and they love getting me into checkmate. Today, one of the students, Miguel Ortega, said something very interesting to me. Between classes he stopped by and before leaving he called back, "Later, Prep!" I was surprised at his comment. He didn't say it in a disrespectful tone. However, my surprise has grown as I have come to consider what he meant by "Prep."

To my Latino students, a "Prep" is one who dresses nicely, is clean cut, academically successful, and so forth. Most of my Latino students do not associate with "Los Preps" of the school. Those whom they categorize as "Preps" are the student body officers, the popular Caucasian students and athletes, and so forth. Clearly Miguel has noticed that I often wear a tie to school. He has recognized that even though I speak Spanish, I also attempt to speak English professionally. He recognizes that I establish relationships with others that are non-Hispanic. I treat everyone equally, so he must infer that because I do so, I am "El Prep." The most intriguing thing about today's incident is that today I realize that as much as I relate with my Latino students, there is still a gap between us. They know that I listen to Mariachi music, that my dad picks fruit for a living for just $10 an hour, and that many of my uncles crossed the border illegally. However, despite all our similarities, my college education and my teaching position create a gap between my Hispanic students and myself. I'm struggling with this set of issues a lot.

Teachability

Carlos's willingness to examine the complexities and contradictions in his own identity evinces great honesty and courage. Acknowledging the complexities of one's own identity can be a disturbing venture that most of us seek to avoid by turning our gazes on others and critiquing them instead of attending to our own issues (May & Yalom, 1995). Carlos's honesty and courage in this matter can be summed up as the quality of "teachability" (an important term and concept in Mormon culture) or willingness to learn from his experiences—in this case, to learn from the feedback given him from his Latino students. Such "teachability" is the *sine qua non* of all deep psychospiritual growth. In this manner, then, Carlos's growth as a teacher can also be linked—both in his reflectivity and classroom practice—to his evolution as an ethical and spiritual being, thereby creating a deep faith-based basis for his pedagogy.

Carlos exposes and explores his identity issues and relationship with the Latino students with great authenticity. However, at this point he only does so within the safe confines of his journal entries. The next logical, though scary, step would seem to be for him to share his internal struggles with his students. In taking this next step, Carlos would be modeling one of the components of Cutri and Ferrin's (1999) model of a nondogmatic spiritual morality—namely, a compassionate desire to connect with self and others in service of the greater good.

Carlos and his Latino students could explore identity options together. In doing so, they might discover that other options exist in addition to the opposite of extremes of either attending "Remedial High" or being caught in the stereotype of "El Prep." Is there another identity option that would remain true to one's Latino identity but also arm both the Latino teacher and student with the tools necessary to succeed in mainstream culture? As Carlos acknowledges his own ability to both change the system at his predominately white middle school and also be changed by it, could he help his students see possibilities for them to positively change the dominant culture at the same time as they are changed *by* it in some positive respects—and remain *Latinos* throughout the entire process?

Pursuing these extensions of a spiritually centered, culturally sensitive approach to these issues may not only help Carlos bridge the gap between him and his Latino students but also help him negotiate the institutional hurdles of a systemically complex school.

Lau . . . and Beyond. . . .

Bilingual instruction in the United States is historically rooted in the Civil Rights Act of 1964, the Elementary and Secondary Education Act of 1965, the Bilingual Education Act of 1968, and the U.S. Supreme Court Decision known as *Lau v. Nichols* in 1974. By these means, schools were informed that they must address the needs of limited English proficiency (LEP) students. However, there were very few suggestions or guidelines given to the schools as to how, precisely, this was to be accomplished. Consequently, LEP programs in American schools are extremely variable from site to site, are often more or less "jerry-rigged," and typically carry low prestige in the culture of the school (Garcia, 2001; Riordan, 2000; Valencia, 1991). Carlos discovered this during his first year as a teacher in his ESL assignment.

September 17, 2001
A month of school has gone by, and today is the first day I recognize the issues facing my ESL students. They are spread out throughout the day. I have one or two in each class, and in one class half of them qualify under this label. My ESL students are amazing kids. They have the courage to come into a completely foreign classroom and make an effort to adapt to the curriculum being taught. Most of them are very quiet. They only speak if spoken to. Rarely do they ask a question or comment during class. I am afraid that their needs are not being met. Really, I know that their needs are not being met!

In my class they often cannot read any of the material I present to them, nor can they grasp the content of our classroom discussion. Some of the second language learners are enrolled in an ESL class here at school. I don't know much about the class, but from what I've seen I'm not very impressed. Suffice it to say that we don't have a full-time faculty member teaching these needy students. In fact, the ESL teacher doesn't even have a college degree. When I ask the principal why, the only response is "funding."

Today I must point the finger directly at myself. I was an ESL student when I first arrived in the United States. I struggled through pull-out programs to eventually reach a mainstream course in junior high school. I've completed my college education, which also includes a minor in teaching ESL. You'd think that I'm the perfect candidate to teach the ESL population, yet today I've recognized my struggle to involve them in my class. I don't know the answers to all the questions regarding their education. I do know that their parents worry but don't know how to help.

I know that their parents feel uneasy when they see their quiet, loveable son or daughter immerse themselves in a culture foreign to their Hispanic roots. The academic culture that their children need to master in order to succeed in today's public school is very distant from them. I need to come up with a better plan than what I have today. I recognize that I'm in an environment where I'm the "expert." Yet, I often find myself without tools and the resources to serve the student I once was.

NOT ONLY CARLOS BUT *ALL* TEACHERS

Having access to the thoughts and experiences of this first-year Latino middle-school teacher compellingly and concretely illustrates some of the major issues and findings in the multicultural literature today and point to areas that should be of interest to all teachers.

First, it is clear that teachers must adopt an authoritative stance with their students—one that communicates the message that they as teachers both care about their students of color and have high academic expectations of them. Second, when a student of color does not perform well despite the teacher's having related to him in an authoritative fashion, there might be nonacademic reasons for this problem. In Carlos's journal, we saw three of those reasons: a) the specific characteristics and perspectives of the subgroup from which the student comes; b) the entry conditions under which the student first enrolled in a public school; and c) pressure from the students' peers which make it seem a cultural betrayal to do well in school. Third, the English instruction that language-minority students get is often haphazard, underfunded, and marginal in the school's culture.

Fourth, to the maximum degree feasible given the (usually limited) funds allotted to schools for LEP-student language instruction, the administration should try to create a program that has clearly defined teaching strategies and academic goals. Staff should also show an interest in its LEP programs, and students who perform well in the LEP programs should be given special recognition in the form, perhaps, of certificates, awards, and other media of schoolwide communication. In this way, these students can be increasingly pulled into the mainstream of academic culture, not pushed out onto its margins (Gamoran, 2000; Hallinan, 2000). Fifth, administrators and other faculty members should be sensitive to both the particular strengths and special challenges of novice teachers of color in order to maximize what those teachers have to offer the school both pedagogically and culturally (Mayes, Montero, & Cutri, 2004).

Finally, we have attempted to show how all of these crucial pedagogical and institutional issues can be handled in a much more profound manner pedagogically, politically, and psychologically if teachers and teacher educators are allowed to frame these questions in spiritual terms. There is a wide variety of legally and institutionally appropriate ways that teachers in the schools as well as teacher educators and students in colleges of education can engage in this spiritual reflectivity. Kniker (1990), Mayes (1998, 1999, 2001a, 2001b), and Nord (1995) have offered many specific suggestions about how to accomplish this. The great benefit of doing so is that teachers' pedagogical, political, ethical and spiritual commitments will increasingly come to interact synergistically in such a way as to make the teacher more sensitive and effective as both an educator and an agent of social change.

The Case for Spiritual Reflectivity

Carlos's concern and vulnerability wrench the hearts of teacher educators and policymakers who are trying to help Carlos and other young visionary teachers like him in their valiant endeavors. The common response of most teacher educators and policymakers to Carlos's dilemmas is to search for better instructional, institutional, or fiscal models for reform. Such externally oriented approaches are of great importance.

However, equally important is the internally oriented process of examining ourselves as teacher educators and policymakers. In doing so, we might well find, along with Carlos, that in many ways we have also become diminished or confused in certain respects and are "without the tools and the resources to serve the [teacher] [we] once [were]." Hence, Mayes (2003) has called for "spiritual reflectivity" in colleges of education for both prospective and practicing teachers as well as for teacher educators who want to engage in such a process (see also Mayes & Ferrin, 2001).

Spirituality as a Motivating and Sustaining Force

Through reflecting on and refining the spiritual foundations of his sense of having been "called to teach" by some deeper purpose or higher power, the teacher may access the ethical and spiritual roots of his pedagogical and political commitments in a special way and, in so doing, both refine and strengthen those commitments (Bullough, Patterson, & Mayes, 2002; Stokes, 1997).

However, it is important to note in passing that the teacher's sense of being "called" can be taken advantage of. Teachers often lack professional prestige and are underpaid. Sometimes they are even considered to be little more than professional babysitters. Teachers certainly do not engage in their undervalued, inadequately compensated work for the money. Nevertheless, even spiritually called teachers, who are trying to nurture what hooks (2000) calls "the light of love in all living beings," deserve to be better compensated financially and professionally than they presently are (p. 71).

Mayes has shown in depth and using a wide variety of examples from various psychological and spiritual perspectives how spiritually reflective processes can take on many forms—none of which require (but which also do not prohibit) specific religious commitments (Mayes, 1998, 2001a, 2001b).

Rather, these forms of reflectivity build upon the individual's personal relationship to a transcendent reality as he uniquely understands it.

This is important because, as Giddens (1991) has pointed out, spirituality is still not only an important issue for most people but is also becoming less formal and more personal. Moreover, we believe that political and pedagogical reflectivity that does *not* include spiritual reflectivity will produce but a pallid picture of the teacher for whom spiritual commitment is an important part of his life and practice. Such partial reflectivity will not involve or transform the teacher's existential complexity. Thus, it will have only a limited value in refining his reflectivity and augmenting his pedagogical and political potency.

Spiritual reflectivity can also help sustain teachers in the face of new and often punishing constraints that are placed upon them in the name of "accountability." Teachers can grow frustrated, angry, and anxious being under the relentless scrutiny of high-stakes "monitoring" of the complex, delicate dynamics of their classes. Spiritual reflectivity can help teachers deal with these pressures by encouraging them to look beyond the daily "politics" of education toward its larger spiritual purposes for them and their students. Spirituality can be a sustaining force when times get tough. Hooks (2000) states, "For many, the strength received from spiritual awakenings has provided a buffer from the personally damaging effects of prejudice, discrimination, and hate" (p. 78). Similarly, a teacher's spiritual commitments can also help him heal the wounds caused in his heart and soul by public mistrust, the daily buffeting of classroom challenges, and the insensitivity of policy restrictions.

Spirituality as *Individual* Social Activism in the Classroom

Lisi and Rios (2005) in their introduction to an issue of the journal *Multicultural Perspectives* focused specifically on spirituality and multicultural education, posing this question:

> How do we, who are multicultural educators, think about and respond to these spiritual and religious aspect of our students' (and our own) identities *but still* abide by principles of pursuing justice, advocating inclusion, affirming difference, and ensuring quality education for all? (p. 1, emphasis added)

The words "but still" implies that focusing on spiritual aspects of our cultural identity is somehow at odds with the work of social justice. We commend Lisi and Rios for looking at multicultural issues in spiritual terms. However, we want to stress our conviction that spirituality and social justice not only *can* but *must* "abide" together, informing and enriching our pedagogical efforts.

The real "stuff" of education—of the school system—is the daily interactions between teachers and students. Teachers and students go about their daily dance, sometimes under distressing circumstances (Kozol, 1991) and almost always following complex, often unwritten rules (Oakes, 2000). Yet they keep dancing! Drop out rates are high, but large numbers of teachers and students still show up each day to school to do the dance. Policy debates and differing theoretical approaches to multicultural education are long in "trickling down" to the dance floor of the classrooms and hallways of schools. After almost 130 years of public schooling in America, it is clear that public schooling in our immensely complex society precludes the possibility of finding any quick or complete answers for *reforming* how the school dance is done.

As Tyack (1974) has so compellingly argued, there is no "one best system." This does not mean that we should not carry on educational policy debates as a society and forge the best programs that we can for our teachers and students. However, we must never lose sight of the fact that what happens in classrooms, on a person-to-person basis, is where the rubber always meets the road educationally. Helping teachers and students catch a higher vision of their daily tasks and duties as more than just mundane, therefore, is crucially important for two reasons: first, it addresses educational issues at their very heart and second, it offers achievable, vital goals that are almost always more immediately important for students and teachers than abstract policy statements which, historically, have had only limited practical effects in classrooms anyway (Cuban, 1993).

In this way, teachers can avail themselves of the many opportunities in the course of a day to interpret their difficult work in spiritual terms that are personally sustaining to them as individuals. This spiritual approach should not make teachers politically passive or blind them to the need for social and institutional change. In fact, we believe that it will make them more energetic yet also more realistic in pursuing political answers. Through small, daily decisions, teachers can change both their and their students' experience of the classroom, with all of its challenges, so that, together, they can grow spiritually and create solid, principled foundations for political action.

Helping Carlos reflect on the spiritual foundations of his practice—all the while doing the same ourselves as teacher educators in ways that are legally and institutionally acceptable in both public and private venues (Mayes & Ferrin, 2001)—offers exciting possibilities for teacher renewal and empowerment at all levels of the teacher's personal, professional, and political life. Carlos's journal highlights some of the major problems facing students and teachers of color in the public schools today. Attending to the experiences and observations of teachers like Carlos is an important step in finding ways to achieve the overarching goal of making our schools challenging and nurturing for *all* of our students.

Conclusion

TEACHING AND LEARNING IN THE TWENTY-FIRST CENTURY

As American society is becoming increasingly diverse, we simply must learn—all of us—to accommodate a variety of cultural worldviews in ways that are healthy and productive. Learning how to do this will lead to more integrated, loving, and balanced individuals. Indeed, it will take people who are themselves holistically integrated to lead others in the salutary world historical direction of cultural tolerance and mutual enlightenment. We believe that the practice of holistic multicultural education can play a role in accomplishing this goal.

The great promise of the twenty-first-century Age of Multiculturalism is that it may be the time in human history when we will all come to understand that there are legitimately different, equally valid, and mutually enlightening ways of being in and acting on the world. Understanding them—indeed, being changed by them in order to become wiser and more whole—should be of paramount educational importance in creating classrooms where students are edified by each other's worldviews. Unfortunately, many teachers, school leaders, policymakers, and citizens in general have not responded to these differences in the most productive ways, and we are currently losing large numbers of young people who feel alienated by school because they have been either ignored because of their differences or mislabeled as "deficient" when in fact they are merely "different." In many cases, this has not led to education at all—but to *anti-education*, discouraging people from developing the best within themselves.

Teachers can take the lead in the noble endeavor of honoring a wide variety of worldviews by examining their own cultural assumptions, beliefs, and biases through *cultural reflectivity*. They can also model for their students what it means to be *ethnographic detectives* who can enter into productive dialogue with members of other cultures so that all can be mutually informed and shaped. In the process, the individual grows greatly in practical efficacy and moral stature. As the famous anthropologist Edward Hall (1973) said, "the best reason for the layman to spend time studying culture is that he can learn something about himself" (p. 32). If teachers strive with students to become as aware as possible of valid cultural differences, and honor and celebrate alternative ways of knowing and learning (*all the while avoiding the two pitfalls of cultural determinism or moral relativism*), then they will help create classrooms in which students can thrive individually and collectively.

Regarding sensorimotor issues, we saw that when teaching and learning honor various cultures' differential sensory preferences, they are also helping each child develop as a multivalent sensory being. A classroom that is multirhythmic—respecting and embodying different cultural views of time and space—will be felt as affirming for minority students in the classroom and will contribute to the liberating holistic health of each child. Another reason for celebrating different sensorimotor modalities is that it creates a wonderfully therapeutic environment for the increasing numbers of children who are coming to our classrooms scared and scarred by a wide variety of traumas that have been physically inflicted on them everywhere from the bedroom to the battlefield. It is of paramount importance that classrooms be physically safe and sensorily rich environments in which children can heal and grow.

At the sociolinguistic level, we presented our strong conviction that schools that take a positive view of a cultural minority student's native language and culture—and thus encourage the student to view her language and culture optimistically—have much greater success in teaching English to her than schools which send her the explicit and implicit message that her native language and culture (the language and culture of her parents, grandparents, other loved ones, and venerated ancestors) is inferior. It is enormously important that we learn to take an "additive" view of bilingualism—where linguistic diversity is seen as a great social resource—not a "subtractive" one—where linguistic diversity is seen as a sort of social pathology that must be eliminated in favor of "English Only." Both currently and historically, some of the strongest and most productive societies have been those where various languages are used.

Of course, there is no doubt that a major item of business in any classroom is the cognitive enrichment of each student. However, it is important to recognize that our cognition is inseparable from our emotions, and that our emotions are inseparable from our cultures. Cognition does not operate mechanically in an existential vacuum. It is integrally related to one's emotional life and cultural predispositions. When teaching and learning respect the emotional and cultural makeup of each child, the classroom becomes a psychodynamically therapeutic space. Again we wish to emphasize that, given the tragic fact that so many children in classrooms today are suffering psychologically from a wide range of personally and politically caused traumas, it becomes doubly important that classrooms are places where— feeling safe, affirmed, and cherished—*all* children can blossom cognitively and emotionally.

A related reason that it is vital for the teacher to be aware of her students' psychosocial complexities (and this does not mean that she can, or even should, try to know all the specific subjective details of these differences) is that she will be better able to: (1) create classrooms where students will eventually feel safe enough to challenge some of their own deepest cognitive and cultural assumptions while entertaining those of their classmates, (2) foster discussions and create activities that allow students to explore their own and each other's emotional and political responses to the "official curriculum," and (3) avoid unproductive classroom confrontations that arise out of gross emotional insensitivity on the part of either the teacher or a student to another student or group of students.

We have also argued that both teachers and students will find their time in the classroom more interesting, exciting, and truly consequential in their lives if they are engaged in learning about the culturally distinct ways in which people view and process information, reason and construct theories, and even justify what is worth thinking about in the first place! Every individual—whether she comes from a dominant or minority culture—sees her world through her cultural schemas, which encourage her to pick, choose, and interpret things in certain ways and not in others. If the message being conveyed to students from a minority culture is that their and their parents' cultural schemas are inferior, many of those students will understandably find ways to subvert—or at least detach themselves from—the life of the classroom.

For example, in spite of the fact that they are so esthetically compelling and interpersonally subtle, Native American and African American styles of cognition and communication are often dishonored and their use is even punished in classrooms where the emphasis must unilaterally and unrelentingly be only on empirical facts, individual competition, standardized test scores, and depersonalized theoretical knowledge. We believe that this is a large contributing factor in the low performance and high drop-out rates among so many ethnic minority students—indeed, among so many students in general! It is our belief that by making classroom environments more colorful, varied, and authentic, holistic multicultural pedagogy can play a role in encouraging students from across the socioeconomic and cultural spectrum not to make the bad choice of leaving school.

John Dewey often said that the public school should be a "laboratory of democracy." We concur with this high ideal. Teachers who are aware of differential sociocognitive styles in instruction and assessment help foster a "pluralistic classroom" that is profoundly democratic. A practical benefit of the pluralistic classroom is that it gives students abundant opportunities to expand their repertoire of cognitive strategies in defining and dealing with problems. It also makes them more flexible, creative, and dynamic *thinkers* and *actors* in a "global village" that is increasingly in need of people who can frame and approach issues from multiple perspectives and in multiple ways.

Another political benefit of such a classroom for students from minority cultures is that it allows them to strike a balance between *learning* the knowledge that is important to succeed in the dominant social order and *analyzing* the dominant social order from their unique cultural perspective. It is our faith that the result of such ongoing analyses—sometimes celebratory, sometimes critical—of the prevailing social order will be the creation of more dynamic, inclusive, and effective ways of interpreting and enacting the noble notion of democracy. This will engender an increasingly humane society that can benefit everyone.

We also want to voice again our belief that it is high time that the teacher's moral and religious commitments—rooted in her sense of the Divine and her relationship to it—be honored in both educational scholarship and school governance, for they often play a significant role in a teacher's sense of "calling" as a teacher as well as her understanding of the goals of education. There are many ways that this can be done in a legally and institutionally appropriate manner. This is important because the ethical and spiritual aspects of one's life are generally the most compelling in shaping how one interprets the world and relates to others. Our case study of a young Latino teacher named Carlos illustrated the advantages of allowing all teachers to reflect on their sense of calling and classroom practices in spiritual terms that are personally meaningful to them.

As teachers ourselves, we are aware that it is no small accomplishment to use the ideas and practices we have presented in this book to address the student's complex nature and needs. But then again, teaching is not a small job. It is a great calling. It is hard to imagine work that is as important as teaching and impossible to imagine work that is more important. The authors of this book believe that the best types of teaching and the most rewarding moments in the classroom (those that are likely to be cherished by teacher and students long after the students have graduated) are most likely to occur when a teacher is teaching in a manner that is holistically sensitive.

Yet, although the teacher's calling is a high one and her potential to shape a student for good is indeed great, it is not necessary that a teacher be "perfect" in order to do her job well. What Winnicott has said about the best type of mothering also holds for teaching—it should be "good enough." It is not neurotic perfectionism but a realistic commitment to doing one's best under given conditions—realizing one's own and other's limitations—that leads to growth in both the teacher and her students.

Students love and respond gratefully to a good-enough, good-hearted teacher who does her practical best on a daily basis (and in the midst of the many other demands being placed on her) to put even a few of the ideas such as those in this book into practice. In this way, the teacher can provide a model for her students to admire and emulate as—under her wise guidance—they grow intellectually, emotionally, politically, and spiritually *with* each other and learn *from* each other. This is a way of teaching and learning that is good for one and all in the twenty-first-century classroom.

Bibliography

Adams, M. (1995). *The multicultural imagination: "Race," color, and the unconscious.* London: Routledge.

Adler, A. (1930). *The education of children.* (Tr. E. Jensen and F. Jensen). South Bend, IN: George Allen and Unwin, Ltd.

Aguessy, H. (1977). Sociological interpretations of time and pathology of time in developing countries. In P. Ricoeur (Ed.), *Time and the philosophies* (pp. 93–105). Paris: UNESCO.

Almon, J. (1999). From cognitive learning to creative thinking. In J. Kane (Ed.), *Education, information, and transformation: Essays on learning and thinking* (pp. 249–269). Upper Saddle River, NJ: Prentice Hall.

Anderson, R. (2000). The notion of schemata and the educational enterprise. In R. Anderson, R. Spiro, & W. Montague (Eds.), *Schooling and the acquisition of knowledge* (pp. 415–431). Hillsdale, NJ: Lawrence Erlbaum Associates.

Anthony, E. (1989). The psychoanalytic approach to learning theory (with more than a passing reference to Piaget). In K. Field, B. Cohler, & G. Wool (Eds.), *Learning and education: Psychoanalytic perspectives* (pp. 99–126). Madison, CT: International Universities Press, Inc.

Anyon, J. (2001). Inner cities, affluent suburbs, and unequal educational opportunity. In J. Banks & C. Banks (Eds.), *Multicultural education: Issues and perspectives* (4th edition) (pp. 85–102). New York: Wiley.

Apple, M. (1990). *Ideology and curriculum.* London: Routledge.

Arredondo, P., Toporek, R., Brown, S. P., Jones, J., Locke, D. C., Sanchez, J., & Stadler H. (1996). Operationalization of multicultural counseling competencies. *Journal of Multicultural Counseling and Development, 24*, 42–78.

Artiles, A. J., Barreto, R., Peña, L., & McClafferty, K. (1998). Pathways to teacher learning in multicultural contexts: A longitudinal case study of two novice bilingual teachers in urban schools. *Remedial and special education, 19* (2), 70–90.

Ashbaker, B., & Morgan, J. (2006). *Paraprofessionals in the classroom.* Boston: Allyn & Bacon.

Au, K., & Kawakami, A. (1985). Research currents: Talk story and learning to read. *Language Arts,* 62(4), 406–411.

Ballantine, J. (1997). *The sociology of education: A systematic analysis.* Upper Saddle River, NJ: Prentice Hall.

Bandura, R. (1986). *Social foundations of thought and action.* Englewood Cliffs, NJ: Prentice Hall.

Banks, J., & Banks, C. (2001). (Eds.), *Multicultural education: Issues and perspectives* (4th edition). New York: Wiley.

Barford, D. (2002). Introduction. In D. Barford (Ed.), *The ship of thought: Essays on psychoanalysis and learning* (pp. 11–16). New York: Karnac Books.

Basch, M. (1989). The teacher, the transference, and development. In K. Field, B. Cohler, & G. Wool (Eds.), *Learning and education: Psychoanalytic perspectives* (pp.771–788). Madison, CT: International Universities Press, Inc.

Belenkey, M., Clinchy, B., Goldberger, N., & Tarule, J. (1986). *Women's way of knowing.* New York: Basic Books.

Benedict, R. (1989). *The chrysanthemum and the sword: Patterns of Japanese culture.* Boston, MA: Houghton Mifflin.

Berger, P. (1967). *The sacred canopy: Elements of a sociological theory of religion.* New York: Doubleday and Company.

Bennett, M. (1993). Towards ethno-relativism: A developmental model of intercultural sensitivity. In M. Paige (Ed.), *Education for the intercultural experience.* Yarmouth, ME: Intercultural Press.

Berger, P., & Luckmann, T. (1966). *The social construction of reality: A treatise in the sociology of knowledge.* New York: Anchor Books.

Berliner, D., & Biddle, B. (1995). *The manufactured crisis: Myths, fraud, and the attack upon America's public schools.* Reading, MA: Addison Wesley.

Bernstein, B. (2000) *Pedagogy, symbolic control, and identity: Theory, research, critique.* Lanham, MD: Rowman and Littlefield.

Bernstein, H. (1989). In K. Field, B. Cohler, & G. Wool (Eds.), *Learning and education: Psychoanalytic perspectives* (pp. 143–158). Madison, CT: International Universities Press, Inc.

Best, J. (2004). *Deviance: Career of a concept.* Belmont, CA: Thomson/Wadsworth.

Block, A. (1997). *I'm only bleeding: Education as the practice of social violence against children.* New York: Peter Lang.

Bloom, A. H. (1981). *The linguistic shaping of thought: A study on the impact of language on thinking in China and the West.* Hillsdale, NJ: Lawrence Erlbaum Associates.

Blos, P. (1940). *The adolescent personality: A study of individual behavior for the commission on secondary school curriculum.* New York: D. Appleton-Century Company.

Boorstin, D. (1985). *The discoverers: A history of man's search to know his world and himself.* New York: Vintage Books.

Bourdieu, P. (1977). Cultural reproduction. In J. Karabel, & A. Halsey (Eds.), *Power and ideology in education* (pp. 487–507). New York: Oxford Press.

Bowles, S., & Gintis, H. (1976). *Schooling in capitalist America*. New York: Basic Books.

Brophy, J. (1997). *Motivating students to learn*. Boston: McGraw-Hill.

Brown, J. S., Collins, A., & Duguid, O. (1988). Situated cognition and the culture of learning. *Educational Researcher*, 18, 32–42.

Bruner, J. (1996). *The culture of education*. Cambridge, MA: Harvard University Press.

Buber, M. (1985). *Between man and man*. New York: Scribners.

Buendia, E., & Ares, N. (2006). *Geographies of difference: The social production of the east side, west side, and central city school*. New York: Peter Lang.

Bullough, R., Jr. (1989). *First-year teacher: A case study*. New York: Teachers College Press.

Bullough, R., Jr. (2001). *Uncertain lives: Children of hope, teachers of promise*. New York: Teachers College, Columbia University.

Bullough, R., Jr., Patterson, R., & Mayes, C. (2002). Teaching as prophecy. *Journal of Curriculum Inquiry,* 32(3), 310–329.

Burke, K. (1989). *On symbols and society*. J. Gusfield (Ed.). Chicago: University of Chicago Press.

Butkowski, I., & Willows, D. (1980). Cognitive motivational characteristics of children varying in reading ability: Evidence for learned helplessness in poor readers. *Journal of Educational Psychology,* 72, 408–422.

Carroll, J. B. (Ed.). (1956). *Language, thought, and reality: Selected writings of Benjamin Lee Whorf*. Cambridge, MA: MIT Press.

Castaneda, L. (1995). The role of social history in research and practice: One Chicana's perspective. In C. Grant (Ed.), *Educating for diversity: An anthology of multicultural voices* (pp. 143–147). Lanham, MD: Rowman and Littlefield.

Castoriadis, C. (1991). Time and creation. In J. Bender & D. Wellerby (Eds.), *Chronotypes: The construction of time* (pp. 38–64). Palo Alto, CA: Stanford University Press.

Chi, M. T. H., Feltovich, P. J., & Glaser, R. (1983). Categorization and representation of physics problems by experts and novices. *Cognitive Science*, 5, 121–152.

Chodorow, N. (1978). *The reproduction of mothering: Psychoanalysis and the sociology of gender*. Berkeley: University of California Press.

Chomsky, N. (1968). *Aspects of the theory of syntax*. Cambridge, MA: MIT Press.

Clift, R., Houston, W., & Pugach, W. (Eds.), (1990). *Encouraging reflective practice in education: An analysis of issues and programs* (pp. 208–222). New York: Teachers College Press.

Cohler, B. (1989). Psychoanalysis and education: Motive, meaning, and self. In K. Field, B. Cohler, & G. Wool (Eds.), *Learning and education: Psychoanalytic perspectives on learning* (pp.11–84). Madison, CT: International Universities Press, Inc.

Collier, V. P. (1995). Acquiring a second language [Electronic Version]. *Directions in Language and Education*, 1. Retrieved April 11, 2006 from http://www.ncela.gwu.edu/pubs/directions/04.htm.

Conger, J., & Galambos, J. (1997). *Adolescence and youth: Psychological development in a changing world*. New York: Longman.

Connor, U. (1996). *Contrastive rhetoric, cross-cultural aspects of second-language learning*. Cambridge: Cambridge University Press.

Cooper, G. (1989). Black language and holistic cognitive style. In B. Shade (Ed.), *Culture, style, and the educative process* (pp. 116–128). Springfield, IL: Charles C. Thomas.

Counts, G. (1932). *Dare the school build a new social order?* New York: John Day.

Cremin, L. (1964). *The transformation of the school: Progressivism in American education, 1876–1957*. New York: Vintage Press.

Cremin, L. (1988). *American education: The metropolitan experience*. New York: Harper and Row.

Crosby, A. (1997). *The measure of reality: Quantification and Western society, 1250–1600*. Cambridge, UK: Cambridge University Press.

Cuban, L. (1993). *How teachers taught: Constancy and change in American classrooms, 1890–1990*. New York: Teachers College Press.

Cummins, J. (1994). Power and pedagogy in the education of culturally diverse students. In *Schooling and language minority students* (pp. 3–49). Sacramento, CA: California Department of Education.

Cummins, J., & Dorson, D. (Eds.) (1997). *Bilingual education*. Boston: Kluwer Academic Publishers.

Cutri R., & Ferrin. (1999). Exploring the moral dimensions of bilingual education. A paper presented at the annual meeting of the National Association for Bilingual Education. January 1999. Denver, CO.

Dennen, J. van der. (1999). *The Darwinian heritage and sociobiology*. Westport, CT: Praeger.

Dewey, J. (1916). *Democracy and education*. New York: Macmillan.

Deyhle, D. (1986). Break dancing and breaking out: Anglos, Utes, and Navajos in a border reservation school. *Anthropology and Education Quarterly*, *19*(4), 354–382.

Dole, J., & Sinatra, G. (1994). Social psychology research on beliefs and attitudes: implications for research on learning from text. In R. Garnes & P. Alexander (Eds.), *Beliefs about texts and instruction with text* (pp. 245–264). Hillsdale, NJ: Elbaum.

Driver, R., Asoko, H., Leach, J., Mortimer, E., & Scott, P. (1994). Constructing scientific knowledge in the classroom. *Educational Researcher, 7*, 5–12.

Dunn, R., Dunn, K., & Price, C. (1977). Diagnosing learning styles: A prescription for avoiding malpractice suits. *Phi Delta Kappan, 58*, 418–420.

Duschl, R., & Gitomer, D. (1991). Epistemological perspectives on conceptual change: Implications for educational practice. *National Association for Research in Science Teaching, 9*(2), 839–858.

Dusek, J. (1994). *Adolescent development and behavior*. New York: Macmillan.

Dweck, C. (1999). *Self-theories: Their role in motivation, personality, and development*. Philadelphia: Psychology Press.

Eisner, E., & Vallance, E. (1985). *The educational imagination: On the design and evaluation of school programs*. New York: Macmillan.

Ekstein, R. (1969). Psychoanalytic notes on the function of the curriculum. In R. Ekstein & R. Motto (Eds.), *From learning for love to love of learning: Essays on psychoanalysis and education* (pp. 47–57). New York: Brunner/Mazel Publishers.

Ellis, R. (2005). Instructed language learning and task-based teaching. In E. Hinkel (Ed.), *Handbook of research in second language teaching and learning* (pp. 713–728). Mahwah, NJ: Lawrence Erlbaum Associates.

Elson, M. (1989). The teacher as learner, the learner as teacher. In K. Field, B. Cohler, & G. Wool (Eds.), *Learning and education: Psychoanalytic perspectives on learning* (pp. 789–808). Madison, CT: International Universities Press, Inc.

Erickson, F. (2001). Culture in society and in educational practices. In J. Banks & C. Banks (Eds.), *Multicultural education: Issues and perspectives* (4th edition). (pp. 31–58). New York: Wiley.

Erickson, F., & Mohatt, G. (1982). Cultural organization of participant structures in classrooms of Indian students. In G. Spindler (Ed.), *Doing the ethnography of schooling* (pp. 132–174). New York: Holt, Rinehart, and Winston.

Ermarth, E. (1992). *Sequel to history: Postmodernism and the crisis of representational time.* Princeton: Princeton University Press.

Ernst-Slavit, G., Moore, M., & Maloney, C. (2002). Changing lives: Teaching English and literature to ESL students. *Journal of Adolescent and Adult Literacy, 46*(2), 116–128.

Fairbairn, W. R. D. (1992). *Psychoanalytic studies of the personality.* London: Routledge.

Fay, B. (1987). *Critical social science: Liberation and its limits.* Ithaca, NY: Cornell University Press.

Fay, B. (2000). *Contemporary philosophy of social science: A multicultural approach.* Oxford: Blackwell Publishers Ltd.

Ferdman, B. M. (1990). Literacy and cultural identity. *Harvard Educational Review, 60*(2), 181–204.

Ferrucci, P. (1982). *What we may be: Techniques for psychological and spiritual growth through psychosynthesis.* Los Angeles: Jeremy Tarcher, Inc.

Field, K., Cohler, B., & Wool, G. (Eds.) (1989). *Learning and education: Psychoanalytic perspectives on learning.* Madison, CT: International Universities Press, Inc.

Foshay, A. (2000). *The curriculum: Purpose, substance, practice.* New York: Teachers College Press.

Foucault, M. (1980). *Power/knowledge: Selected interviews and other writings, 1972–1977.* New York: Pantheon Books.

Frazer, J. (1935). *The golden bough: A study in magic and religion.* New York: The Macmillan Company.

Friedman, T. (2000). *The Lexus and the olive tree.* New York: Anchor Books.

Freire, P. (2001). *Pedagogy of freedom: Ethics, democracy, and civic courage.* Lanham, MD: Rowman and Littlefield.

Gamoran, A. (2000). Is ability tracking equitable? In R. Arum & I. Beattie (Eds.), *The structure of schooling: Readings in the sociology of education* (pp. 234–240). Mountain View, CA: Mayfield Publishing Company.

Garcia, E. (2001). *Hispanic education in the United States: Raices y alas.* Lanham, MD: Rowman and Littlefield.

Gardner, H. (1999). Are there additional intelligences? The case for naturalistic, spiritual, and existential intelligences. In J. Kane (Ed.), *Education, information, and transformation* (pp. 113–131). Columbus, OH: Merrill/Prentice Hall.

Gardner, H., & Hatch, R. 1989, http://www.infed.org/thinkers/gardner.htm, 12/06/2006.

Garner, R. (1990). Do readers change their minds while reading persuasive text? An unpublished paper. Vancouver, WA: Washington State University.

Gass, S. M., & Selinker, L. (1994). *Second language acquisition: An introductory course*. Hillsdale, NJ: Lawrence Erlbaum Associates.

Gauvain, M. (1995). Thinking in niches: sociocultural influences on cognitive development. *Human Development, 38* (1), 25–45.

Gauvain, M. (2001). *The social context of cognitive development* (vol. 4). New York: The Guilford Press.

Gay, G. (2000). *Culturally responsive teaching: Theory, research and practice*. New York: Teachers College Press.

Gee, J., Michaels, S., & O'Connor, M. (1992). Discourse analysis. In M. LeCompte, W. Millroy, & J. Preissle (Eds.), *The handbook of qualitative research in education* (pp. 227–291). London: Academic Press.

Gelberg, D. (1997). *The 'business' of reforming American schools*. Albany: State University of New York Press.

Gibson, M. (1988). *Accommodation without assimilation: Sikh immigrants in an American high school*. Ithaca, NY: Cornell University Press.

Giddens, A. (1990). *The consequences of modernity*. Palo Alto, CA: Stanford University Press.

Giddens, A. (1991). *Modernity and self-identity: Self and society in the late modern age*. Palo Alto, CA: Stanford University Press.

Giddens, A. (2002). *Runaway world: How globalization is reshaping our lives*. London: Profile.

Gilligan, C. (1982). *In a different voice: Psychological theory and women's development*. Cambridge, MA: Harvard University Press.

Giroux, H. (1983). Theories of reproduction and resistance in the new sociology of education: A critical analysis. *Harvard Educational Review, 53*(3), 257–293.

Goffman, E. (1997). *The Goffman reader.* C. Lemert & A. Branaman (Eds.). London: Blackwell.

Gonzalez, N. (2001). *I am my language: Discourses of women and children in the borderlands*. Tucson: University of Arizona Press.

Greenspan, S. (1989). Emotional intelligence. In K. Field, B. Cohler, & G. Wool (Eds.), *Learning and education: Psychoanalytic perspectives on learning* (pp. 209–244). Madison, CT: International Universities Press, Inc.

Grossman, H. (1995). *Teaching in a diverse society.* Boston: Allyn and Bacon.

Gurevich, A. J. (1976). Time as a problem of cultural history. In Ricoeur, P. (Ed.), *Cultures and time* (pp. 229–243). Paris: UNESCO.

Hall, E. T. (1973). *The silent language*. New York: Doubleday.

Halliday, M. (1975). *Learning how to mean*. London: Edward Arnold.

Hallinan, M. (2000). Tracking: From theory to practice. In R. Arum & I. Beattie (Eds.), *The structure of schooling: Readings in the sociology of education* (pp. 218–223). Mountain View, CA: Mayfield Publishing Company.

Hansen, J. (1979). *Sociocultural perspectives on human learning: An introduction to educational anthropology*. Englewood Cliffs, NJ: Prentice Hall, Inc.

Haynes, J. (2005). Stages of second language acquisition. Retrieved April 11, 2006, from http://www.everythingesl.net/inservices/language_stages.php.

Heath, S. (1983). *Ways with words: Language, life, and work in communities and classrooms*. Cambridge, UK: Cambridge University Press.

Hendricks, G., & Fadiman, J. (Eds.). (1976). *Transpersonal education: A curriculum for feeling and being*. Englewood Cliffs, NJ: Prentice Hall, Inc.

Herrnstein, R., & Murray, C. (1994). *The bell curve: Intelligence and class structure in American life*. New York: Free Press.

Hewitt, J. (1984). *Self and society: A symbolic interactionist social psychology*. Boston: Allyn and Bacon.

Hill, J. (1969). The unconscious mind in teaching. In R. Ekstein & R. Motto (Eds.), *From learning for love to love of learning: Essays on psychoanalysis and education* (pp. 79–94). New York: Brunner/Mazel Publishers.

Hinkel, E. (Ed.). (2005). *Handbook of research in second language teaching and learning*. Mahwah, NJ: Lawrence Erlbaum Associates.

Hofstede, G. (2001). *Culture consequences*, 2nd ed. London: Sage.

Holland, R. (1986). Learner characteristics and learner performance: Implications for instructional placement decisions. In B. Shade (Ed.), *Culture, style, and the educative process*. (pp. 167–183). Springfield, IL: Charles C. Thomas.

hooks, b. (2000). *All about love: New visions*. New York: Harper Perennial.

Jencks, C. (1992). *Rethinking social policy: Race, poverty, and the underclass*. Cambridge, MA: Harvard University Press.

Jones, M., Jones, B., & Hargrove, T. (2003). *The unintended consequences of high-stakes testing*. Lanham, MD: Rowman and Littlefield.

Jones, R. (1968). *Fantasy and Feeling in Education*. New York: New York University Press.

Joseph, P., & Burnaford, G. (1994). *Images of schoolteachers in twentieth-century America: Paragons, polarities, complexities*. New York: St. Martin's Press.

Jung, C. (1956). *Symbols of transformation: An analysis of the prelude to a case of schizophrenia*. R. Hull (Trans.). Princeton: Princeton University Press.

Jung, C. (1959). *The archetypes and the collective unconscious*. Princeton: Princeton University Press.

Jung, C. (1974). *Psychological types*. Princeton: Princeton University Press.

Jung, C. (1978). *The structure and dynamics of the psyche*. R. Hull (Trans.). Princeton: Princeton University Press.

Kampf, C. E. (2005). *Kumeyaay online: Dimensions of rhetoric and culture in the Kumeyaay web presence*. Doctoral dissertation awarded by the faculty of the University of Minnesota.

Kaulback, B. (1989). Styles of learning among Native children: A review of the research. In B. Shade (Ed.). *Culture, style, and the educative process*. (pp. 137–149). Springfield, Illinois: Charles C. Thomas.

Klein, M. (1975 [1932]) *The psychoanalysis of children*. A. Strachey (Trans.). New York: Delacorte Press.

Kirman, W. (1977). *Modern psychoanalysis in the schools.* Dubuque, IA: Kendall/Hunt Publishing Co.

Kniker, C. (1990). Teacher education and religion: The role of foundations courses in preparing students to teach about religions. *Religion and Public Education, 17(2),* 203–222.

Kohut, H. (1978) *The search for self: Selected writings of Heinz Kohut: 1950–1978.* P. Ornstein (Ed.), Madison, CT: International Universities Press.

Kornhaber, M. (2004). *Multiple intelligences: Best ideas from research and practice.* Boston: Pearson/Allyn and Bacon.

Kozol, J. (1991). *Savage inequalities: Children in American schools.* New York: Harper.

Krashen, S. (1981). The "fundamental pedagogical principle" in second language teaching. *Studia Linguistica, 35(1–2),* 50–70.

Krashen, S. (1982). *Principles and practice in second language acquisition.* New York: Pergamon Press.

Krashen, S. (2003). *Explorations in language acquisition and use: The Taipei lectures.* Portsmouth, NH: Heinemann.

Lado, R., & Fries, C. (1958). *English sentence patterns: Understanding and producing English grammatical structures.* Ann Arbor: University of Michigan Press.

Laing, R. D. (1967). *The politics of experience.* New York: Ballantine Books.

Lee, P. (1997). Cultural dynamics: Their importance in culturally responsive counseling. In C. C. Lee (Ed.), *Multicultural issues in counseling: New approaches to diversity* (pp. 15–30). Alexandria, VA: American Counseling Association.

Levi-Strauss, C. (1987). *Anthropology and myth.* New York: Blackwell.

LePage, A. (1991). Creation, spirituality and the reinventing of education. In R. Miller (Ed.), *New directions in education: Selections from holistic education review* (pp. 267–275). Brandon, VT: Holistic Education Press.

Lieberman, A. (Ed). (2003). *The Jossey-Bass reader on teaching.* New York: Wiley.

Linde, C. (1993). *Life stories: The creation of coherence.* New York: Oxford University Press.

Lindh, K., Gashi, L. M, Kuittinen, E., & Varis, V. (2003). Developing a Training Program for Intercultural Learning on the Web—Starting Points and Challenges. Proceedings from the First International Conference on Educational Technology in Cultural Context (ETCC), p.120.

Lisi, P., & Rios, F. (2005). Editors' introduction. *Multicultural perspectives*, (7)4, 1.

Littner, N. (1989). Reflections of early childhood family experiences in the educational situation. In K. Field, B. Cohler, & G. Wool (Eds.), *Learning and education: Psychoanalytic perspectives on learning* (pp. 825–850). Madison, CT: International Universities Press, Inc.

Macdonald, J. (1995). *Theory as a prayerful act: The collected essays of James P. Macdonald.* B. Macdonald (Ed.). New York: Peter Lang.

Macias, J. (1987). The hidden curriculum of Papago teachers: American Indian strategies for mitigating cultural discontinuity in early schooling. In G. Spindler & L. Spindler (Eds.). *Interpretive ethnography of education: At home and abroad.* Madison, CT: International Universities Press, Inc.

MacIntyre, A. (1985). *After virtue: A study in moral theory.* Notre Dame, IN: University of Notre Dame Press.

MacLeod, J. (1987). *Ain't no makin' it: Leveled aspirations in a low-income neighborhood.* Boulder, CO: Westview Press.

Marx, K., & Engels, F. (1978). *The Marx-Engels reader.* R. Tucker (Ed.). New York: W.W. Norton and Co.

Matute-Bianchi, M. (1986). Ethnic identities and patterns of school success and failure among Mexican descent and Japanese-American students in a California high school: An ethnographic analysis. *American Journal of Education, 95*(1), 233–255.

May, R., & Yalom, I. (1995). Existential psychotherapy. In R. Corsini & D. Wedding, (Eds.), *Current psychotherapies* (pp. 262–292). Itasca, IL: F. E. Peacock.

Mayes, C. (1998). The use of contemplative practices in teacher education. *Encounter: Education for Meaning and Social Justice, 11*(3), 17–31.

Mayes, C. (1999). Reflecting on the archetypes of teaching. *Teaching Education, 10*(2), 3–16.

Mayes, C. (2001a). Cultivating spiritual reflectivity in teachers. *Teacher Education Quarterly, 28*(2), 5–22.

Mayes, C. (2001b). A transpersonal developmental model for teacher reflectivity. *Journal of Curriculum Studies, 33*(4), 477–493.

Mayes, C. (2003). *Teaching mysteries: Foundations of a spiritual pedagogy.* Lanham, MD: University Press of America

Mayes, C. (2005a). *Jung and education: The educational ideas of C .G. Jung.* Lanham, MD: Rowman and Littlefield Education Press.

Mayes, C. (2005b). Teaching and time: Foundations of a temporal pedagogy. *Teaching Education Quarterly, 32*(2), 143–160.

Mayes, C., Blackwell Mayes, P., & Sagmiller, K. (2003). The sense of spiritual calling among teacher education program students. *Religion and Education, 30* (2), 84–109.

Mayes, C., Blackwell Mayes, P., & Williams, E. (2004). Critique as homiletics. *International Journal of Leadership in Education, 7*(3), 293–296.

Mayes, C., & Ferrin, S. (2001). Spiritually committed public-school teachers. Their beliefs of spiritually committed public school teachers concerning religious expression in the classroom. *Religion and Education, 28*(1), 75–94.

Mayes, C., Montero, F., & Cutri, R. (2004). First-year Latino teacher. *Multicultural Education, 12*(1), 2–9.

McLaren, P. (2003). *Life in schools: An introduction to critical pedagogy in the foundations of education* (3rd ed.). New York: Longman.

Miller, J. (1983). *The educational spectrum: orientations to curriculum.* New York: Longman.

Miller, J., & Seeler, W. (1985). *Curriculum: Perspectives and practices.* New York: Longman.

More, A. (1989). Native Indian students and their learning styles: Research results and classroom applications. In B. Shade (Ed.), *Culture, style, and the educative process.* (pp. 150–166). Springfield, IL: Charles C. Thomas.

Morrow, R., & Torres, C. (1995). *Social theory and education: A critique of theories of social and cultural reproduction.* Albany: State University of New York Press.

Nickerson, R. (1985). Understanding understanding. *American Journal of Education, 93,* 201–239.

Nieto, S. (2002). *Language, culture, and teaching: Critical perspectives for a new century.* Mahwah, NJ: Lawrence Erlbaum Associates.

Nisbett, R. E. (2003). *The geography of thought: How Asians and Westerners think differently . . . and why.* New York: The Free Press.

Noddings, N. (1984). *Caring: A feminine approach to ethics and moral education.* Berkeley: University of California Press.

Noddings, N. (1995). Care and moral education. In W. Kohli (Ed.), *Critical conversations in the philosophy of education* (pp. 137–148). New York: Routledge.

Nord, W. (1995). *Religion and American education: Rethinking a national dilemma.* Chapel Hill: University of North Carolina Press.

Nowotny, H. (1989). Mind, technologies, and collective time consciousness: From the future to an extended present. In J. G. Fraser (Ed.). *Time and mind: Interdisciplinary issues* (pp. 197–216). Madison, CT: International Universities Press.

Oakes, J. (2000). The distribution of knowledge. In R. Arum & I. Beattie (Eds.), *The structure of schooling: Readings in the sociology of education.* Mountain View, CA: Mayfield Publishing Company.

Ogbu, J. (1987). Variability in minority school performance: A problem in search of an explanation. *Anthropology and Education Quarterly, 18,* 312–334.

Ong, W. (2002). *Orality and Literacy: The technologizing of the world.* New York: Routledge.

Ovando, C. (2001). Language diversity and education. In J. Banks & C. Banks (Eds.), *Multicultural education: Issues and perspectives* (4th edition). (pp. 268–292). New York: Wiley.

Ovando, C., Combs, M., & Collier, V. (2006). *Bilingual and ESL classrooms: Teaching in multicultural contexts.* New York: McGraw-Hill.

Pai, Y., & Adler, S. (2001). *Cultural foundations of education* (3rd edition). New York: Merrill/Prentice Hall.

Pearson, G. (1954). *Psychoanalysis and the education of the child.* New York: Norton.

Peller, L. (1978 [1958]). The development of the child's self. In E. Plank (Ed.), *On development and education of young children: Selected papers* (pp.55–88). New York: Philosophical Library.

Pepper, F., & Henry, S. (1989). Social and cultural effects on Indian learning style: Classroom implications. In B. Shade (Ed.), *Culture, style, and the educative process.* (pp. 33–42). Springfield, IL: Charles C. Thomas.

Piaget, J., & Inhelder, B. (1969). *The psychology of the child.* New York: Basic Books.

Piers, G., & Piers, M. (1989). Modes of learning and the analytic process. In K. Field, B. Cohler, & G. Wool (Eds.), *Learning and education: Psychoanalytic perspectives on learning* (pp. 199–208). Madison, CT: International Universities Press, Inc.

Pfister, O. (1922). *Psycho-Analysis in the service of education, being an introduction to psycho-analysis.* London: Henry Kimpton.

Pintrich, P., Marx, R., & Boyle, R. (1993). Beyond cold conceptual change: The role of motivational beliefs and classroom contextual factors in the process of conceptual change. *Review of Educational Research, 63,* 167–199.

Popkewitz, T. (1997). The production of reason and power: Curriculum history and intellectual traditions. *Journal of Curriculum Studies, 29*(2), 131–164.

Posner, G. J., Strike, K. A., Hewson, P. W., & Gertzog, W. A. (1982). Accommodation of a scientific conception: Toward a theory of conceptual change. *Science Education*, 67(4), 498–508.

Postman, N. (1969). *Teaching as a subversive activity.* New York : Delacorte Press.

Pratt, D., Kelly, M., & Wong, W. (1999). Chinese conceptions of 'effective teaching' in Hong Kong: Towards culturally sensitive evaluation of teaching. *International Journal of Lifelong Education, 18*(4), 241–258.

Purpel, D., & Shapiro, S. (1995). *Beyond liberation and excellence: Reconstructing the public discourse on education.* Westport, CT: Bergin and Garvey.

Ravitch, D. (1983). *The troubled crusade: American education, 1945–1980.* New York: Basic Books.

Ravitch, D. (2000). *Left back: A century of failed school reforms.* New York: Simon and Schuster.

Rawls, J. (1999). *A theory of justice.* Cambridge, MA: Harvard University Press.

Redl, F., & Wattenberg, W. (1951). *Mental hygiene in teaching.* New York: Harcourt, Brace and Company.

Remen, R. (1999). Educating for mission, meaning and compassion. In S. Glazer (Ed.), *The heart of learning: Spirituality in education* (pp. 33–49). New York: Jeremy P. Tarcher.

Richards, B. (2006). Education in the Third Reich. Unpublished manuscript. Provo, UT: Department of Educational Leadership and Foundations, Brigham Young University.

Riordan, C. (2000). *Equality and achievement: An introduction to the sociology of education.* New York: Longman.

Rivers, Wilga. (1978). *A practical guide to the teaching of English as a second or foreign language.* New York: Oxford University Press.

Roberts, T., & Clark, F. (1975). *Transpersonal psychology in education.* Bloomington, IN: The Phi Delta Kappa Educational Foundation.

Robinson, B. (1999). Asian learners, western models: Some discontinuities and issues for distance educators. In R. Carr, O. Jegede, W. Tat-meg, & Y. Kin-sun (Eds.), *The Asian distance learner* (pp. 33–48). Hong Kong: Open University of Hong Kong.

Rogers, P. C. (2006). Exploring cultural competence in the lived experience of instructional designers. *Dissertation Abstracts International, 67* (02), 529. (UMI No. 3205627).

Rogoff, B. (2003). *The cultural nature of human development.* New York: Oxford University Press.

Rokeach, M. (1979). *Understanding human values: Individual and societal.* New York: The Free Press.

Rorty, R. (1999). *Philosophy and social hope.* New York: Penguin.

Sabbah, H. (2005). *Gender issues in Islamic schools: A case study of two schools in the United States.* An unpublished dissertation. Provo, UT: Department of Educational Studies and Foundations, Brigham Young University.

Sadker, M., & Sadker, D. (2004). *Failing at fairness: How America's schools cheat girls.* New York: Charles Scribner's Sons.

Salzberger-Wittenberg, I. (1983). *The emotional experience of learning and teaching.* London: Routledge and Kegan Paul.

Sapir, E. (1929). *Language: An introduction to the study of speech.* New York: Harcourt Brace.

Saracho, O. (1983). *Understanding the multicultural experience in early childhood education.* Washington, DC: National Association for the Education of Young Children.

Sardello, R., & Sanders, C. (1999). Care of the senses: A neglected dimension of education. In J. Kane (Ed.), *Education, information and transformation: Essays on learning and thinking* (pp. 226–237). Columbus, OH: Merrill/Prentice Hall.

Schipani, D. (1988). *Religious education encounters liberation theology.* Birmingham, AL: Religious Education Press.

Schutz, W. (1976). Education and the body. In G. Hendricks & J. Fadiman (Eds.), *Transpersonal education: A curriculum for feeling and being* (pp. 104–110). Englewood Cliffs, NJ: Prentice Hall.

Serow, R., Eaker, D., & Ciechalski. J. (1992). Calling, service, and legitimacy: Professional orientations and career commitment among prospective teachers. *Journal of Research and Development in Education* 25(3), 136–141.

Shade, B. (1989). (Ed.). *Culture, style, and the educative process.* Springfield, IL: Charles C. Thomas.

Shawaker, T., & Dembo, M. (1996). *The effects of efficacy building instruction on the use of learning strategies.* Paper presented at the annual meeting of the American Educational Research Association, New York.

Skinner, B. F. (1968). *The technology of teaching.* New York: Appleton-Century-Croft.

Skinner, B. F. (1971). *Beyond freedom and dignity.* New York: Knopf.

Slavin, R. (1990). *Cooperative learning: theory, research, and practice.* Robert E. Slavin. Englewood Cliffs, NJ: Prentice Hall.

Slife, B. (1993). *Time and psychological explanation.* Albany: State University of New York Press.

Slowinski, P. T. (2002). Exploring cultural competency for TESOL professionals: A proposed conceptual model. (Doctoral dissertation, Brigham Young University). *Dissertation Abstracts International, 63* (04), 12–34.

Solano-Flores, G., & Nelson-Barber, S. (2001). On the cultural validity of science assessments. *Journal of Research in Science Teaching, 38*(5), 553–573.

Sommers, C. H. (2000). *The war against boys: how misguided feminism is harming our young men.* New York: Simon and Schuster.

Spindler, G. (1963). *Education and culture: Anthropological approaches.* New York: Holt, Rinehart, and Winston.

Spindler, G., & Spindler, L. (1992). Cultural process and ethnography: An anthropological perspective. In M. LeCompte, W. Millroy, & J. Preissle (Eds.), *The handbook of qualitative research in education* (pp. 52–92). London: Academic Press.

Spodek, B., & Saracho, O. (1981). Teachers' cognitive styles. *Educational Forum*, 45, 153–159.

Spring, J. (1976). *Educating the worker-citizen.* New York: McGraw-Hill.

Spring, J. (2000). *The intersection of cultures: Multicultural education in the United States and the global economy.* New York: McGraw-Hill.

Spring, J. (2006). *American education* (12th ed). New York: McGraw-Hill.

Spronk, B. (2004). Addressing cultural diversity through learner support. In J. Brindley, C. Walti, & O. Zawacki-Richter (Eds.), *Learner support in open, distance and online learning environments* (pp. 169–178). Oldenburg, Germany: Bibliotheecksund Informationssystem der Universität Oldenburg, 2004.

Stafford, A. 10/29/06: http://www.mnsu.edu/ emuseum/cultural/ language/ whorf. html

Stevens, A. (2000). *Archetype revisited: An updated natural history of the self.* London: Routledge.

Stokes, D. (1997). *Called to teach: Exploring the worldview of called prospective teachers during their preservice teacher education experience.* An unpublished dissertation. Salt Lake City: University of Utah.

Sue, D. W., Ivey, A. E., & Pederson, P. B. (1996). *A theory of multicultural counseling and therapy.* Pacific Grove, CA: Brooks Publishing Company.

Tetreault, M. K. (2001). Gender bias: From colonial America to today's classrooms. In J. Banks & C. Banks (Eds.), *Multicultural Education: Issues and Perspectives,* 4th edition (pp. 125–151). New York: Wiley.

Tharp, R. G. (1989). Psychocultural variables and constants: Effects on teaching and learning in schools. *American Psychologist*, 44, 349–359.

Tillich, P. (1956). *The essential Tillich.* New York: Macmillan Publishing Co.

Ting-Toomey, S. (1999). *Communicating across cultures.* New York: Guilford Press.

Tinney, M.-V., Morgan, B., & Rogers, P. C. (2006, October). *How designers can connect different cultural expectations of teacher-student relationships in online courses.* Presented at the Association of Educational Communications and Technology (AECT), Dallas, TX.

Trent, J. (1994). *Inventing the feeble-minded: A history of mental retardation in the United States.* Berkeley: University of California Press.

Tyack, D. (1974). *The one best system: A history of American urban education.* Cambridge, MA: Harvard University Press.

Valencia, R. (Ed.). (1991). *Chicano school failure and success: Research and policy agendas for the 1990s.* London: Falmer Press.

Valli, L. (1990). Moral approaches to reflective practice. In R. Clift, W. Houston, & M. Pugach (Eds.), *Encouraging reflective practice in education: An analysis of issues and programs* (pp. 39–56). New York: Teachers College Press.

Valsiner, J., & van der Veer, R. (2000). *The social mind: Construction of the idea.* Cambridge: Cambridge University Press.

Van Lier, L. (2005). Case study. In E. Hinkel (Ed.), *Handbook of research in second language teaching and learning* (pp. 195–208). Mahwah, NJ: Lawrence Erlbaum Associates.

Vosniadou, S. (1991). Designing curricula for conceptual restructuring: Lessons from the study of knowledge acquisition in astronomy. *Journal of Curriculum Studies, 23,* 219–37.

Vosniadou, S., & Brewer, W. (1987). Theories of knowledge restructuring in development. *Review of Educational Research,* 57, 51–67.

Vygotsky, L. (1986). *Mind in society: The development of psychological functions.* Cambridge, MA: Harvard University Press.

Wade, J. (1996). *Changes of mind: A holonomic theory of the evolution of consciousness.* Albany: State University of New York Press.

Wax, M., Wax, R., & Dumont, R., Jr. (1964). *Formal education in an American Indian community: Peer society and the failure of minority education.* Prospect Heights, IL: Waveland Press.

Weiten, W. (1998). *Psychology themes and variations.* Pacific Grove, CA: Brooks/ Cole Publishing Company.

Wertsch, J. (1985). *Vygotsky and the social formation of mind.* Cambridge, MA: Harvard University Press.

Wexler, P. (1996). *Holy sparks: Social theory, education and religion.* New York: St. Martin's Press.

Whitmore, D. (1986). *Psychosynthesis in education: A guide to the joy of learning.* Rochester, VT: Destiny Books.

Whitrow, G. (1988). *Time in history: The evolution of our general awareness of time and temporal perspective.* Oxford: Oxford University Press.

Williams, R. N. (1987). Can cognitive psychology offer a meaningful account of meaningful human action? *The Journal of Mind and Behavior,* 8(2), 209–222.

Willis, P. (1977). *Learning to labour.* Aldershot, UK: Gower.

Wilson, W. (1987). *The truly disadvantaged: The inner city, the underclass, and public policy.* Chicago: University of Chicago Press.

Winnicott, D. W. (1992). *Psychoanalytic explorations.* C. Winnicott, R. Shepherd, & M. Davis (Eds.), Cambridge, MA: Harvard University Press.

Woods, P. (1992). Symbolic interactionism: Theory and method. In M. LeCompte, W. Millroy, & J. Preissle (Eds.), *The handbook of qualitative research in education* (pp. 337–404). London: Academic.

Wool, G. (1989). Relational aspects of learning: The learning alliance. In K. Field, B. Cohler, & G. Wool (Eds.), *Learning and education: Psychoanalytic perspectives* (pp. 747–770). Madison, CT: International Universities Press, Inc.

Yogananda, Paramahansa. (1946). *Autobiography of a yogi.* Los Angeles: Self realization fellowship.

Zachry, C. (1929). *Personality adjustments of school children, with an introduction by William Heard Kilpatrick.* New York: Charles Scribner's Sons.

Index

About the Authors

Clifford Mayes is an associate professor of education at Brigham Young University in the Department of Educational Leadership and Foundations. He earned a PhD from the University of Utah in the cultural foundations of education and a doctorate from Southern California University for Professional Studies in psychology. Cliff grew up in a highly multicultural setting with a population including Native Americans, Hispanic Americans, African Americans, and Caucasian Americans in the outskirts of Tucson, Arizona, in the 1950s and 1960s. He taught at universities in Panama and Japan throughout the 1980s and speaks Spanish. His research centers around the psychosocial dimensions of teaching and learning. He and his wife, Pam, have three wonderful children — Liz, Josh, and Dana.

Ramona Maile Cutri earned her PhD in Education from U.C.L.A. She is an adjunct professor of teacher education at Brigham Young University, where she teaches multicultural theory. Her academic interests include the spiritual/moral dimensions of multicultural and bilingual education and exploring these in both theoretical and pragmatic ways. She has taught in the public schools. Her other-than-academic interests include raising two lovely children with her husband, Chris, (who was born in Argentina and is a filmmaker and professor in the School of Fine Arts at Brigham Young University), running, reading, and yoga.

P. Clint Rogers is a visiting research associate at the Rollins Center for eBusiness at Brigham Young University. He holds a doctorate in instructional psychology and technology, with specific research interests in the cultural dimensions of online learning. Currently, he is facilitating cooperative research projects involving the United States and China in collecting, assembling, and making available high-quality digital educational content via mobile technologies. He is also associated with the PhD program in educational technology at the University of Joensuu in Finland, where he coordinates a team of PhD students from China, Africa, and Europe in researching the ethical and multicultural aspects of educational technology.

Fidel Montero is a graduate of Brigham Young University's master's program in educational leadership and is currently a doctoral student at Columbia University, Teachers College. Fidel has worked as a middle school teacher, school improvement consultant at all three levels of public schooling, and secondary school administrator. His research and practice emphases include school improvement, Hispanic community involvement, and at-risk student interventions. Mr. Montero is an immigrant to the United States and during his youth faced the challenges of a new culture, poverty, and learning English as a second language.